The World of
SILK
Priscilla Lowry

Also by the Author

*The Secrets of Silk:
From the Myths & Legends to
the Middle Ages*

*The Secrets of Silk:
From Textiles to Fashion*

St John's Press, Auckland, New Zealand 2014
© Priscilla Lowry, 2014

Priscilla Lowry, DipTch. BA, MA (London)
Email: priscilla.silkroad@gmail.com
Website: www.priscillalowry.co.nz

Priscilla Lowry asserts her moral right to be identified as the author of this work.

All rights reserved. No part of this publication may be reproduced or transmitted in any form or by any means electronic or mechanical, including photocopying, recording, information storage or retrieval system, except for brief reviews, without prior permission in writing from the publishers.

The majority of the pictures are the copyright of the author. Every effort has been made to contact copyright holders for all the other images. The author and publisher apologizes for any omissions which they will be pleased to rectify at the earliest opportunity.

ISBN 978-0-9941063-0-8

A catalogue record for this book is available from the National Library of New Zealand.

Cover Illustration: Japanese Geisha wearing Kimono
Design and layout: Nick Turzynski, redinc. Book Design, Auckland

Contents

Prologue 6

Chapter One: Sericulture 9

Chapter Two: Silk in Japan 25

Chapter Three: Silk in Korea 45

Chapter Four: Silk in India 63

Chapter Five: Silk in Thailand 83

Chapter Six: Silk in South-East Asia 99

Chapter Seven: Silk in the Balkan and post-Soviet States 117

Chapter Eight: Silk in the United States 141

Chapter Nine: Silk in England 161

Chapter Ten: Old World, New World 181

Chapter Eleven: Silk in China 201

Chapter Twelve: Science and the Future 223

Chapter Thirteen: Practical: Sewing with Silk 237

Bibliography 252

Index 258

Prologue

This book, *The World of Silk*, is the third in the series on the history of silk. Like the other two, it is complete in itself, and yet it gives the opportunity to expand some of the topics introduced in the earlier books and to add any new research that has become available. It highlights both the similarities and differences between each country and their response to the changing world situation for silk and sericulture. Each chapter focuses on a particular country and explores its history, unique culture and priorities, problems and solutions. Irrespective of the way each has responded, it is still the people who make the story of silk come alive and each person has a special story to tell.

So often someone has said, 'Where does silk come from?' and my response has been India, China or wherever, and they have said, 'No, where does it really come from?' It seems such a cheap answer to say: 'The silk moth lays eggs, the silkworm eats mulberry leaves and spins a cocoon, then turns into a silk moth.' There is just so much more to the story than that, so this book begins with a review of that extraordinary process of change and metamorphosis. This will set the stage and have the added advantage that the part of the story that is common to every country will not have to be repeated.

Following the general pattern of the way silk has spread from ancient China, the first chapters are on silk in Japan, then Korea and India. Silk was well suited to both tropical and subtropical regions, so the next chapters are on Thailand, South-East Asia, Turkey and the post-Soviet states. The dream of establishing sericulture in England

and the United States met with mixed results and that led to their move from sericulture to manufacturing. 'Old World, New World' looks again at the changes to silk and sericulture in Europe and includes Central and South America and South Africa. China has come full circle and is once more the world's leader and this chapter looks at some of the most recent developments. The penultimate chapter draws together some of the exciting scientific developments and explores the future for world silk. Lastly, there is a practical section, as in the other two books, this time on sewing with silk.

Since my return to New Zealand from the UK, and the publication of the second edition of the first book, *Silk: From the Myths and Legends to the Middle Ages*, my silk world has expanded with teaching, workshops and exhibitions, *Silk: Deconstructed, Reconstructed*, 2008 and *Off the Wall*, 2012 with Joan Taylor. There have also been long journeys co-hosting groups of intrepid adventurers across the Old Silk Road, following in the footsteps of Marco Polo, exploring the amazing tombs, textiles and treasures, and meeting the people who are not just involved but dependent for their most basic income on the changing world of international silk and sericulture.

The last ten years have been some of the richest and most rewarding, and I owe so much to my students and colleagues at the University of Auckland. Although technically my topic is Medieval History, silk has always been part of the story, be it women's work, fashion, social change, science, art, illuminated manuscripts, health or business. So it is to my family, friends and colleagues that I offer my heartfelt thanks for all their help and for the endlessly stimulating questioning, exploration and comments.

Today, the sun shines, the tide is in, and the garden sparkles: it has to be the perfect day to share my love of silk with you.

Priscilla Lowry
Devonport, Auckland
April 2014

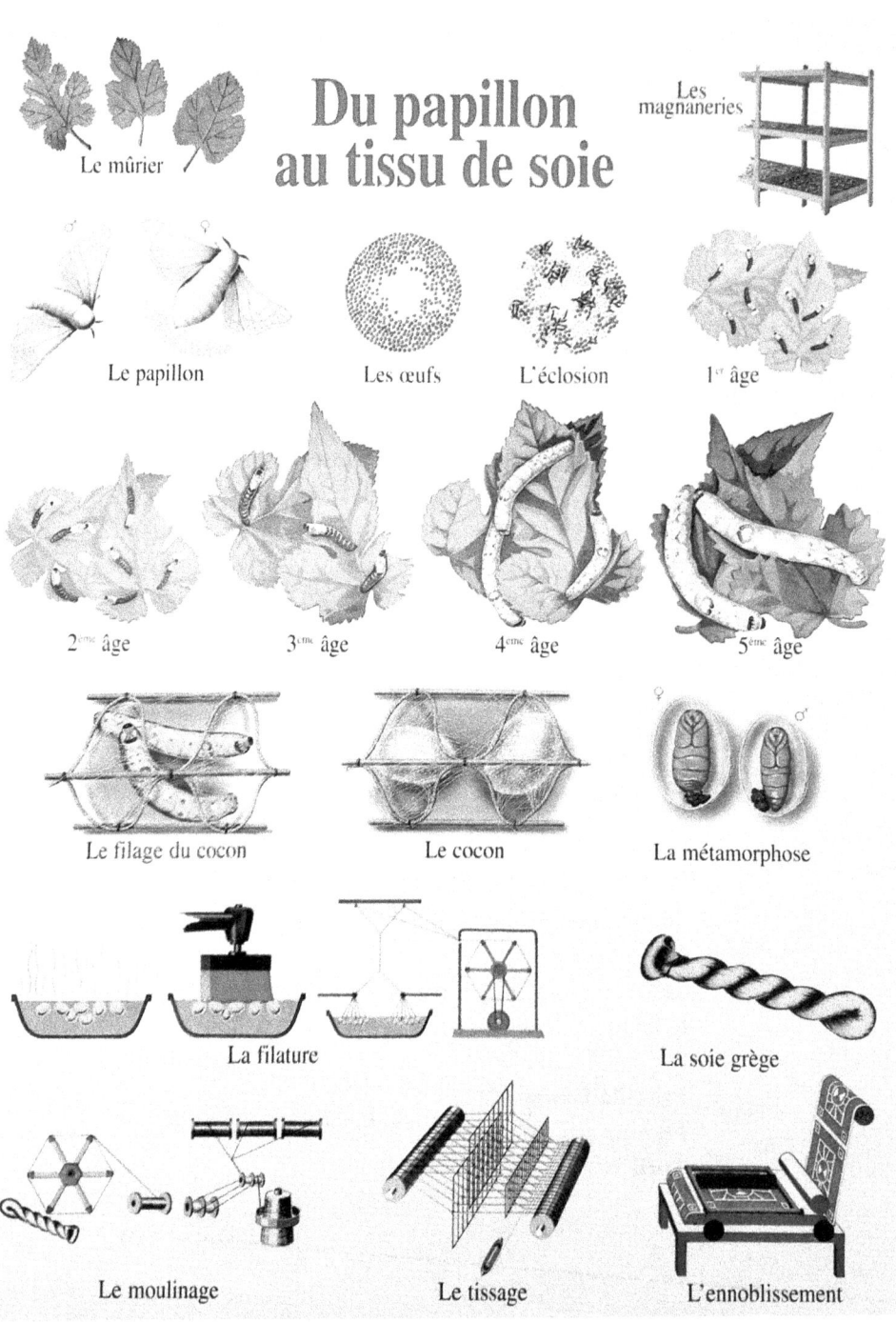

French life cycle poster showing the development of the silkworm from the hatching of the egg, to the spinning of its cocoon, boiling to free the thread from the cocoons, twisting the yarn, throwing, weaving and screen printing the fabric.
Source: La Magnanerie de Saillans, Drome, France

CHAPTER ONE

Sericulture

So, first of all to answer the question, 'Where does silk really come from?' There are two main kinds of silk: the white mulberry silk, known as *Bombyx mori*, which contributes around 95 per cent to world production and the wild, honey-coloured tussah silks.

The production of all silk can be divided into two main areas: the caring and feeding of the silkworms until they spin their cocoons, known as sericulture, and the unwinding of the silk from the cocoons to make thread, weave it into fabric and market it, known as silk manufacture. Both parts can be done in a domestic situation within the home, but silk can also be produced on a massive scale and almost entirely industrialized with large egg hatcheries, artificial feeding and mechanized reeling, throwing, spinning, dyeing, weaving and finishing. In addition, there are all the associated activities and processes, including developing new foodstuffs, fertilizers, scientific discoveries and international marketing.

Watching a wriggling black speck emerge from a miniature egg and grow into a large plump caterpillar, then spin a silk cocoon and disappear, to finally re-emerge as a silk moth, is a miracle. The silkworm has gone through four stages in its life cycle: egg, larva or caterpillar, then pupa or chrysalis, and finally moth. About 20,000 *Bombyx mori* eggs, weighing 11 g, can be contained in a small round box 8 cm in diameter. This is usually all a farmer can manage each hatching or season. Within four weeks, these tiny black specks will have feasted on mulberry leaves and grown to 10,000 times their original size. At every stage they are entirely dependent on their carers to feed and look after them while they go through four periods of eating, sleeping and moulting, known as instars, before they spin their cocoons, complete the pupa stage and emerge as a silk moth.

In warm climates like southern India and Thailand, silkworms are multi-voltine. They tend to be smaller and production can be almost continuous, with up to seven hatchings a year. In cooler climates where the summer is shorter, the silkworms are uni-or bi-voltine. They have only one or two hatchings each year and a period of hibernation or diapause until the weather warms into spring. Usually, the fewer the hatchings, the longer it takes for the silkworms to mature and this results in larger cocoons, giving a greater length of quality silk. Every country is different. The different species and hybrids, along with the varied climate and conditions, the amount and quality of the mulberry and the time it takes to complete the cycle, all make the development of silk in each country unique.

The life cycle

The *Bombyx mori* silk moth is completely domesticated and takes up to 16 hours to lay between 250 and 600 eggs. This coincides with a temperature of between 23 and 27°C, when new leaves start appearing on the mulberry trees. In the egg hatchery, the silk moth will lay her eggs onto special paper or in a tray. After eight days the eggs crack open, and the tiny silkworms will start feeding on the finely shredded fresh mulberry leaves. Initially, like babies they have to be fed every two hours, day and night. After three days they stop feeding, take a nap for 24 hours, and when they wake up, they emit a tiny drop of goo from their tail to attach themselves to a handy leaf. They will then, like a snake, take some hours to moult, by splitting and shedding their outer skin.

After they have moulted, they look for food. A fine mesh is laid over their container and it is covered with freshly picked and finely chopped leaves. The silkworms crawl up through the mesh and start feeding again. The bottom of the container is removed and the half-eaten leaves and detritus discarded. The trays are disinfected, because

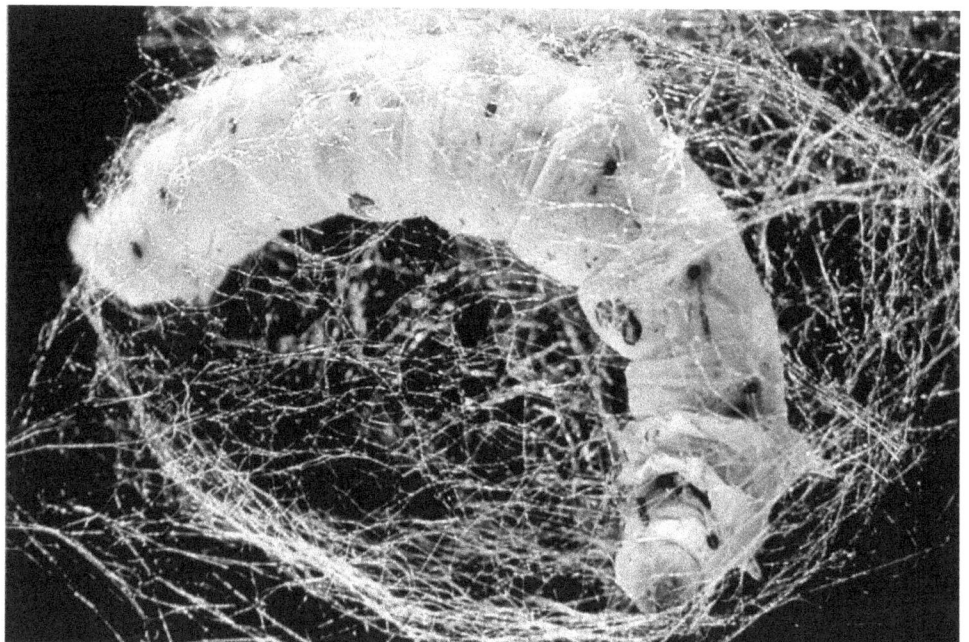
Silkworm spinning its cocoon from the outside, gradually enclosing itself.

hygiene is of prime importance. At each of the four instars when they feed, moult and shed their outer skins, the mesh, container and leaves are a little larger and the silkworms feed for a longer period, until the last instar when they feed continuously for eight to ten days.

Silkworms are fragile creatures and can easily get sick and die. They must be screened to keep out predators like uzi fly, mice or wasps and kept quiet and free from all strong smells like cigarettes or garlic, changes in temperature or humidity. Wilted leaves and droppings must be removed along with dead and diseased silkworms because they can turn chalky or become viscous and contaminate the healthy ones. A very light, gentle touch is required so that the silkworms will flourish. The surprise is the noise. The sound of silkworms eating is like the fizzing of lemonade, and the atmosphere has a warm, slightly sulphurous smell. They now require a very large protected space or container, up to 4 m x 1 m, and a constant supply of large fresh mulberry leaves. In total, it takes between 23 and 27 days from the time the eggs hatch until the silkworms grow to their maximum size of around 10 cm, when they are now ready to spin their cocoons.

The cocoons

The silkworms are now plump and a speckled ashy-grey-green in colour. When they are ready to spin their cocoons, they raise their heads and start looking for a suitable place to attach the first threads. It is all rather experimental at first and the silk is often uneven and breaks, but the silkworm perseveres. It touches its head against a tepee of twigs, bunches of straw or bamboo framework, offered as a support for the cocoons, and begins to spin its silk. Each country uses a different system. This silk floss will form a network to allow the silkworm to settle down to spin a continuous thread, twisting its head in a figure-of-eight movement and working from the outside to the inside. Gradually it encloses itself over 48–72 hours.

The silk thread comes from two long silk glands lying on either side of the alimentary canal. The spinneret is near its mouth and the two fine streams of silk, the *brin*, are held together by a gum called *sericin*. The liquid silk, called *fibroin*, hardens on exposure to air to form a silk filament. It is between 500 and 1600 m long, depending on the silkworm species, the quality of leaves it has eaten and the season. During this period, the silkworm will shed its skin for the last time within the cocoon, leaving it with its brown inner skin, and become a pupa or chrysalis. It is amazing that such a large silkworm can fit inside a small cocoon, but as it spins, it empties its silk glands and contracts. The cocoon takes three to four days to complete and although it is thick and feels firm, it is actually porous, allowing the silkworm, pupa and moth to breathe.

During the next ten-day period of metamorphosis, the silkworm changes from a pupa to a silk moth. The strong jaws, alimentary canal and silk glands that have been so important to it as a silkworm are of no further use and will atrophy. What it will need as a silk moth are wings, compound eyes and functioning gonads to produce eggs or sperm and these will develop within the pupa.

It is essential that the cocoons are sold or stifled before this can happen and the moth breaks the threads of the cocoon to emerge. The cocoons are immediately collected and sent to either the cocoon auction to be sold, or the silk filature where the silk will be reeled off the cocoon. At the same time, the cocoons will be weighed and sorted, and the finest and most perfect of the species will be kept for breeding.

The silk moth

When the silk moth is ready to emerge, it will emit a brown enzyme to dissolve the end of the cocoon, and will scratch away with its front legs until it has made a hole. In commercial sericulture, the top of the cocoon is usually cut off at the pupa stage. Having an open-ended cocoon does not seem to affect the pupa at all and makes it easier for the moth to emerge and save its energy for mating. The silk moth will crawl out of the cocoon and stand on it, gradually filling its ashy-grey wings with air to dry them. Adult moths have a wingspan of up to 5 cm and the females, being full of eggs, have larger bodies. The female moth emits a pheromone, or sex attractant, that gets the neighbouring males very excited. They leap about and flutter, but neither moth can really fly. The male, often with help from the 'silkmother' or attendant, attaches himself to the female, tail to tail, and fertilizes her so she can settle down and lay her eggs.

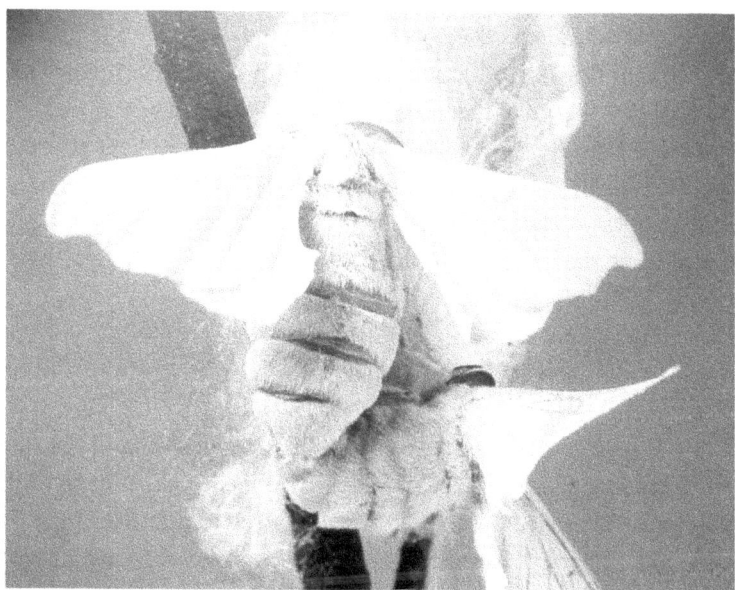

Silk moths mating, tail to tail, with a yellow cocoon in the background, surrounded by the loosely spun silk floss that had attached the cocoon to the supporting twig.

Around 50 moths are placed on a tray. Some countries place each pair of moths onto a sheet of blotting paper, divided into squares and surrounded by a metal ring like an egg poacher, to ensure they stay together and the eggs can be counted and checked.

With mating and egg laying complete, the silk moth's job is done. They cannot see and do not have functioning mouthparts or an alimentary canal so they can neither eat nor drink. Offering them tasty mulberry leaves, drops of dew or cosy nests will have no effect, as they cannot live more than three to five days. They are not designed to. At this stage, the moths are crushed and chemicals added to test for any possible sign of disease, especially the highly infectious pébrine disease. If it is detected, the entire batch of eggs will be destroyed instantly.

Commercial egg hatcheries

The trend these days is to build special hatcheries to ensure that the eggs are laid in controlled and hygienic conditions and are tested to be disease free. The eggs from each mating are labelled, checked and washed in a dilute solution of hydrochloric acid. This kills any pathogens and delays the eggs from hatching. They are then dried, chilled and stored until required. Uni- or bi-voltine eggs may have been laid at the end of the previous season and kept at a temperature below 10°C to hold them over until the next spring. Eggs that are required for hatching now are placed on trays or racks with tender mulberry leaves and cared for until the third instar when they are delivered to the farmer to complete the feeding.

Candling and sorting the cocoons

There is barely ten days between spinning the cocoon and the silk moth emerging, so when the cocoons arrive at the filature or factory, they must be sorted quickly, by spreading them over a strongly lit table to be 'candled' to check the condition of the silkworm inside. The girls work extremely fast, sorting them into three main groups. The top 5–10 per cent of the cocoons that are perfect in every respect and true to that particular species are set aside for breeding.

Covered trays of silk cocoons at the Sericulture Research Station near Bangalore, India. The cocoons will go on to the filature to be reeled or to the driers so they can be stored.

Any poor, weak, damaged, diseased, stained or irregular cocoons are separated out, along with the double ones where the silkworms have got tangled together while spinning their cocoons, and those where the silkworm has died within.

The bulk of the cocoons are either sent on to the reeling factory, or snuffed, dried and stored. Different methods are used for shrinking and drying the pupa inside. Some cocoons are left out in the hot sun or smoked over a fire, some industrialized countries use a slow oven, microwave or steam, and occasionally chemicals are used. Drying kills the pupa and evaporates the moisture that would otherwise cause the cocoons to rot. In some societies, the pupa is a delicacy and after they have been removed from the cocoon, they are freeze-dried and sold in the local market or eaten as a snack with chilli, garlic salt and shallots or roasted in banana leaves with herbs and spices. Oil can also be extracted from the pupa and used in the cosmetic industry. The discarded pupa is a rich source of protein, an excellent fertilizer or feed for the fish or animals.

Reeling

The cocoon contains three grades of silk. The strong outer floss silk tends to be short and irregular, compared with the innermost silk that is extra fine, fragile and broken. The most valued silk is the continuous filament that comes from the middle section. This reeled silk is called raw silk because it still has some of the sericin gum in it. Reeling can be done in the home or village filature or at one of the enormous reeling factories. In the domestic or village setting, a small wood fire is built under a cauldron of hot water and the cocoons soaked to soften the gum to free the silk so it can be unwound. When the thread breaks, it is replaced from another cocoon. It is a highly skilled job to catch the silk thread off each cocoon, and ensure that the same number of ends are joined in to form a consistent and even thread. The process is continuous and monotonous and some domestic reelers work in pairs, with one handling the cocoons in the very hot water, joining in the threads, and the other turning the reel continuously to wind it into skeins. In large commercial filatures, each reeler can look after a bank of steaming basins of soaking cocoons, adding in the fibres and attending to the whirling reels.

Hotan woman boiling cocoons and drawing off the silk fibres to be wound onto a reel, just beyond the boy on her right.

Commercial filature, Suzhou, In the steamy, hot atmosphere the attendant captures the threads off the soaking cocoons so they can be automatically drawn onto the reels above. In the foreground are some cocoons still with their pupa.

Throwing

The reeled silk is too fine and loosely twisted for general use, so it is re-reeled and passed under tension through a *croissure*, or cross, and through a number of 'eyes' to squeeze out the excess water and smooth the fibres. They are then twisted and doubled repeatedly to the desired thickness and strength, a process called throwing. This comes from the Anglo-Saxon word 'thrawn' meaning to twist and is similar to plying. Other processes follow, and the silk is soaked in a hot soap solution, or a mixture made from the ash of a variety of local plants. It is washed, sometimes bleached using a local material like shen shell powder, or more usually hydrogen peroxide, then dried before winding into skeins or onto cones. To make it easier to identify the different grades or styles of silk, the skeins are tinted with a non-permanent dye before they are packaged into 'books' of 25 to 30 tightly twisted skeins. Throwing is a prolonged and highly technical process that determines the quality, weight and final use of the yarn, known as filament silk.

The finest, hard-twist filament silk is called *organzine* and is used on top grade, industrial computerized looms for the warp or lengthwise

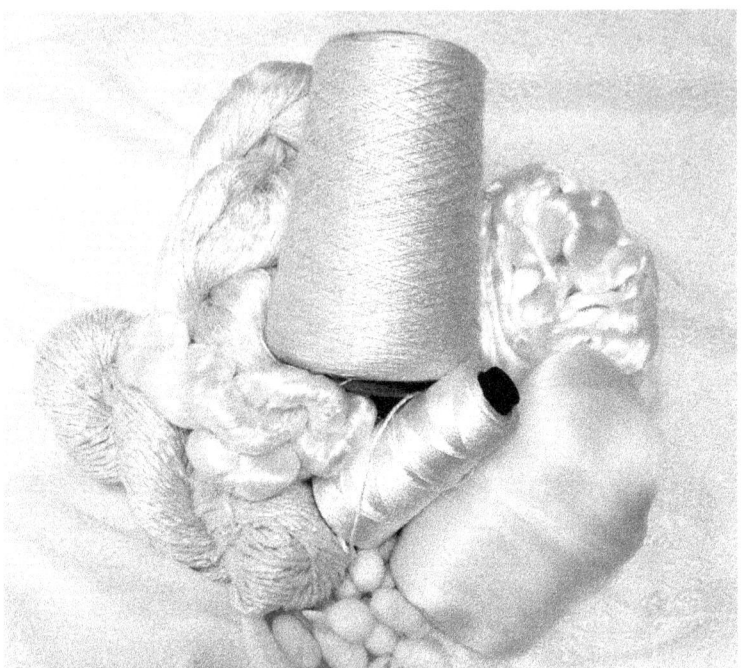

Bombyx mori yarns and fibres, bottom left to right, Handspun silk, skein of filament silk, machine spun and plyed silk, singles on a cop, A1 grade silk tops ready for spinning, cone of thick knitting grade silk, silk filament stiff with its gum or sericin and *Bombyx mori* cocoons, some with their tops cut off allowing the moths to emerge, all lying on a length of cloqué or 'blistered' silk.

threads that take the greatest strain during weaving. Other softer twists are needed to produce a whole variety of woven fabrics. Most of the sericin is removed during the boiling, but some fabrics like crepe de Chine are woven 'in the gum' with at least a percentage of the sericin retained. Finishing processes can also involve stretching, calendering through heated rollers, weighting with metal salts and starching to improve the lustre and reduce creasing.

Waste silk

Everything other than reeled filament silk is called 'waste silk', which is rather a misnomer, because all silk has value. The broken threads, discards from the various machines and all the poor-quality cocoons are collected and the raw silk is washed and dried. The best of this silk is carded and combed. These two separate processes are designed

Waste silk, piled up in Phetchabam, Thailand ready to go to a specialist spinning and weaving factory.

to straighten the short and broken fibres. Carding can be done domestically using hand-carders — two wooden battens with wire hooks that are drawn over the fibres to straighten them and get rid of any extraneous matter. The silk is then formed into a fluffy sausage shape called a *rolag*, ready for spinning. In large factories, the matted silk is fed repeatedly between drum rollers, covered with hooks, to separate and straighten the fibres. The best is cut into uniform lengths of around 10 cm, combed again and separated into different grades. The silk is then packaged and sold to spinners, both domestic and commercial, who spin it into threads of various grades of spun silk.

The poorest quality waste silk is grey and tacky and appears to be of an almost irredeemable quality. These fibres can be little better than floor sweepings, the very last little knotty bits left over from the carding and combing processes. When this waste silk arrives at the factory, the bale is broken apart, often with a pick-axe because the gum has set solid. The broken silk fibres are boiled again to remove more of the sericin, before being dried, carded and tightly spun. It can then be woven into a soft and pliable noil fabric with a dull finish that takes the dye beautifully, and wears like a soft, knobbly cotton. One of noil's distinguishing features are the tiny flecks of black or brown, the last remnants of the silkworm's skin, shed within the cocoon.

Schapping is an old European system, once used on waste silks to remove sericin. The dirty, gummy silk is left to ferment until the sericin can be washed away in a local mountain stream. It produces a superior quality thread but the smell can be terrible and the process has to be done well outside the village.

Other useful waste silks come from the discarded, degummed cocoons left over after the breeding moths have emerged. These cocoons cannot be reeled as their tops have been cut off at the pupa stage, breaking the continuous thread. The whole cocoon is then boiled to soften it, then stretched out over a hooped frame, to make what is known as a *mawata* cap. The top section, cut off from the cocoon, is also boiled, stretched and pegged into a square to form a *mawata* hankie. Both caps and hankies make superb featherweight filling for duvets and jackets.

Wild tussah silk

There are hundreds of species of wild silkworms, and many are from the *Saturniidae* family. In general, wild silk moths are much larger than *Bombyx mori*, some with a wingspan of over 25 cm. They live in forests all over the world, but few produce usable silk. The lovely golden lustre, so characteristic of wild tussah silk, is the result of the silkworm's preference for leaves with a high tannin content, like tannin in tea. Many religions are opposed to killing any living creature and their communities prefer harvesting wild silk where the silk moth has escaped and flown free.

Tussah silkworms are uni- or bi-voltine and their eggs have a period of diapause over the winter. Some of the cocoons are hard and compact and require soaking for six to eight hours in a soda ash solution and steaming for another six hours to soften the sericin. Most cocoons are sold to local merchants who set the price and dominate the industry, although there are movements to support cooperatives where the people can have more control.

Tussah is the general name for wild silks, and India and China have a number of both tropical and temperate breeds that produce commercial quantities of silk. In India especially, the remote jungle

A selection of wild tussah silk cocoons of different colours and textures, some with a peduncle to attach it to the tree on which the silkworm has fed.

people are very protective of both their silkworms and forests, and the men patrol them constantly to scare predators away. India has some semi-domesticated tussah breeds of wild silkworms they call tasar. Some are lime green and live in the thick jungles of Bihar, Madhya Pradesh and Orissa. The *Antheraea paphia* silk moths lay their eggs in 'leaf cups' made of folded leaves, hung in the asan or other native trees.

Some wild silkworms first spin a handle or peduncle, and their cocoons hang on trees like fruit. They are collected and the cocoons tied together into long ropes. When the female moths emerge, they are tied by one leg onto strips of paper and rehung back on the trees. The female moths emit a strong pheromone that will attract a mate from up to 4 km away. After mating, the female moths are taken back indoors to lay their eggs.

Muga, *Antheraea assamensis*, is only produced in Assam in northern India where the silkworm feeds on the local laurel and magnolia trees. Its silk is golden or amber coloured and currently the government is supporting the village of Sualkuchi to develop a species that can be semi-domesticated. Assam also has an eri silk moth that came originally from China and has now spread to Cuba, Egypt, Uruguay and Europe. It is a subspecies of *Samia cynthia ricini*, is semi-domesticated and feeds mainly on castor oil leaves. Its cocoons are either white or brick red and cannot be reeled but are washed, carded and spun like cotton.

China also has many wild silks, and probably the best known are the Chinese tussahs from Shantung (Shandong) and Antung. The *Attacus atlas* spins a very large cocoon that is unreelable, but the silk fibre can be carded and spun. *Antheraea pernyi* is an oak tussah that has been found all over China since the Han dynasty, 206 BCE–220 CE, especially in Liaoning where almost 70 per cent of Chinese tussah silk is produced.

The *Saturnia pyretorum* silkworm is a giant silk moth that has been bred since 885 CE in China and was brought to Hainan Island by the Japanese early in the twentieth century. The silkworms feed mainly on the Liquidambar formosana and Cinnamomum camphora plants. Before the silkworm spins its cocoon, an ancient technique is used to carefully remove the silk glands. They are soaked in vinegar, washed and stretched. They are used for leads on fishing lines and the protein-packed silkworms are sometimes eaten as a delicacy.

Tensan silk comes from the wild Japanese oak silk moth *Antherea yamamai*, and has been semi-domesticated in Japan for more than 1500 years. It produces green- or yellow-tinted cocoons, depending on how much light the pupa was exposed to. It has spread to Taiwan and parts of Russia and China, and in some places has become a pest, but in Japan, where labour costs are high and sericulture has almost disappeared, it is cultivated and used for a few precious ritualistic items.

Mulberry orchards

The mulberry can be a tree or a bush. They are hardy and versatile and can grow wild or be cultivated in orchards. They will grow in most areas, in between other crops, provide shade for people and animals, and produce delicious fruit. Although there are hundreds of varieties, the *Morus alba*, or white mulberry, is the silkworm's first choice. The tougher black mulberry, *Morus nigra*, was grown in England during the reign of James I, 1601–25, but the silkworms did not thrive. The *Morus multicaulis* was promoted in America around 1850 as the perfect tree for sericulture but caused a financial panic when it failed, a situation similar to tulipmania

Mulberry leaves & fruit, with a silkworm feeding on Morus alba leaves, the preferred mulberry and showing its fruit in various stages of ripeness.

in Europe two hundred years before.

These days, moriculture, or growing mulberry trees, is a separate and highly specialized part of sericulture. The many hybrid species are grown from seed or cuttings to suit each climate or soil, and for the needs of the silkworm at each stage. Mulberry trees take some years to establish before they can be systematically picked to feed the silkworms. The leaves are usually harvested in the early morning, before dawn when it is still cool. Machines are rarely used other than on large commercial orchards, and it is a constant battle to pick enough of the right leaves and get them to the silkworms before the leaves wilt. Men and boys usually care for the mulberry, grafting and weeding, fertilizing and later picking the leaves or sawing off the branches and delivering them to the rearing houses. Sericulture involves the whole family, and in most successful communities, the profits are returned to sustain the income and lifestyle of the whole community.

Over the centuries, each country or district has cared for its silkworms and adapted its resources to fit both the silkworms and their carers. The different breeds or hybrids, the climate, land, culture and people made for an enormous variety, and these differences form the fascinating story of *The World of Silk*.

Furisode kimono with Paulownia Tree and Phoenixes, late 18th c, shibori tie-dyed with silk and metallic thread embroidery on red-orange figured silk satin.
Source: Los Angeles County Museum of Art, gift of Miss Bella Mabury

CHAPTER TWO

Silk in Japan

Exquisite, gorgeous silk! So much a part of our vision of Japan with its sumptuous kimono, decorated with fragile orange blossom, sprays of autumn leaves, pine cones and fans.

But Japan did not always know the secrets of silk, and in 200 BCE it was still a capital offence in China to divulge how the precious thread was unwound from the silk cocoons. Perhaps the knowledge travelled to Japan when a Chinese prince was exiled for some misdemeanour and sought asylum in Japan. Perhaps he offered silkworm eggs as a priceless gift in exchange for sanctuary, or in revenge, angry at his treatment by the Emperor or court? Other accounts tell of wars and include an exchange of silk workers, captured and taken as slaves from China and Korea. A Japanese chronicle tells of a Chinese emperor who had included silkworm eggs among the gifts he had exchanged with a Japanese envoy. The Japanese had long known about luxurious silk fabrics. What they did not know was how the silkworm was cared for, to enable it to spin a cocoon suitable for unreeling. This was the secret of sericulture that was so highly prized.

The value of this information was immediately recognized in Japan and sericulture was placed under the control of the Emperor's trusted officials. The Imperial Silk Workshop was set up using Chinese methods and gradually the techniques were mastered to produce exquisite fabrics for the court. The nobles delighted in the softness, lustre and luxury of silk that fitted in so well with the fine aesthetic feelings of the Japanese hierarchy.

In areas where the climate was suitable for growing both mulberry trees and silkworms, the local lord directed that his peasants be trained in all aspects of sericulture. It was seen as women's work because it could be handled within the home, alongside all the other chores and responsibilities of feeding and looking after the family and animals. It was labour-intensive and all the family, from the youngest child to the elderly, were at times involved in caring for the silkworms. The family valued sericulture because it brought in a little cash to pay their expenses. For the authorities, it was a reliable source of tax revenue.

Even after the establishment of sericulture in Japan, the wearing of silk was severely controlled and restricted to people within the inner court. Most people wore clothes made from cotton or hemp in either a poncho style, made up of two pieces of woven fabric with a neck opening, or a jacket with either pants or a skirt. The Japanese were initially very impressed by the Imperial Chinese dress code and the refinements of the court, but gradually China and Japan drew apart and followed their own artistic traditions.

By late in the Asuka period, 552–710, it was fashionable for men to tattoo and paint their faces to reinforce their family identity and rank. The nobility adopted the Chinese jacket, with its left to right closing, a long skirt, lacquered shoes, hats and bamboo combs in their hair. Women wore baggy pants and a long loose jacket with a tiny skirt, like a ceremonial apron, worn at the back. The last vestiges of this skirt still remain in the formal bridal clothes worn by a Japanese princess.

The Japanese kimono, like the Chinese jacket, crossed from left to right, the men's way in the West. It was considered very poor form and a sign of barbarism to cross any garment from right to left, unless the wearer was moving from one 'profound state' to another. Traditionally, a corpse was dressed in white with the robe crossing to the left, indicating their movement to the afterlife. In the same way, a bride crossed her robe to the left as she signalled the end of her life as a maiden and moved from her family and single status to that of a married woman in her husband's home.

During the Nara period, 710–794, silk gowns took a romantic turn

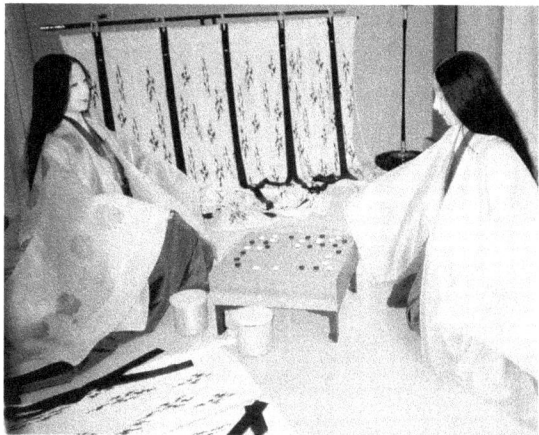

Above: Ladies playing Go wearing their *juni hitoe*, or 'twelve unlined robes', eighth–eleventh century, the epitome of elegant, static grace, and subtly of mood, built up layer by layer in beautiful fine silk.

Left: Ancient patchwork kimono, loosely tied at the waist and covered with a long *haori* coat, Yokohama Museum.

when the court ladies, to emphasise their wealth, style, refinement and leisure, started wearing over their pants not one but a number of sheer silk gowns. The subtle shading and layers showed at the cuffs and front opening, combining colours in the most poetic way, and presenting an exquisite idea of leaves fluttering in autumn, plum blossom or birds' wings. This was known as *juni hitoe*, or 'twelve unlined robes'. By the Heian period between 794 and 1185, up to 20 robes were being worn at once and a whole raft of rules and customs had evolved. The knowledge was only available to the elite in the innermost circles of court life. It was a static grace, a picture of perfection, as it was not easy to conduct one's life and keep each layer in position, with just a suggestion of each colour showing at the edge.

It was during this time in the eleventh century that Murasaki Shikibu wrote *The Tale of Genji*. It was written in the form of a diary with poems, and has become a classic. It tells a delightful story of a woman's experience in the closed and sophisticated world of the Emperor's court. Full of political and sexual intrigue, vice and manipulation, it draws its tale from both life in the court and the harsh realities of provincial Japan. The book includes descriptions of beautiful silk clothes and silk-stringed instruments. It enchanted its readers, as it was full of magic and delight that drew them into a lifestyle that was quite outside the range of most women's experience.

The samurai period

The Muromachi period, 1336–1573, saw the introduction of new silk fabrics, especially silks from Ming China. These included *kinran*, and a golden brocade called *donsu*, a silk damask called *chirimen*, a heavy crepe, and *kaiki*, a flat woven silk taffeta. The Japanese valued beautiful fabrics very highly and felt that gems, silver and gold were cold in comparison. They relished the lovely feel, the subtle colour combinations and the refinement of designs featuring birds and flowers. The most exquisite Japanese silks had been made in the Imperial workshops, but during the early Muromachi period, this monopoly collapsed and the development of silk textiles moved out of the control of the court and into private hands.

The samurai had originally been provincial warriors attached to their lord, the *damyo*, but over time they increased in power and

Man's padded jacket with paualoni leaves, short rounded sleeves and *mon*, or family crest, on each shoulder.

influence. They became an elite military class, with specific duties and privileges and a strict code of honour. They wore ceremonial silk gowns and used silk for cords and ties on their armour. Under their leader the Shogun, they took control of the government and moved the Imperial capital away from Kyoto, believing that it had become increasingly decadent. They instituted more stringent controls over the people to demonstrate social differences and personal status, including sumptuary laws to control articles of dress, style, material, hairstyles and items used in the home. Merchants and artisans were instructed not to wear padded silk clothing, and their wives were prohibited from wearing fancy dyed silks, heavy with embroidery. Farmers and other workers were forbidden to wear any striped, patterned and brightly coloured materials, especially silk. The samurai were particularly critical of the *juni hitoe*, or 'twelve unlined robes'. Now the ladies of the warrior class were directed to wear only a single gown, or at most, two or three over-gowns.

In response to samurai controls, there developed an aesthetic known as *eki*. This was very chic, a superb understatement. It severely limited ostentation and display and kimono outwardly conformed. A heavy silk crepe in a narrow range of dull colours was often chosen. Only simple patterns of varying stripes, dots and checks

Group of kimono silks. Subdued *eki*-style silk, *shibori* dyed green crepe, 'dappled faun' dyed tussah silk, printed satin twill, printed *chirimen* silk.

were permitted, but luxury could be exploited secretly by having the lining exquisitely hand-painted or made in a brilliant exotic silk. It suggested a double standard of modesty and ostentation, secretive and inviting subterfuge, and in the end both men and women's clothes could be just as expensive and elaborate as before.

For centuries, a woman's long glossy black hair had been her crowning glory. As women started putting up their hair, the short sleeves on the kimono developed into long, swinging sleeves and women gradually stopped wearing wide-legged pants under their open gowns. Japanese garments do not have buttons, zips or domes and as the robes needed to be closed firmly and hitched and folded up to the right length, a tie around the waist replaced the ancient apron. Over time, this cord was covered with a wider sash called the *obi*. By the sixteenth century the *obi* was up to 15 cm wide for men and 30 cm for women. It became fashionable to choose a stiffer, heavier, tapestry-weave silk that could be folded into many exotic shapes. The *obi* was the one area where the colours, width and patterns could be influenced by fashion trends and reflect the social position of the wearer. It now became more elaborate and the focus of the garment. Over the years, questions have been raised as to whether or not fashion mirrors social values, oppression and control, noting the way the kimono wraps tightly around the body, flattening the bust and restricting free and active movement. Many Japanese women may have appeared controlled and oppressed but they have always wielded considerable power within the home and the women's world.

In 1603, Ieyasu Tokugawa became Shogun and established a new government around the court in Kyoto, controlling nearly 300 feudal clans all over the country. The Edo period that followed brought internal peace to Japan for two and a half centuries. It was a consumer society with every kind of luxury available and once more fabrics were blatantly luxurious. At its height, at the beginning of the eighteenth century, there were 10,000 employees working 7000 looms, including draw-looms with a draw-boy on the top pulling the strings, needed to make the most exotic gold and silver silk brocades.

Meiji Restoration

In 1867, the Shogun returned power to the Emperor, the Meiji Restoration was realized and the government moved the capital from Kyoto to Tokyo. The Meiji Emperor was passionate in his desire to make Japan the equal of Europe and to catch up in the shortest possible time. He believed that if his people could emulate European styles of dress and include even a modest item, such as a watch or waistcoat, it would show that the wearer was modern and enlightened. Japanese men were required to adopt a Western suit when doing business and women were encouraged to wear Western dress and to learn to dance. It became known as the Rokumeikan period, named after a very chic dancehall in the International Sector. There were cultural exchanges, and knitting became a craze in Japan. In Europe, artists were drawn to Japanese styles that

Japan embraces foreign dress 1887. Two ladies doing their best to conform to the new edict, even to playing a western organ to accompany their singing. Japanese lyrics were sung to western tunes and were popular during the Rokumeikan period.
Source: Museum of Fine Arts, Boston.

influenced painting and design. Japanese influence could also be seen in clothes, gardens, architecture and food.

Many Japanese women found it very difficult to emerge from the anonymity and security of their homes into mixed company and wear foreign, full-skirted dresses with their low décolletage. Inevitably perhaps, the drive to modernize was followed by a limited reversion to local styles and the kimono made a comeback. Gradually, men accepted a Western style for work while still wearing kimono at home. Suits were more comfortable when sitting on chairs at the office, but at home where tables were low and people sat on the floor, kimono just felt better. Smart young women who wore Western dress to go to the office could see little reason to wear the more complex and restricting kimono, even at home. The wearing of Western clothes spread to include military and factory uniforms. Schoolgirls wore a mixture, with a midi blouse and a long traditional skirt, while the housebound housewife made little or no changes at all.

The Meiji period had seen the abolition of feudal regulations, and some small drapery shops grew quickly into larger department stores offering more and more Western goods. The Takashinmaya Store expanded with a mass market for silk kimonos, drapery and *obi*. It concentrated on stripes, *ikat*, and single-colour plain weaves, woven on a traditional treadle loom. Timeless Japanese designs were printed on the different silks along with *yuzen* and other more complex printing techniques and powerful new chemical dyes offered new and sometimes raucous colour combinations. The introduction of modern fibres and fabrics gradually pushed the far more expensive silk kimono into the special category of art or investment. They were now only worn on important occasions like New Year celebrations, graduations, weddings and funerals. This led to kimono made of chemically dyed, man-made fibres becoming available as cheap ready-mades in the shops.

Kimono

Traditionally, the New Year celebration of the year when a girl turned 13 was the occasion for wearing a *furisode*, her first kimono, with long, swinging sleeves. Usually it was light and colourful, patterned

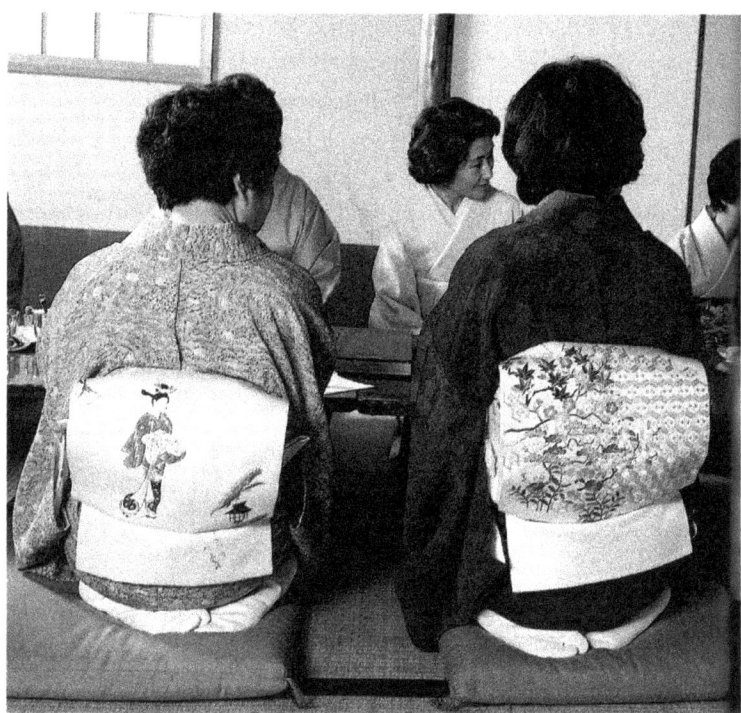

Ladies wearing kimono with *obi*. It is still popular for ladies who practise tea ceremony, flower arranging and other traditional arts to wear kimono.

throughout, with a wide tight *obi* that flattened her chest and covered her middle from underarm to waist. When she married, she gave up the girlish long sleeves and wore a shorter sleeved kimono, called a *tomesode*, often in more subtle colours. The pattern was now restricted to the shoulders and towards the hem and her *obi* sat a little more comfortably. An older woman chose still more sober colours, sometimes black with a small pattern, and a richly painted, embroidered or dyed design only in the lower sector and hem.

Today, kimono is worn by many leisured older women who practise traditional Japanese arts, such as the tea ceremony, classical music or flower arranging. A relatively informal kimono might be made in a dull-finished shantung or other raw silk. A more formal kimono is indicated by lustrous silk and restrained colour and pattern. The addition of the *mon*, or family crest, on each shoulder at the front and centre back further heightens the formality. These may be worn on occasions where an informal kimono would be quite inappropriate. The *mon* is like a round seal containing a stylized representation of flowers, birds, animals, stars or waves. It is a point of recognition for a noble family, usually handed down through the matriarchal line from mother to daughter.

The classic kimono evolved within strict rules. The sensitive interaction of colour, pattern and decoration contain hidden messages reflecting the age, gender and refinement of the wearer, and the status, wealth and occupation of the family, especially the most senior male. A silk kimono is commissioned like a work of art from a specialist shop. The woman is accompanied by women friends and relatives who ensure that she makes the right choices. This takes time and cannot be rushed, so an appointment has to be made with the principal, a kimono expert, and the customer is guided at all stages.

In the kimono shop, tissue paper protects little bolts of white silk fabric, stacked on open shelves. The silks are of different weights and weaves and all are around 35 cm wide and approximately 12 m long. One by one, each bolt of fabric is opened and compared, its texture and woven pattern considered. The resident designer then makes suggestions as to the colour that the silk is to be dyed. There are many restrictions: some pale or light colours are only suitable for young girls or casual occasions, and only married or older women wear black. Tension mounts as to the choice of pattern, its placement and the techniques to be used, including any printing or embroidery. Popular dyeing techniques include *yuzen*, a form of resist dyeing, or *shibori* where the fabric is stitched and tied, and *kanoka*, in which the whole fabric is covered with tiny, tied dots.

The sense of balance, harmony, design and appropriateness of the kimono are discussed at length as well as its cost. A commissioned silk kimono outfit could cost more than $10,000 and the family honour is at stake because even today, the beauty of the kimono is a subtle but public declaration as to the status, wealth and power of the family. It has the advantage also of being timeless, and on each occasion that it is returned to the kimono specialist for cleaning, it will be taken apart completely, cleaned and hand sewn again, and its size adjusted if required. The excess fabric is never cut away, just folded into the seams so that it can be refitted to accommodate the changing figure.

Family at Yokohama, The young mother is wearing a full kimono, with obi, obi tie and scarf, and carrying a little bag, this particular Sunday morning in Yokohama.

In the colder months between late September and April, a lined kimono called *awase* is worn. It is often a heavy silk crepe de Chine, lined with a lighter crepe or silk mousseline. The lightweight unlined *hitoe* or *ro* kimono is worn in summer from May to early September. There are hundreds of designs and they are chosen for their seasonal significance. This may be pine for January, irises for May, cherry blossom for spring, little trout for summer, and maple leaves in autumn. Many colour combinations are considered to be appropriate, such as pale-green layered over deep wine, embroidered with pine cones for January. Some patterns are obviously part of the natural world, but others like fans, cartwheels and bridges are considered to be auspicious. A more casual kimono, a *yutaka*, often dyed with indigo, is the favourite. Unlike Western fashion, Japanese design is chosen not to stand out, but to be subtle, to harmonize with one's surroundings, both natural and social, and to be appropriate for the season and event.

The geisha

The geisha follows a traditional and valued vocation. She is a highly skilled professional. She begins as an apprentice geisha, a *maiko*, and over many years she will be trained and guided in every aspect of her work to be an intelligent and exquisite companion, able to entertain and enchant the businessman. She will require many and varied kimono during her working life. Every part of her outfit is prescribed and must be understood and adhered to if she is not to cause derision or offence. She takes special care at all times with the many requirements relating to the colour, pattern, design, seasonality and appropriateness of her kimono. For special occasions she will wear her 'top drawer' kimono, her *desho*, literally her 'going out wear'. This is a trailing black kimono with five crests and an exquisite pattern, dyed and embroidered towards the hem. She will also have a range of less formal kimono. These are very similar to any other woman's special kimono, but with subtle differences.

Geisha and *maiko* are wearing nearly identical 'top drawer' kimono, except the young *maiko's* wooden-soled shoes, or zori, are higher, as is her *obi*. The white make-up and elaborate black wig with delicate hair ornaments along with the deep fall of the geisha's collar at the back are signs of their profession as refined, professional entertainers.

Under the kimono the geisha wears a wrap-around underskirt and cotton bodice. The kimono is kept closed by a stiff, formal *obi*, tied tightly around the waist and formed into an exotic 'boxy pouf', or other shape at the back. An *obi* scarf is tucked in around the top, with an *obi* cord around the middle, and an *obi*-dome covering the knot. This is the only piece of jewellery she wears, other than a watch. Her collar, the *eri*, forms an extra lining around the neck. On her feet she wears white cotton slit-toed *tabi* socks and *zori* wooden clogs. Her hair is hidden under a black lacquered wig, embellished with jewelled hair decorations, and her face is very carefully made up with the traditional white mask, black-ringed eyes and small red mouth. It is not until she turns around that the main difference becomes apparent. The *eri* collar of the geisha dips sharply down at the back, revealing the nape of the neck which has for centuries been considered by the Japanese as a highly erotic zone.

The geisha wears her kimono and *obi* with a particular style and flair, and turns it into an art form. On one level she can be credited with keeping the traditions of kimono alive, although no self-respecting woman would ever wear her kimono in such a way, especially showing the nape of her neck, something that proclaims the woman as a geisha.

The Japanese silk girls

The Japanese silk girls were another group of working girls. It began as part of the drive to bring Japan into the modern world, making it a strong country, able to compete with the West. The Meiji Emperor recognised that Japan had silk, a product that was highly sought after and valued by the West, so in consultation with his interior ministers, a plan was devised to centralize and modernize the silk industry. The problems included unregulated production and distribution and the erratic quality of yarn produced in the villages.

A team of people were trained to go into silk-growing districts and talk first to the village leader and then to the senior man in each household. They were to sell the idea that honour could be brought to the village and to the family if their daughter was chosen to go

Sericulture farmhouse in Gunma Province. The whole top floor of the house is given over to caring for the silkworms. The mulberry trees along with the neatly stripped stems are cut, stacked and dried for winter firewood. In 1995 there were only three remaining farmers in the district doing sericulture.

to train in one of the new factories, called a silk filature. The costs involved in transporting, housing and keeping the girls while they were in training would gradually be paid out of the girl's wages and any surplus money would be sent back to the head of the family. It was an enticing offer, and many peasant families with too many daughters and mouths to feed leapt at the chance, not really appreciating that their daughter would be under a strict contract and control for many years.

The first group of young girls were fêted and made to feel very special, and their families felt privileged that they were doing their bit to rebuild Japan into a strong and forward-thinking nation. As more girls were required, there were examples of strong-arm tactics, bribery and fees being siphoned off by agents and certainly, many fathers did not really understand the contracts they were signing.

The girls quickly discovered that they had to work between 13 and 14 hours a day, sometimes up to 17 hours, under a fixed-pay system. The girls were graded daily as to their skill and speed, so their wages fluctuated, but the company allowed only a certain amount for wages and competition was encouraged for that money. Part of their salary was deducted to repay their initial contract, part paid for their mandatory board in the dormitory, and if there was any over, it was sent back to their family. In the village, the family's honour and reputation was at stake so everyone tried to work harder and the average output rose — but only the factory owner benefited.

Although there were many desperately unhappy girls in the factories, there were others who loved the work, appreciating the freedom from the drudgery of farm work and the obligation to marry an uneducated local boy with the possibility of repeated pregnancies. The vast majority of girls accepted the back-breaking work, their hands constantly in very hot water, the long hours, harsh controls and bleak living conditions in the dormitories. They enjoyed the companionship and eventually even had a little pocket money once the initial fees had been repaid.

For some, the horror of having to return to the village at the end of their contract was sufficient to draw them towards the deeper companionship of a 'girls' club'. This was similar to becoming a Beguine, a celibate working woman in a close community, and her commitment was similar to a marriage. These girls' houses were very common. Once her debts were repaid and she could leave the factory dormitory, she might choose to take the final step in becoming part of this community and go through the 'haircutting ceremony' sealing her commitment. Usually the girls chose houses where there were women they had known and lived with in the mother-house and bonds frequently grew deeper over the years. It took enormous strength and courage to make this decision, to reject marriage and cut themselves off, despite pressure from their families, friends and factory managers. Many families treated their daughters as social outcasts because they had expected them to keep sending wages home or to return to the farm, to marry and look after them.

Silk filatures and mills

One of the first silk mills to be redeveloped as a model silk filature was at Tomioka in Gunma Province, about 100 km northwest of

Tokyo. It was established in 1872 by the Meiji government to teach modern silk-reeling methods using machinery newly imported from France. Japanese silk at the time had a poor reputation for quality, and this reflected badly on Japan as an international silk supplier. Initially, there were 150 silk-reeling machines, containing 300 basins, employing around 400 women to operate them. Wada Ei, 1857–1929, was one of the girls recruited in 1873 to become a silk worker at the Tomioka filature. Her life became well known when her diary was published, telling the story of her time at the silk mill. She was the daughter of a samurai and under contract before becoming one of the trainers in her own prefecture. The government awarded Wada Ei and her colleagues medals for their skill and dedication with the special title 'Women Spinners' Victory Battalion'. She later went to the Saijo Village Silk Reeling Factory at Matsushiro in Nagano Prefecture, where she married an army officer. He died in 1913 from wounds sustained in the Russo-Japanese war. She began writing the *Tomioka Diary* many years later and it was published by her son after her death, leading some historians to doubt its total authenticity.

Gradually, the quality of the silk produced by the Tomioka mill improved and it began to enjoy a good reputation overseas, but the business was always in debt even after constant efforts to reduce costs. The government decided to privatize the mill and transferred the business to the Mitsui Finance Group in 1893, the first of a series of changes of ownership until it was finally closed as a working mill in March 1987, but retained as a historical site.

Nishijin in Kyoto was also an old and important silk centre. Kyoto had a very large No theatre and geisha community so there was a constant demand, both locally and internationally, for exquisite silks. By 1872 the traditional textile trades, widely dispersed throughout the countryside, were in decline. Between 1881 and 1885, Japan suffered a serious depression so the Meiji government introduced radical new ideas and European technology. Promising students were sent to France to learn new methods, especially to Lyon where the Jacquard looms were causing such a stir. Some of the students had great difficulties with the language and customs of the Europeans, and found the freer behaviour of the local students quite shocking, so different from Japan.

Tomioka silk factory, very superior, clean and light, but still the girls were under a harsh contract with long hours, competing for limited pay.
Source: J P Devoize with the authorization of Mr Verney

Recovery was aided by a large order from the Imperial Palace for silk fabrics woven on the newly imported Jacquard looms. They used chemical dyes and blended European rococo styles with traditional Japanese designs. Design schools were set up to produce the pattern cards required by the Jacquard looms and production increased as the new looms took only half as long to weave a complex length of cloth as the old system, which had used a draw-loom with a draw-boy pulling the strings.

From the beginning of the twentieth century, to increase self-sufficiency, the government set about controlling all areas of sericulture, mulberry production, reeling, throwing and weaving, but there were problems when traditional methods were in conflict with the new technology. The hand-looms were not suitable for complicated figured and patterned silks and the Jacquard loom was far too expensive for the individual owner to buy. As a result, most of the weavers wove plain white silk that was in high demand. The *Debata*, or Putting Out system, was still common. In this arrangement, the company or master craftsman owned the yarn and the loom that was set up in the individual weaver's home. The weaver tied the yarn and the card chain onto the loom and did not pay rent, but everything, including the final product, belonged to the master or company. The weavers were paid for the work by the scroll piece or belt. Every member of the family contributed and in 1984, 71 per cent of all looms in Nishijin were still worked in the *Debata* system.

Special dyeing units were set up to use chemical dyes, but the science of dyeing was not well understood and if the colours were unstable, the silk was rejected by the international market. There were instances of inadequate quality control and the silk content being less than 100 per cent and therefore not true to label, which further discredited Japanese silk abroad.

The government later tried to regenerate the Nishijin Trading Company, which resulted in a very different industry. The new company was to be a cooperative, which should have made it more acceptable to the workers but in fact alienated many of them as it was not a style of employment that they understood or valued. The government opened additional ports to assist the industry, but these policies actually took business away from Nishijin. Silk thread became scarce and expensive and many of the silk weavers left to look for other work. The final straw, as far as the remaining workers were concerned, was the directive to close down their guild, the Nakama, which had been functioning intermittently since 1745.

Around 1865 a disease called pébrine had rocked the world. It decimated sericulture in every silk-growing country except Japan. It was highly infectious and attacked the silkworms causing them to wither and die before they had a chance to spin their cocoons and emerge as fully developed silk moths ready to lay eggs. It was not until the French scientist Louis Pasteur found a method of isolating and identifying the disease that the worldwide silk industry began to slowly rebuild, but most countries never regained the production they had lost. During that time Japan set the world standard for disease-free eggs and was the only country able to supply the world market.

To safeguard its enormous financial commitment to the silk industry, successive Japanese governments kept the price of silk artificially high to recompense their farmers and keep them loyal politically.

The hostess at a health spa in Gunma Province plans the meal with her guest. The guest is wearing an indigo dyed yukata, supplied by the guesthouse to be worn after soaking in the hot, natural spa. The house, high up in the mountains had originally been an old silk establishment.
Source: Y Nobeta.

Gradually, the standard of living rose, and elderly farmers died, but their families did not want to continue with sericulture. Silkworms are finicky, fragile creatures, susceptible to many diseases, and require unrelenting care for an unpredictable income. With fewer farmers involved in sericulture, there was no need politically to support them and the artificial price controls were removed. When China repeatedly reduced the price, Japanese silk could no longer compete on the world market. Today, sericulture as an agricultural crop has all but disappeared, but fine silk using Chinese yarn is still woven for a very discerning market.

Couple wearing traditional hanbok. A woman wearing a short, tight-fitting jeogori (jacket) and a chima skirt held out with many petticoats. With his baji trousers, the man is wearing a durumagi or traditional topcoat.
Source: Sunny Yang

CHAPTER THREE
Silk in Korea

Korea is said to have a history of over 4300 years. The earliest people were nomads who sheltered in caves, hunted wild animals, fished and gathered edible roots and berries for food. They used skins, tree bark, leaves and other fibres to make their clothing, with dried intestines for thread and needles made from the fine bones of fish and birds. Archaeological relics have been found, including axe heads, scrapers, jewellery and spindles for spinning. Loom weights, dated to around 2000 BCE, have been found at the Gonggui-ri site in Pyong-an Province in Northern Korea.

During the Bronze Age, known as the Ancient Choson period, and the later Iron Age, the nomadic Puyo people settled around the river basins of Northern Korea. As their weapons and organization became more effective, they began to cultivate the land and plant rice, hemp and mulberry trees to feed the silkworms to make *myungju*, or silk. Sericulture seems to have developed also in the Mahan area, between 300 and 200 BCE, with the arrival from China of immigrants, colonizers and slaves who were experienced in sericulture. *The Chronology of Korean History* notes that the Puyo people of this period wore coarse white undyed jackets and trousers with straw sandals and their hair drawn into a topknot, or *sangtu*.

Long sleeved dancers, Muyong-chong mural painting. Men and women are all wearing baji pants, the women under their pleated chima skirts and the men with their durumagi jackets, Tomb of Dancers in Guknaesong (Tung-gu) Koguryo 5thc.

The tombs at Gogureo, now in modern China, offer a valuable record of clothing styles worn in Korea between 100 BCE and 300 CE. Painted murals show dancers wearing full pleated skirts and *durumagi*, overcoats with extremely long flapping sleeves that waved as they danced. Men and women were warmly dressed for the cold weather, wearing long, tight-sleeved jackets with left-to-right closing in the Chinese style, short, tight trousers and riding boots. In the paintings, some men are wearing *baji* trousers, with *hwa* boots or silk and leather shoes, a hat and a *dae*, or girdle, coloured according to rank. Some noble women are wearing what looks like beautiful silk garments, with precious jewellery, bracelets, rings and necklaces. Jackets varied in length but over time they became shorter, and both men and women wore wrap-around skirts that developed into the *chima*. These two garments, the short jacket and gathered skirt, would later develop into the *hanbok*. This was an abbreviation of the term *Han-guk boksik*, or 'Korean attire', and became the national dress.

Since the Neolithic period, embroidery has been an art and a highly valued skill. The ideas probably originally came from China and by the first century BCE, gold and silver leaf was incorporated to make the embroidery sparkle. Leisured noblewomen were expected to be skilled needlewomen, having been taught to sew from childhood. Gradually, as they learnt these techniques, they became experts at making the exquisite ceremonial robes.

By the second century BCE, the Chinese had already infiltrated into the Korean peninsula, bringing their culture and setting up military colonies. In 108 BCE, the Chinese Emperor Wu-di sent additional troops in a final attempt to subdue the people of the peninsula. A first-century CE Korean document records requests to supply large quantities of fine silks in reparation, so the silk industry was almost certainly well established by this time.

The three kingdoms, 57 CE–668 CE

Despite the Chinese military invasion, the local hierarchy still recognised and admired China as a sophisticated and ancient society. Gifts of Chinese hats, silk robes, embroidered fabrics and rank badges were highly valued and the local officials continued to wear them when conducting important political or trade negotiations. When the Chinese were finally expelled, they left open one border trading post at Lelang, an important conduit through which trade, goods and ideas flowed. Tombs at Lelang have yielded valuable finds including exquisite silk textiles. Tomb number 212 contained the remains of a husband and wife, both dressed in Chinese-style silk garments and wrapped in silk burial cloths, surrounded by precious items, including little bolts of silk.

Queen Seondeok, who reigned from 632 to 647, was queen in her own right, being the oldest child of King Chinp'yong. She held her authority through what was known as the hereditary bone rank system, similar to degrees of royal blood. The kingdom at the time had no prejudice against women rulers and Confucianism, which is strongly male oriented, currently had little influence. Queen Seondeok was pro-T'ang and is remembered for the way she constantly sought peace for her country, promoted education and built temples and an observatory. Graves of the time have revealed gorgeous jewels, pendants, crowns, earrings and necklaces.

Queen Seondeok was followed by Queen Jindeok, who reigned 647–654. With the help of her general, Kim Yushin, she was able to strengthen Silla's defences and greatly improve her kingdom's relations with T'ang China. Her efforts laid the foundation for the unification of the three kingdoms of Silla, Baekje and Goguryeo.

She encouraged the court and civil servants to wear formal, Chinese T'ang-style silk robes with left-to-right closing. Noblemen wore baggy trousers tied at the ankles, with tunic-style jackets cuffed at the wrists and belted at the waist. Each distinct group in society wore specific colours and designs showing rank and class and it was around this time that noblewomen began to wear full-length cullottes and wide-sleeved, hip-length jackets belted at the waist. Elaborate hats made of silk, white birch, horsehair or bark were decorated with gold and silver embroidery. Beautiful textiles were one of Queen Jindeok's great interests and she was celebrated for her beautiful silk embroidery. According to the *Samgook Sagi*, when she died the Chinese Emperor Gaozong sent a gift of 300 bolts of silk to her funeral.

In 668, the three kingdoms consolidated into the Unified Shilla, 668–935 CE. Buddhism was declared the national religion, while Daoism, Confucianism and Shamanism all flourished. People's beliefs infused their art with an appreciation of nature, the seasons and colours. A Confucian school had been established in 372 to teach the Chinese characters and the classics, and these remained the basis of Korean education up to the nineteenth century. Literary sources also record details of architecture, science, religious rituals, painting and sculpture. The beautiful silk textiles were highly prized, but sericulture was the work of country folk, taken for granted and rarely mentioned. During King Yurinisaryong's reign in the ninth year of the Shilla Dynasty, a weaving contest was arranged between two groups of noble ladies with the princess as judge. This happy occasion ended with singing and dancing and a celebratory meal organised by the losers.

Under the Unified Shilla, Korea had a golden age of peace and prosperity. Increasing trade with T'ang China brought new ideas, opportunities and luxuries. The nobility became increasingly indulgent and even people of lower rank enjoyed an improved standard of living, with some relaxation of the strict social controls. In 834 CE, the Shilla King, Hongdok, sought to manage the uneven distribution of wealth and opportunity through the introduction of sumptuary laws. These attempted to control the extravagance of the upper class, including the wearing of expensive embroidered silks, but the court failed to appreciate the extent of the heavy tax burden

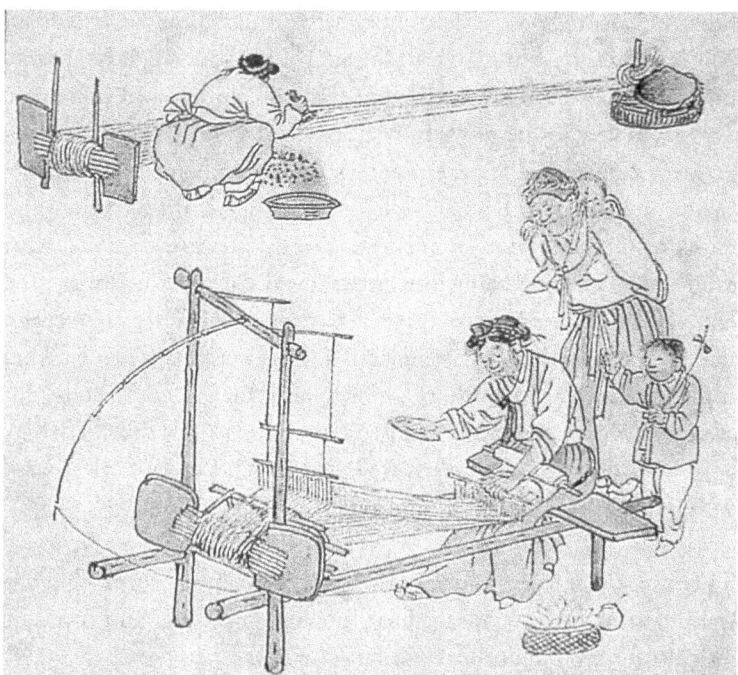

Woman weaving using a well set up loom, tensioned by the strap around her hips. She is lifting the heddles to change the shed with her left hand and throwing the shuttle with her right. The woman in the background is preparing a warp and brushing it to ensure the warp threads are separate and under the same tension, or brushing on a paste to strengthen the threads during weaving. 18thc genre painting by Tanwon (Kim Hong-do).

that the common people endured, and an extended period of unrest followed. Eventually, the rebel leader, General Wang Kon, seized the opportunity to force the last Shilla king to surrender peacefully in 918 and the general established the new kingdom of Koryo, 918–1392.

The Koryo kingdom

The name Koryo, from which 'Korea' is derived, means 'high and clear' and was now used for the whole peninsula. General Wang Kon immediately set out to promote unity and harmony. He married a Shilla princess, protected the Buddhist monks, initiated a civil service, freed slaves and reorganized the government. This resulted in peaceful development and increasing trade with China, but over the next 300 years, periods of domestic unrest continued and there were repeated external threats, especially from the Mongols. For a brief time Korea was a vassal state of Mongolia, and the Korean king was pressured to marry a Mongol princess and their heirs were forced to live in Peking and adopt Chinese clothes and hairstyles. This was a very astute move by the Yuan court, as the royal children grew up steeped in Chinese rather than Korean culture. This had a lasting influence on Korean style, especially regarding clothes and rank. Women had to avert their faces in mixed company and wear a *nuhwool*, an enveloping veil of stiffened silk over a frame. The materials to be used for each type of garment were designated and the colours and patterns stipulated for each season. The weather could be bitterly cold in the north and so some garments for ceremonial occasions were made in thick, luxurious fabrics. These gorgeous silk costumes were often padded and lavishly decorated with gold thread, jade and embroidery.

To ensure there was a continuous supply of silk, the farmers in the warmer areas were encouraged to grow mulberry trees and combine sericulture with their other farming activities. It was mostly women's work, but at busy times every member of the family helped to collect the mulberry leaves and keep the silkworms clean, warm and fed. A huge variety of silk was produced. As well as rough, country reeled and woven silks, there were beautiful satins, twills and plain weave. *Sa* was a lightweight, transparent, gossamer summer silk, woven into an openwork pattern similar to gauze. *Ra* was a more complicated version, often incorporating densely woven stripes. The secret of the open weave was the use of highly twisted fine warp threads, used in pairs with the weft threads inserted between them. This gave the fabric openness and stability making it both beautiful and cool to wear. Koreans gave gauze romantic names, such as flower-patterned *sa* and *yongmun-sa*, a dragon silk. The designs were woven, embroidered or hand-painted onto the silk. Some silk weaves like *sookgosa* were soft, some were stiff like organdie and the very best quality was called *gap-sa*. The half-silk *hang-ra* was similar and could incorporate fine ramie or cotton. Heavier, opaque, expensive silks like *dan* could be satin or damask weaves with multi-coloured motifs, while pongee silk was a plain weave sometimes with a *Bombyx mori* warp and tussah weft.

During the reign of King Gongmin, 1351–74, Korea became a tributary state of Ming China, 1368–1644. It was a period of rising

Picking mulberry leaves to feed the silkworms, 19thc woodcut, clearly shows the skirts held out by the many petticoats. The unmarried and younger women are wearing yellow samhoejang jackets with red chima with their hair in a chignon or braided.

internal conflict and corruption between the powerful monks and the aristocrats. There were terrifying raids by northern 'Red Turban' nomads and external attacks from Japanese pirates. The prime function of the king was not to rule or govern his country but to act as the supreme intermediary between Heaven and Earth. He had to conduct sacrificial rites to restore and maintain the celestial balance and it was essential that he wore the appropriate robes when conducting these rituals to ensure the return of health and good fortune to his people. These ceremonial robes were called *jei-bok* and had to be perfect in every detail. His full court robe was made of yellow cloud-patterned silk brocade, the yellow representing the centre of the universe. It was lined with soft red silk in the winter. Other gowns were of patterned black silk gauze, lined with red or dark-blue silk displaying nine, and later twelve, sacred and auspicious symbols. Some *sa* silk gowns were left unlined for summer. The robes had long wide sleeves and a white neckband that fastened at the right side of the chest with a long *goreum* bow, embroidered with motifs representing good fortune.

The focus of the gown was a specially embroidered medallion called a *bo*. This was attached to the shoulders, chest and back, and featured a five-clawed dragon embroidered in gold. The *bo* sometimes displayed other mythical animals or birds and it was usually made of the same colour and silk as the robe. The *bo* of the royal family were round, denoting Heaven, while those of courtiers were square, the Earth sign, but it was the number of claws on the dragon on the royal robes that had the greatest significance. On his head the king wore a black silk cap or mortarboard, called a diadem. This was richly embroidered and encrusted with floral ornaments, with a cascade of beads front and back. The strings of beads were believed to protect the king from seeing undesirable sights, while the silk cords or ribbons tied over his ears protected him from hearing anything that could be offensive. He wore a girdle with white or green jade plaques and ceremonial aprons front and back, red leggings, socks and silk shoes, and finally in his hand he held a precious white jade tablet.

The Yi or Choson Dynasty, 1392–1910

In 1392, the Yi or Choson Dynasty conquered the Koryo kingdom. It was founded by an ex-Goryeo general named Yi Seonggye and his descendants ruled Korea for over 600 years. With the change of dynasty, Buddhism lost favour and Confucianism became the ruling ideology, guiding the social and political structure of government, court and every aspect of people's lives. Confucianism emphasised strict rules, land reform, education and peace. The great Code of Administration of 1485 carefully laid out explicit rules governing all ranks and their relationship to each other, even to the depiction and details of the garments that should be worn by each group within society.

People were born into one of four heredity classes. The highest level under the king was the *yangban*, an elite group of nobility both civil and military that was based on achieved scholarship and official position rather than on wealth. The *chungin* were literally the 'middle people', a privileged class of petty bureaucrats and other skilled workers who kept the system operating. The *sang-min* formed the third group and included tenant farmers, craftsmen and merchants who paid taxes and served in the military. The lowborn, the *chuhn-min*, included slaves, shamans and entertainers, prostitutes, Buddhist monks, butchers and grave-diggers. Heredity status was enforced by strict rules and social conventions so there were few opportunities to change one's station in life.

Confucian Scholar's ceremonial robe made of sa silk, consists of three parts, the red coat, the blue coat and the apron, 19thc Chosen dynasty.
Source: Powerhouse Museum and Museum of Korean Embroidery.

Silk in Korea   53

The elite, the *yangban*, had few restrictions as to the colours they might wear, but generally, young girls wore bright colours and more subdued colours were worn by older men and women. Natural dyes were rare and special, so the use of red, yellow and purple was limited to the upper classes. The law required commoners to wear white, undyed clothes and hemp was the most common fibre. White was also worn by old people and for mourning clothes, but for special occasions such as weddings, people were permitted to wear dull shades of pink, light green, grey or charcoal. Boys wore a coloured coat, maybe light green or purple, while girls wore a brightly coloured *chogori* and red *chima*. Girls also had little decorative purses with pendants attached and large ribbons in their pigtails.

Over the period of the Yi Dynasty, a unique Korean culture emerged in the way the people wore their clothes, ate at low tables sitting on the floor on silk cushions, and slept, covered with an *eebul*, or quilt, on a *yo* mattress that was rolled up and stored during the day. Their clothes were suitable and appropriate for the lifestyle, and hard work, filial piety and modesty were the highest values.

Hanbok

The *hanbok* consisted of a full gathered skirt, the *chima* that was hitched up over the bust and tied under the arms with two long sashes. The *juhgori* jacket included many variations, with contrasting material on the cuffs and underarm gussets and with sleeves curved at the bottom. The jackets tended to be shorter than they had been in the Koryo period, 935–1392, but they were always fastened on the right side with a large single bow called a *goreum*. Under the gathered *chima* women wore many underskirts and a pair of long, full bloomers, a one-piece shift and a little under-jacket, smaller than the *juhgori*. Men continued to wear roomy *baji* pants bound at the ankles, with coats, hats and boots. Both men and women wore *durumagi*, the long outer coat, so necessary in Korea's cold winters. Their full baggy pants and skirts used lots of fabric to emphasize their wealth and position. In summer the fabric was silk, hemp or ramie, but for winter the jackets could be double layered, with additional padding for extra warmth.

As *hanbok* have no pockets, both men and women carried a purse, or *jumeoni*. These could be round, pleated or triangular, and closed with a drawstring. They were embellished with elaborate knots and tassels that varied according to the person's status or gender. The only items of jewellery were hairpins, rings or a *norigae*, a knotted pendant of silk, gold or semi-precious stones that was attached to the hair, the *goreum* or the collar.

The *git* was the band of fabric that trimmed the white inner collar. It was stiffened with paper and tacked into place so it could be easily removed for laundering. Cotton was easy to wash, but ramie had to be pounded with a heavy wooden stick on a smooth shiny stone to release the starch that gave it its crisp, glossy finish. When the *hanbok* needed to be cleaned, it was taken apart completely and sometimes the fabric was reversed if it had become stained. Nothing was wasted and the old thread was used for tacking or mending. After years of wear, the fabric was finally cut up and used for children's garments and favourite pieces were incorporated into gifts, patchwork wrapping cloths and other special items. Well-worn cotton and hemp made lovely babies' nappies, aprons, dishcloths and cleaning rags.

Beautiful ceremonial chests were used to store the valuable clothes, accessories and jewellery. Each chest was unique, and fitted with a variety of drawers and compartments with brass or cast-iron motifs and fittings. The symbolism of the motifs was important and in Korea, flower, bird or butterfly motifs meant a life filled with joy and happiness. There were small chests to contain cosmetics, including rouge, powder and lipsticks, combs, camellia oil for the hair, mirrors and brushes. Charcoal was used on the brows and crushed balsam flower was combined with new leaves and alum to dye the fingernails red.

In elite households, the wives and women were separated from the men and secluded in a walled inner compound. It was here that they had the leisure to do the exquisite embroidery. They not only made clothing, but purses and baby socks, pillowslips and hair ribbons incorporating motifs of good fortune. They also made gifts for special celebrations such as those to mark 100 days after the baby's birth, weddings, or a sixtieth birthday. This was a very significant day in Korean culture as it marked the end of the 60-year cycle in the Asian zodiac and was regarded as an important signifier of a long life.

At court, the king and noblemen were not restricted to the number of wives or concubines they could have, although there was only one queen or empress. Women did not have a social life outside the compound and sericulture played an important part in their lives. A secret garden in the Changdok Palace was set aside for the royal women to raise silkworms and weave silk. They spent many hours sewing luxurious and multi-layered court garments that featured the ten Chinese characters of longevity, or other auspicious symbols, including the lotus, peony and chrysanthemum, pairs of cranes, birds and butterflies.

Celebrated women and scholars

There was one group of women called *gisaeng* who were professional court entertainers. They were not prostitutes but beautiful, cultured young women who lived under the protection and patronage of the crown. Hwang Jini, 1506–60, was so celebrated for her charm, beauty and exceptional intellect that she was known as 'Myeongwol', which means Bright Moon, and her life was portrayed in novels, operas and films. Her exotic silk gowns and the sadness and tragedies in her life inspired her sensitive poetry. *Gisaeng* were trained to sing, dance and converse from the age of ten and as they matured were often called upon to entertain envoys or take a wife's role as hostess. They wore a green robe with a bright floral crimson silk skirt with the wide band around the chest, tied at the back. Both hands were covered by extra long, narrow sleeve extensions, which floated alluringly as they danced. In their long black hair they wore two very large embroidered red silk ribbons with an exclusive gold stamped design. The position of the *gisaeng* in society was protected until the fall of the Yi Dynasty in 1910, after which the best that many could hope for was to become the valued concubine of a wealthy official or businessman or open a small teahouse or restaurant.

It was very difficult for a cultured and talented woman to gain an honoured place in society yet Shin Saimdang, 1504–51, became

Gisaeng, secluded, private world of professional court entertainers. 18thc genre painting by Shi San (Yoo Un-hong). Gisaeng were known for their beauty and refinement. They wrote poetry, sang and danced and were valued and protected by the court. Hwang Jinee was one of the best known and her story has been the basis of many novels, poems, films and TV scripts.

a legend. She had been highly educated in classical Confucian studies and after marrying and bringing up seven children, her exquisite embroidery, poetry, painting and calligraphy was publicly recognised and a statue erected to her in Saljig Park in Central Seoul. Her third child, her son Yulgok, showed great talent and he like other sons of aristocrats in the Yi Dynasty went to a private school from the age of seven to prepare for life as a scholar or a high-ranking civil or military official. These children had to learn the many details of statesmanship, scholarship and etiquette. The gentleman scholar was highly respected and spent his days on official duties, memorizing the Analects of Confucius, composing poetry or practising calligraphy. He had a special room, separated by paper screens and positioned near the gate of the house. Inside there were scrolls, musical instruments, bonsai and large embroidered silk-covered floor cushions and arm rests, all in muted tones. The quiet contemplative atmosphere was enhanced by books and favourite *object d'art*, lacquerware, celadon and exquisite writing implements. The most distinguished scholars were entitled to wear the scholar's robe with deep, flared sleeves, made of white silk edged with black. The student's robe was pale blue or green in winter. In spring and autumn, silk was replaced by cotton and in summer by ramie.

The noblemen's clothes had to conform to strict rules as to colour, design, length of sleeve, rank badges, girdles and shoes. Rank badges identified each person's position in the hierarchy. They featured a variety of divine or mythical birds and animals, including tigers and leopards, valued for their strength and courage. One of the most valued was the crane carrying a piece of the sacred bullocho plant in its beak, symbolizing eternal youth. The badges were loosely stitched on to the garment and could be easily removed if the official fell from grace.

The foremost social values of integrity in men and chastity in women were reflected in the way people dressed. Before marriage, both men and women wore their hair in long pigtails. Once married, men's hair was knotted into a topknot while the women twisted theirs into a ball at the nape of the neck securing it with a *pinyo*, a long, decorative pin which varied according to the wearer's class and status. Red, white, blue, yellow, black or green were symbolic and the colours of all clothes carried meaning. *Chima* skirts were made the same size, often finely pleated with embroidered or woven bands on the bottom, and shoulder straps to make them easier to wear. It was a very versatile garment and served as a wrap, a coverlet, mat for sitting on, or as a head-cover. Many working women found a shorter *chima*, with less fullness, more practical.

Hanbok have undergone many changes over the centuries, responding to fashion trends that dictated loose or tight sleeves, square-cut neckbands and long or extremely short *juhgori*. Until recently there were strict sumptuary laws, but fashionable women always experimented with new colour combinations, lengths and embellishments, pushing the boundaries of what is considered acceptable. These days, many young women choose to get married in a white Western-style dress but many still wear traditional style — a pink *hanbok* for the engagement ceremonies and a yellow *chogori* and red *chima* for the wedding. With the traditional *hanbok*, a bride wears a ceremonial flower crown on her head and decorates her clothes with pendant trinkets. On other occasions, colour is less restrictive and fabrics include embroidered, hand-painted, or gold-stamped silk.

A timeless favourite has been the use of patchwork, often in fine stiff silk organza. The large patchwork squares in clear colours are

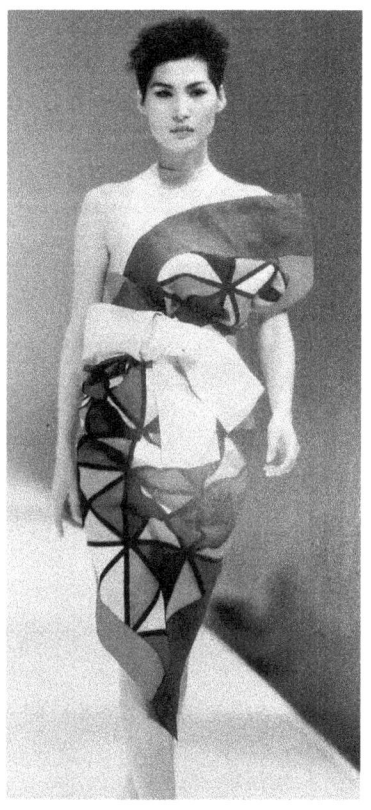

Above: Oppo, fine sa silk patchwork wrapping cloth, used for wrapping clothes, 19thc Chosen Dynasty.
Source: Powerhouse Museum and Museum of Korean Embroidery.

Right: Some modern designers are taking the essence of the traditional hanbok and re-inventing it to stunning effect. This patchwork mosi joagbo in ramie has a large goreum bow.
Source: Kazou Ohishi.

stitched together to form harmonious patterns, and look wonderful when made up into a little jacket or large square patchwork called a *bojagi*. It is common for many to be owned and used as covers, wrappers for gifts, headdresses or mats. Today's designers increasingly seek inspiration from the *bojagi* and *hanbok* to create fashions with a uniquely Korean flair. They incorporate the lines and cut of the ancient clothes and accessories into their designs, and use traditional fabrics such as silk, hemp and ramie. Many department stores have boutiques specializing in a new generation of *hanbok*, made from man-made fibres for everyday wear.

Sericulture in modern Korea

There have been some dramatic changes in the supply and use of silk in Korea. These days only the most expensive *hanbok* are made in silk, most of which is imported from China and only woven or

One of the many stands at the Suwon Symposium for Alternative Products from Sericulture, 2000 showing some of the new foods being developed from the silkworm, including bread, cakes, biscuits and pasta. At the very end of the table, pupa are being lightly pan-frying in sesame oil.

Two hostesses wearing hanbok with the author at the Suwon Symposium for Alternative Products from Sericulture 2000. In the background are some of the many stands displaying the many new innovations and developments.

Another stand at the Suwon Symposium, this time with oils, mulberry tea and icecream, drinks, pharmaceuticals.

finished in Korea. Korean silk is two and a half times dearer to produce than Chinese silk. This has meant that the production of silk fibre for yarns and fabrics has ceased to be commercially viable, and alternative products have had to be developed to utilize the skills of the sericulture farmers and their extensive mulberry orchards. Exciting work has been done at Suwon University and the Food Technology Institute to develop alternative food and medicinal products.

The government and the Department of Sericulture in South Korea have sponsored many programmes both in the universities and in the field to raise the standard of sericulture, the quality of the eggs, cocoons and mulberry. There have been a number of initiatives to cooperate with Northern Korea, share information and give practical and financial help. One of their successes is the collection and drying of fully developed fourth-stage silkworm to produce a protein powder that can be added to bread, cakes, biscuits, buns and pasta to substantially increase their nutritional value. There is little difference in the taste or texture but a marked difference it its food value, making it a new and valuable product.

For many generations the pupa has been recognised as a good food source and today it is freeze-dried, or fried in oil, to form a nourishing protein-packed snack. There are ongoing experiments to inject the pupa with enzymes for use as a medium to produce a much valued liquor that is the basis of energy, medicinal or tonic drinks. An alcoholic drink, similar to whisky, has also been produced. Mulberry branches have been turned into walking sticks and mulberry leaves are powdered to make tea with special medicinal qualities or added to ice cream. Most of the products are directed towards the Asian market, but applications have been made to the American Food and Drug Organisation for worldwide distribution.

Three Bengali girls in sari, wearing jamdani and brocade saris with a little choli blouses, a long scarf and their wealth in gold chains and bangles. Early 20thc.
Source: Royal Commonwealth Society.

CHAPTER FOUR
Silk in India

Exotic, vibrant, flamboyant India! Everywhere there is colour, a melding of different cultures and religions, wealth and poverty, and a history that goes back to the beginning of time. Discussion can be intense as to exactly when sericulture was first established in India and whether it was the domesticated mulberry silkworm the *Bombyx mori***, or the native tasar, muga or eri silk.**

Certainly, wild native silkworms were in the Indus Valley, Harappa and Chanhu-daro before 2000 BCE and silk was mentioned in the Mahabharata and the Ramayana, the epic Hindu poems composed before 300 BCE. By 200 BCE adventurous Indian merchants were known to have travelled long distances overland to remote Chinese towns, to Kashgar, Turfan and Yarkand where mulberry silk was already well established. The Bodo people from Central Asia migrated to Assam via Burma or Tibet around 140 BCE, and they firmly believe it was their ancestors who brought the knowledge of silk to India. Buddhist missionaries, including the monk Hsuen Tsang, c602–664, who journeyed between China and India searching for ancient Buddhist texts, observed that tasar was one of the most common fabrics worn. Buddhist temples have records of precious gifts of silk textiles, but again, this is not conclusive proof that these silks were from native Indian silkworms rather than Chinese *Bombyx mori*.

Extant examples of Indian silk fabrics are rare, because in the extreme climate, the fibres disintegrate, so the oldest surviving fragments of authentic Indian silk are fifteenth-century Jain silk embroideries.

Indian sailors pioneered sea routes and established trading communities in Canton, throughout Indonesia, Thailand and Cambodia. The *Periplus Maris Erythreae*, a maritime record of regional trade, described indigo, silk and cotton from the weaving centres on the East Indian coast at Barbaricum, Malabar and Coromandel. Indian sailors went as far as the Mediterranean, and Indian silks and muslins were exported to Rome where they were known as *textalis ventalis* or 'woven air'. By 1498, Vasco da Gama had discovered a faster route to India around the Cape of Good Hope, and this led to the establishment of Indian coastal trading colonies.

A period of unrest followed until the battle of Panipat in 1526 when the victor, Mohammad Barbur, 1483–1530, successfully founded the dynasty that became the Mughal Empire, 1526–1858. The luxurious Mughal court required vast amounts of gorgeous silk and gold textiles, and the production of reeled and woven silk greatly increased. The silk trade was flourishing and the royal weaving workshop at Delhi, called a *karkhanah*, employed over 4000 silk weavers. The court travelled frequently between palaces, so workshops, looms and foundries, tents, wall-hangings, cushions and all the paraphernalia of the court had to be easily dismantled, packed and transported. Exotic textiles were perfect, as they could be rolled, bagged then reassembled to set the stage for the glory that was the Mughal court.

During the seventeenth century the inheritance laws decreed that land could only be ascribed for life and not handed on. At death, all land would be claimed in taxes so the nobility were perfectly happy to spend everything they owned. They commissioned vast public works, colossal buildings, luxurious palaces and sumptuous gardens. They surrounded themselves with every conceivable luxury, including the most exquisite and costly voided silk velvets and brocades. These luxurious textiles made in the royal workshops had large designs emblazoned with gold and silver. The nobles valued these superb textiles, and saw them as a suitable reflection of their power and superiority, and so they encouraged the development of sericulture and silk weaving to ensure their continued supply.

Indian miniature of the Mughal court on the move, travelling in style with a decorated camel and elephant. The long strings of pearls denote their wealth.

England wanted to gain access to the exotic Indian silks, spices, cottons, Kashmir shawls and silk embroideries, and so the East India Company was established in London on 31 December 1600. The first trading station was set up at Surat in Gujarat in 1612. This was an important port for pilgrims bound for Mecca and there was always a ready market for the beautiful silk and gold textiles. The next post to be opened was at Madras in 1639, then Bombay, now Mumbai, in 1688 and Calcutta in 1690. Unfortunately, England only wanted raw silk to process in their own mills, so they prevented the local people in Bihar from spinning and weaving their silk cloth for local use and sale. This almost reduced a thriving industry and population to peasantry. The trade was further unbalanced, this time in India's favour because India had no interest in English wool and therefore required payment for silk in silver bullion, which put a great strain on the English economy. Despite these difficulties, the production of silk continued to expand in India and by 1796 their silk industry was producing two million pounds of silk fibre, with exports of over 656,000 pounds per annum.

By the eighteenth century Benares, later called Varanasi, had developed into an important silk-weaving centre, specializing in the heavy figured silk and gold brocades set on a deep red, blue or green ground. Highly skilled Muslim weavers wove these silk fabrics on large draw-looms. The designs included intertwining floral motifs and distinctive panels of upright leaves, and were exactly to the Mughals' taste. Nevertheless, most of the beautiful saris were woven on simple hand-looms, including lightweight plain fabrics, lampas and tissue silks.

Gujarat

The Parse were Persians who arrived in Gujarat during the eighth century, after fleeing from Muslim persecutions and enforced conversions in their homeland. They settled happily and adopted local clothes and languages, but maintained their Zoroastrian religion and ethnic identity. Originally, they were boat builders and traded with China. They imported Chinese silk, including a thin ribbed gauze, a heavier crepe de Chine called *ghara* and a Chinese-style satin called *gaj*. Later, these silks were embroidered in China in an elaborate and delicate mixture of eighteenth-century Chinese 'trade' designs featuring people and bridges, with local Indian motifs of birds, flowers and animals.

During the 1850s and 1860s, the British colonial administration began to apply stringent trade rules, which curtailed the importation of Chinese embroideries. This had a devastating effect on all the associated local textile industries. The Parse avoided these conflicts and developed good relations with the British. They began emulating them and many Parse became very rich, which aroused some antagonism and jealousy between themselves and the local people.

The English favoured the soft colours and smaller patterns of their homeland and the Parse moved from the bright colours associated with Gujarat into soft pastels and sober blacks and whites. *Broderie anglais*, embroidered with tiny motifs, was brought to Gujarat from Christian convents in Goa and lacy patterned silk became all the rage for wedding saris. Concurrently, a group of immigrant Chinese began producing embroidery known as *chinai*. These designs had a Chinese flavour and featured strings of birds and flowers in white against a coloured background. The women made garments and shawls, embroidered with fine silk floss and added borders to saris and children's dresses.

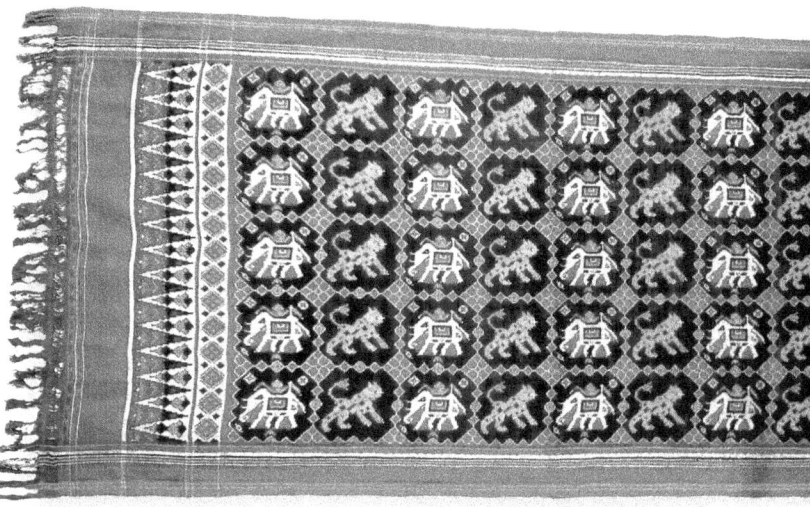

Double ikat patola design of tigers and elephants, Gujurat.

A specialty of Gujarat was *patola*, another of the *ikat* dyeing methods. The word comes from *mengikat*, meaning 'to tie or bind', and each community had its own variations. *Patola* was an extremely refined and time-consuming method of tie-dyeing both the warp and weft threads into bundles before they were woven. Rubber bands or dye-resist string was used to tie the threads and then both warp and weft sets of threads were dyed, untied and retied for each colour change. The warp was then threaded onto the loom in the proper sequence and the fabric woven using the second set of dyed threads. This double *ikat* produces minute spots and complex traditional patterns in the finished cloth. *Patola* designs have been identified in wall paintings in South Indian temples, in Kerala and Tamil Nadu, and valued for their purity, sacred and magical properties. They fall into three main types: geometric Muslim designs, Islamic architecture, and naturalistic flowers and plants. Designs can also include dancing animals, elephants, tigers and parrots, often placed on a bold lattice ground. For the wealthy and upper caste families, *patola* was the supreme textile and has always been associated with the most important occasions, weddings and sacred rituals. Unfortunately, few families remain in Gujarat that can produce the exquisite reversible *patola* silk saris and so more recently, weavers in Orissa and Andhra Pradesh have captured the market with their *ikat* saris.

Bandha is another method of *ikat* dyeing, usually done by women on already woven fine silk georgette or loosely woven mill cotton. This time it is the woven fabric that is stretched out tight and, working from the underside using a sharp spike or pointed fingernail, each spot is firmly tied with fine dye-resist string. This leaves a pattern of little white rings after the fabric has been dyed. The lightest colour is applied first, and the tying process is repeated before each colour is added. Sometimes the pattern is drawn on the fabric with an impermeable substance like wax, gum, paste, resin, starch or mud that is later removed by brushing, ironing or washing. Woodblock printing has always been an Indian specialty. In one method the fabric is laid out flat, and then tight strings, soaked in a water-based dye, are flicked onto the cloth, leaving guide lines that are later filled in with hand drawn designs or patterns using a stencil or wooden printing block. In the Kutch area of Gujarat these lovely fabrics tend to be dyed in dark and natural colours but the bright colours of Rajasthan have their own sacred meanings.

Dyeing, especially with natural dyes, is an ancient art that requires both skill and experience to produce all the vibrant and subtle shades. The dyers were usually from lower caste families, but different aspects of dyeing and the embellishment of the cloth involved many other castes. India has over 300 dye-yielding plants and indigo and madder red are most commonly available. Some are especially colour-fast on silk, so fugitive or non-colour fast dyes require a mordant. The word comes from the Latin word *mordere* meaning 'to bite'. These mordants can be made from local plants or chemicals like alum, salt, caustic soda or vinegar. In the hill country, the local people use ashes and urine to prepare and dye the tougher tasar silks. The petals of the safflower plant yield a fugitive yellow but if treated with a mordant produce a fine yellow especially on silk. Different shades of yellow and orange are associated with spring, asceticism and the Sadhus who have given up their caste to lead a holy life. White was seen as ritually pure so was associated with the Jains and Brahmin caste. It was also the colour of mourning, so it was rarely worn at weddings, except by Parses and Christians. Weavers in Southern Berhampur weave figures on silk brocades, dyed with a brilliant red dye produced by the lac insect, *Lacifer lacca*. Red is the colour of joy, celebrations, lovers and brides. Sober blues and black bring memories of rain-filled clouds and water. Among some Hindus, they are considered inauspicious colours of sorrow and bad luck and associated with the ritualistically impure process of fermenting indigo, but blue is widely worn these days, and even seen to offer protection from the 'evil eye'.

The introduction of chemical dyes in the 1890s was a severe blow. The livelihood of the dyers, the associated crafts and the families who grew the dye plants, was virtually wiped out and that had a demoralizing effect on the whole community. The bright, often harsh colours of the chemical dyes lacked the time-honoured emotional and poetic significance of traditional dyes. The new dyes appeared to have many advantages because they were easy to use, not dependent on climate or growing conditions and could provide a quick income, but all too often the dyes faded and many exports were rejected. Without a clear understanding of the chemical process, these dyes were unstable and they gained a poor reputation that was only slowly improved with experience and greater quality control.

Silk weaving

There has been hand-loom weaving in virtually all areas of India from time immemorial. Bhagalpur in the hill country was famous for its tasar silk mills, and has been thriving since the first European merchants arrived in the sixteenth century. The quality of the woven cloth is defined by the evenness of colour, texture and fineness. *Tasars* can be blended with other silks, cotton, ramie or synthetics to make a variety of fabrics and this can keep the cost down and result in some wonderful textures from superfine to thick, gritty upholstery fabrics. Some tribal women in Assam and Orissa still weave the exquisite *eri* silk saris at home, using a primitive back-strap loom. The men tend to work in a commercial workshop on power looms or a pit loom, where the weaver sits on the ground with his feet on the treadles in a pit under the loom.

The textile industry declined in the nineteenth century, crushed by competition from the more sophisticated European companies using advanced technologies and Jacquard looms. Some hand-looms were modernized and some commercial centres set up dobby and Jacquard looms using punched cards to automatically insert the pattern. To keep up with world standards, the government started introducing new apprenticeship schemes offering training

Pit weaving, the dyed ikat warp is being woven in a simple tabby weave on a two shaft loom.

Wild silks, Eri silk moths tied onto long strings or kharikas so they don't fly away before they mate.
Source: Spin-off Spring 2000.

and quality control in all aspects of sericulture, growing, production and marketing.

Mashru textiles of silk and cotton were made for the Muslim communities because of religious restrictions that prohibit wearing silk next to the skin. *Mashru* means 'permitted' and these fabrics were made with a silk warp completely covered with a cotton weft in a satin weave, and resist dyed into a wavy pattern. Mashru textiles are now mostly concentrated in Kutch, Patan and in Uttar Pradesh. Hand weaving fine floral silk chiffons and georgettes began in Mysore in the 1930s and 1940s in an attempt to capture the growing French chiffon market, but today the designs are screen-printed. Karnataka also produces specific silks for other regions such as the silk *bandhani* for western India and silk *jamdani* for Bengal. The most important Tamil silk-weaving towns are Kanchipuram

Zari embroidery exquisitely done on silk using gold thread in a variety of stitches and styles. It was a bridal sari that was later burnt to retrieve the gold, and only a little saved as a sample.

and further south, Kumbakonam and Thanjavur. They specialize in heavy silks with rich gold borders, woven with tightly twisted three-ply silk and thick *zari* threads.

Zari and embroidery

Metallic *zari* threads need to be very flexible and are made by coating a silver bar with gold, and then drawing it out until it is extremely thin, beating it flat and winding it around a core of red, white or yellow silk. *Zari* is associated with many ethnic groups and especially the wealthy Muslim communities in the western regions. The formal figured silk saris known as *pukai* in Kornad often incorporate *zari* embroidery and have become known as temple saris, because originally they were made as temple gifts.

Sometimes *zari* threads were used for traditional gold jewellery, or as a thick thread to couch down with silk floss on heavier silks. It could be sewn directly onto fine silk georgette or chiffon, or pulled through the fabric to create flat knots to form a floral pattern. Another technique was to stamp silk velvet with a hot iron and add gum arabic, dusting it with gold powder to make rich hangings and screens. Tinsel silks, using the cheaper flaked mica, were used on the odhni, or half saris, worn in the western states of Gujarat and Haryana.

Mochi embroidery had been done since the seventeenth century by the cobblers and leather workers of Kutch and Saurashtra. They developed the art of using silk floss to do fine chain stitch embroidery for the court, merchants and land-owning castes. They used an *ari*, which is a fine stiletto with a small hook that was probably adapted from the cobbler's awl. It worked like a tambour hook, so that the thread, held below the work, was hooked through the fabric. It was a feature of embroidered *ghaghra* or skirt pieces, bodices, children's caps, borders and special hangings to honour Lord Krishna. It was at its height in the late nineteenth and early twentieth century, but with independence and the breakdown of the court, *mochi* embroidery has almost completely disappeared.

Traditionally, the women of the embroidery caste displayed their patchwork quilts and other beautiful embroideries during local festivals. For the high excitement of a wedding, embroidery on silk subtly establishes the status of both families and that of the wealthy guests, the merchants, government and business people. Indian tradition puts a high value on the dowry, gifts of richly embroidered textiles, silk hangings for the new home, jewellery and household items. Many gifts are wrapped in a large decorated cloth called a *chakla*, which features highly coloured embroidery, using specific stitches and metal and mirror work that identifies the caste and culture of the family.

Embroideries have become so popular that standards have dropped, and much of the embroidery these days is made for tourist and export markets in cramped factories. There are still experienced embroiderers doing beautiful work, but much has been replaced by machines that can do chain and satin stitch. There are still centres of excellence, especially involving beadwork. Often it is done by a group of men who sit around the fabric, which is stretched out on a frame, allowing each man to bead his section of the design.

Indian style

India has vast climatic and cultural extremes and diversity. The draped sari developed because it was so appropriate for the climate and lifestyle of the women and because some Hindus believed that to cut cloth made it impure. Cotton was the major fibre but silk always offered luxury. Saris were woven in many weights and qualities, regional designs and decoration. A North Indian terracotta sculpture from the Shunga period, around 250 BCE, shows a woman wearing a draped garment made from an uncut length of cloth, similar to those worn by the Indian temple dancers. Other wall paintings and sculpture from the period of the Graeco-Indian Gandaran civilization around 300 CE show women wearing draped saris. It was traditional for women of all castes to wear a cotton sari, but silk was the prerogative of upper caste women. In some areas she was required to cover her head while in others it was not necessary. The sari varies in length from four to nine metres and can be up to a metre wide. There are three parts: the selvedge borders, the field or middle section, and the *pallau* or decorated end. The richest saris tended to be longer and wider, as were those designed to drape over trousers. Cheap cotton saris worn by the labourers were often rather short and skimpy. It was the practice to cremate the dead wrapped in a sari and so few have survived.

Each region throughout India has its own distinctive style. The impressive Paithani silk saris of Maharashtra are decorated with a gold dot or coin motif. Gorad saris are made with unbleached and undyed silk, with small striped end-pieces, while in Karnataka, the finest saris are made of Mysore silk crepe. Gujarat's specialty was a *kinkhab* or 'woven flower' brocade with small motifs in horizontal rows against a brilliant purple, red or green background.

Most saris require the woman to wear a short tight bodice and a long underslip into which the sari is pleated and pinned. There are over a hundred different ways to wear a sari and these days the trend is to drape it in the *nivi* style. It's graceful and flattering to most figures and was made popular by glamorous Bollywood stars. Also popular is the *salwar sharmees* or Punjabi suit, with loose trousers, tight in at the ankle and a long over-tunic and *odhani* or *dupatta* scarf. In Rajasthan and Gujarat the *ghagra choli* is traditional, with its long full skirt with a rich border around the bottom, and tight short sleeved top and veil.

Men traditionally wear a loose shirt with their *lungi* or short sarong, pyjamas, or wrapped pants called a *dhoti*. Assamese men wear a *lungi* or waist wrapped skirt and an upper wrap or shawl, a *chadar*, usually left its natural colour of white, cream or pale brown, although some woven silks incorporate the lovely golden muga silk for decoration. The *sherwani* is a long fitted, buttoned coat with a Nehru collar. It can be a spectacular garment and very glamorous, especially when made of gorgeous silk brocade. It is worn with tight trousers, often at weddings, and the groom's *shewani* could be in rich cream or ivory silk brocade, embroidered in gold or silver and sometimes worn with long strings of large pearls.

Indian beadwork, dyeing and printing have an international reputation and have enthralled many fashion designers. Ritu Kumar, a Kolkata-based designer, revived traditional hand-block printing and opened her first boutique in Delhi in 1966. She was inspired by royal costumes from the Mughal era, added embroidery and contemporary flair, and 'ethnic chic' hit the headlines and

An exquisite pink dupioni silk sari worn in the Nivi style with an end piece of red and green shot with gold, and gold borders.

A cream silk sherwani, rich with sequins, diamonte and pearls. Wedding sherwani were traditionally white or cream brocaded silk and heavily embroidered.

74 THE WORLD OF SILK

influenced a whole generation. Many of the 1980s designers concentrated on *haute couture* but the next decade saw a dramatic growth in the retail industry as local designers began making for the *prêt-à-porter*, or ready-to-wear, market. Television and movies have added their glamour, and in 1996 the Fashion Design Council of India was established. India Fashion Week in Delhi enabled many designers to break with tradition, introduce 'cocktail saris', pastel colours and gorgeous chiffons, satins and nets. They focused on lustrous Indian silks in stunning colours, using natural and chemical dyes and especially batik and block printing, to offer their high fashion worldwide. As the industry became more professional, many Western countries saw the advantage of cheap labour to have their garments made in India.

Sericulture

Agriculture plays a vital part in the rural economy of India, and sericulture is practised in more than 60,000 villages. It is a cottage

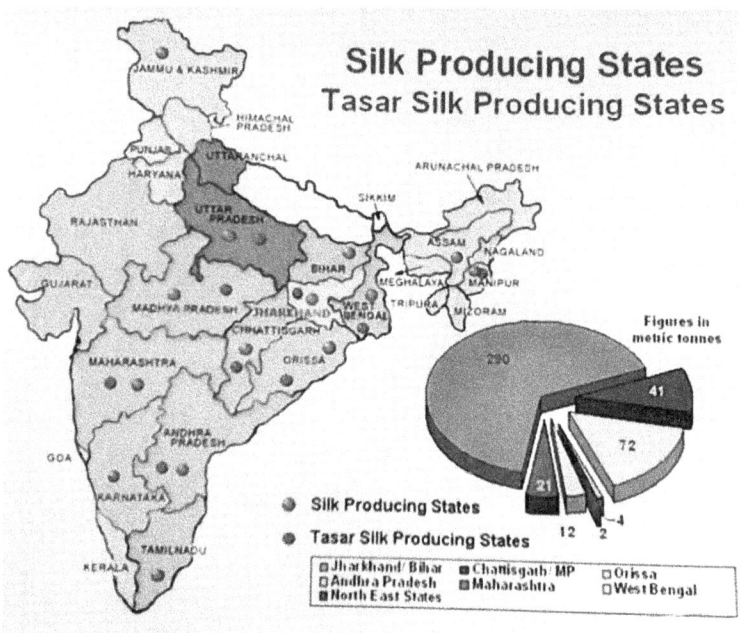

Map of sericulture in the various regions of India, where both *Bombyx mori* and tassar are grown, and their share of the total production.
Source: Department of Industry Jharkhand, India.

industry, traditionally done by women, but it usually involves the whole village, from the youngest to the oldest. The womenfolk rear the silkworms, while the men and boys work in the fields and attend to the mulberry trees. Depending on the village and its traditions, there can be fairly strict divisions of labour where the men do the 'skilled' tasks in the fields and the women the 'unskilled' tasks of caring for the silkworms, and when the tasks are shared, women work under the supervision of men. Many villages practise purity rituals to ensure a good yield, so when a family member dies, a girl reaches puberty and during women's menstrual cycles, the 'polluted person' is not allowed into the rearing house. The family may also practise *samrani* and offer a gift or incense during the silkworm's first stages, and perform a day-long *puja* to Lord Ganesh and distribute sweets in thanks for a good yield. Productive land can be scarce and weather and incomes erratic, so sericulture can supply an additional cash income and fit in with both the family and the demands of the land.

India is the second largest producer of raw silk after China and Indians are the largest consumers of silk. Over seven and a half million people are involved in some aspect of sericulture, growing the silkworms or mulberry trees, unwinding or twisting the threads, dyeing or weaving it, marketing or selling it. *Bombyx mori* silkworms are widely grown in most areas of India, especially in the tropical southern states of Karnataka, Andhra Pradesh and Tamil Nadu. These silkworms are multi-voltine and are produced almost all year round, in comparison with the wild tasar silks that are harvested only once or twice a season. Many areas produce both mulberry and tasar silks.

The native wild silk moths are the eri, the muga, and oak tasar. These Saturniidae or wild species are generally associated with the subtropical tribal forested regions of the lower Himalayas in the northeast, in Jharkhand, Chattisgarh, Andhra Pradesh and Orissa, along with neighbouring Jammu and Kashmir, West Bengal and Bihar. These wild silks are highly valued and the young men patrol the forests with guns and slingshots to scare predators away. The silk moths fly freely, choosing specific trees to feed on and lay their eggs. The tasar moths produce a wide variety of different cocoons. They can be hard or soft, loose or fluffy, and come in a variety of colours from dark brown to bright red or gold. The local people have traditional methods of collecting and harvesting the cocoons and because the silkworm has to break through the cocoon to emerge, the broken fibre cannot be reeled, and is hand carded and spun in the villages. Some is high quality, but most is very variable. The cellular structure of tasar silk is flat and ribbon-like, and the fibres stick together, so fully automated reeling techniques are difficult. In many areas in northern India, the young girls thigh-roll the silk to produce the spun thread, but these days they are encouraged to roll the silk over a ball rather than their leg. There can be a lot of waste and most silk is washed, carded and spun before being woven into fabric.

The eri tasar moth from Assam and Orissa feed on the castor oil plant, spin open-ended cocoons and have become partly domesticated. The female moths are caught as they emerge from their cocoons and tied onto long strips of paper. When the male moth mates with her, the eggs are laid on the paper, ready to be collected, washed and kept cool until the next hatching. Almost all the world's muga silk is produced in the Brahmaputra Valley in Assam, as attempts to cultivate it elsewhere have failed. It feeds on a wide variety of local trees, and its rich golden colour is more lustrous than other wild silks and it has always been expensive.

Around two thirds of tasar silk comes from Bihar although much is woven in Orissa and West Bengal. It has always been tribally based but has become a significant cottage industry for many non-tribal rural villagers and weavers' cooperatives that weave a plain tasar fabric called *sania*. It is the choice of Brahmins, Jains and other orthodox Hindu groups, who avoid killing any living creature and prefer wild tasar silkworms like *Antheraea pernyi*. They emerge naturally from their cocoons and are considered ritually pure so the fibre does not even need to be washed before being used for the swings and ropes used in sacred or ceremonial occasions like the Krishna festival at Sawan. Natural 'unpolluted' silk is also worn during the important rites of food preparation and service. This special silk was called *mukta*, which means 'freedom', and was produced in the holy city of Benares, now Varanasi. The recent introduction of *Antherea proyeli* and *A. ricini* that feed on the *Quercus* oak trees produces the finest tasar silk with a lovely golden lustre.

Bombyx mori and mulberry culture

The multi-voltine species of *Bombyx mori* produce most of the country's silk. The cocoons tend to be smaller and produce less silk per cocoon than the bi-voltine silkworms, but with temperatures between 17 and 30°C, five to six crops a year are the norm. The cocoons are mostly white or gold, but the colour is in the sericin gum that surrounds the fibres and is removed by boiling, leaving lustrous white silk. They are grown extensively in the tropical states of Karnataka, Mysore, Bangalore, Andhra Pradesh and West Bengal.

Traditionally in southern India, it is Hindu families who rear silkworms to the cocoon stage. They obtain the second- or third-stage silkworms from the Government Egg Hatcheries and all the family work to keep the fragile creatures clean and fed with fresh mulberry leaves. In villages like Ramanagaram near Bangalore, the cocoon auction functions almost every day in the year. The Hindu farmers

Cocoons arriving by bicycle at the cocoon auction Ramanagaram, near Bangalore. The Hindu families care for the mulberry orchards and developing silkworms and bring the cocoons into the auction.

bring in their cocoons to be weighed and sold and the auctioneer walks around among the bins, selling the cocoons to the Muslim villagers. The Muslim families run the filature as a cooperative, boiling the cocoons to loosen the silk thread and winding, washing and packaging it for the throwsters and weavers. It is a symbiotic arrangement between the Hindus and Muslims that is harmonious and works very well in the community, and everyone benefits.

In Karnataka and West Bengal, over a million hectares of land are used to raise mulberry as a bush or tree, producing up to 35 tonnes per hectare of leaf every year. There is no waste and shoots are collected for next year's planting, the stripped branches are fed to the cows and goats, and the delicious fruit made into pies and drinks. Any remaining twigs and branches are used for fuel. With usable land at a premium, mulberry trees can also be grown between other crops.

Jammu and Kashmir

Jammu and Kashmir are in the sub-Himalayan region of northern India, and the valleys are an excellent area for uni-voltine and bi-voltine silkworms. These silkworms are reared only once or twice a

At the cocoon auction at Ramanagaram near Bangalore, the Muslim families bid for the cocoons, bought in by the Hindu families who have grown them to the cocoon stage.

year between May and June. They take longer to mature, require more leaves and have a long period of diapause or hibernation, but the cocoons are larger and of superior quality and greater length.

There has been sericulture in Jammu and Kashmir for centuries, yet the Governor in Srinagar during the Afghan period, 1752–1819, was indifferent to its development and the mulberry trees were cut down to clear a large area for horse racing. In 1819, the new ruler, Maharaja Ranbir Singh, recognized sericulture and made silk a state monopoly to boost its development. He imported new machinery and scientific methods from Europe, had 127 rearing houses built in all parts of the valley and offered exemption from state labour to any village people raising silkworms.

The silk industry in Kashmir was devastated in 1878 by the pébrine disease that had spread from India. Sericulture was virtually the only cash crop available to the farmers and it took years for the industry to recover. The Department of Sericulture improved the infrastructure with new mulberry nurseries, silkworm seed stations and silk reeling and weaving factories. Kashmir was briefly able to supply silk to Mysore, Bengal and Karnataka, and even Europe, but that left little raw silk for the Kashmir industry. In 1892, Thomas Wardle from England was invited to reorganize sericulture on modern lines. Unfortunately, there was opposition from the workers and the industry failed to compete with China and Japan on the international market. Recently there has been resurgence with funding, loans and government support and new silk cocoon auction markets, set up by the Sericulture Department to buy and sell local silk cocoons.

The Indian Institute of Carpet Technology in Srinagar has developed a silk carpet, the first of its kind, using reeled mulberry silk produced in Kashmir. Silk carpets are a real growth area, especially as filament silk, rather than poor quality spun silk, is being used. It has the added advantage of losing very little pile when washed and is more durable than carpets made of spun silk. Filament silk is glossier and does not need chemicals to increase its natural lustre, and so far it has been well received on the international market, and offers a unique product for Kashmir.

The local Muslim community filature, everyone works and the financial rewards are returned to the community.

The government research institutions are committed to raising standards and introducing new ideas, technologies and methods, but in general, the quality and the productivity still does not compare to China. There is a constant call for a more professional approach and improved supply of quality mulberry, separate rearing houses and better management during rearing. Quality control, marketing systems and improved scientific methods are being developed to check diseases, especially *grasserie*, *flacherie*, *pébrine* and attacks by uzi fly. India is second only to China in the amount of silk it produces but that is still insufficient for domestic demand.

Sericulture woodcut of a wealthy Thai family involved in all aspects of sericulture, including boiling cocoons, weaving, spinning, and dyeing of yarns.

CHAPTER FIVE
Silk in Thailand

Thai history

Thai silks are probably the best known, most easily recognizable and the most vibrant of all the silks. The glorious colours sing and the wonderful textures combine to stunning effect, making Thai silk unique. This ancient land has been a melting pot of many ethnic groups, immigrants and conquerors. The earliest Tai people came from Southwest China, and they combined with other ethnic groups, and from the twelfth century their land was known as Siam. Since then, the name Thailand has been increasingly used and in 1939 it became the formal name of the country.

Archaeological sites have gradually revealed their treasures. One of the oldest sites in South-East Asia, thought to be over 3000 years old, displayed a complex civilization where the people cultivated crops and produced ornaments and bronze tools. Small bundles of silk threads have been found in the extensive ruins of Nong Han and Ban Chian where the designs on pottery include silkworms, silk cocoons and mulberry leaves, suggesting that sericulture was already established. Temple paintings near Chiang Mai have murals of royalty wearing gorgeous jewellery and gold and silk garments.

At U-Tong in central Thailand, clay stamps used for printing on textiles have been found, along with figurines wearing beautiful silk and cotton wraps and ankle-length sarongs.

Sericulture is village based, domestic and agricultural so it is rare for it to appear in important documents. A Chinese envoy, Cho Ta-Kuan, who had spent time in the city of Angkor in Cambodia noted in his journal dated 1296 that although the Cambodians were not involved with sericulture, the Tai settlers were growing mulberry trees, raising silkworms and weaving silk cloth. By the fourteenth century the Tai people were teaching the Khmers to weave silk, especially the highly intricate *ikat* designs, or *matmi*, made by tie-dyeing the yarns before weaving. Ayutthaya was the capital from 1350 to 1767 and its records describe the procedures and the care needed for looking after silkworms.

From the earliest days, there have been marine silk routes. They served both local and foreign traders who transported goods by sea, from as far away as the Greek and Roman empires. The ancient route through the Straits of Malacca to the South China Sea became infested with pirates and increasingly hazardous. To avoid this danger the traders had to unload their goods and drag them 50 miles overland, across the peninsula. The preferred sea route therefore, started on the west coast of Thailand and ended on the southern shore of the Gulf of Thailand, in Surat Thani. Over the years, trading stations like Hoi An grew into port cities, thriving centres of local and foreign trade. Cultural exchanges were established between India, China, Japan, Portugal and the Middle East. The small ships carried silks and ceramics, embroideries and velvets and these were traded for local dyestuffs, blankets and floral textiles. Marine silk routes were always hazardous and littered with the wrecks of boats, sunk by hidden rocks, buccaneers and bad weather, leaving their valuable cargoes on the sea floor, lost forever.

From the fifteenth century it was the Muslim sailors and merchants who dominated the trade in Indian textiles. The main routes included Coromandel, Burma Ayutthaya, Sumatra and Java and it took around six months to travel there and back to Madras. By the end of the fifteenth century, the Portuguese had taken over this trade but in the seventeenth century, it was the Dutch and English

Sepia photo of two court women from the time of King Rama IV 1851–68, wearing pha-sin skirts and their silk sabai thrown over the shoulder.
Source: Thai National Archives

who exchanged European goods with the Middle East, India, China and Japan. In Thailand, silk cloth was by now firmly established as a valuable trade item and bartered alongside other goods from the neighbouring courts of Cambodia and Burma. Agents collected the beautiful silk textiles made by the weavers and dyers who lived in the wooden houses along the *klongs* and waterways. They traded them for hand-dyed *patola*, a double *ikat* silk, and other extremely valuable brocaded silks and cottons imported from India. Thai and Cambodian designs merged with Indian patterns and as their fame spread, they were copied and woven in Japan, Persia and China.

In 1608, King Ekatotsarot of Ayutthaya sent a Thai emissary to the Netherlands with a gift of fine silk for the Stadholder. In 1685, another ambassador was sent, this time to France, and this court official wore gorgeous garments that so impressed Louis XIV, 1643–1715, that *ikat* designs and patterns were adapted and copied by the silk designers at Lyon. After the destruction of Ayutthaya by the Burmese army in 1767, when the royal family and thousands of citizens were taken hostage or killed, the new capital of Bangkok was finally established under King Rama I, 1737–1809. The king was keen to rebuild his city, modernize the industry and promote international trade. After import restrictions were lifted, there were so many textiles, drapes, cushions and clothes flooding the market that sumptuary laws and a strict dress code were decreed so that no one's silk garments, ritual items or jewellery could outshine the monarch.

By the nineteenth century, Thailand was flourishing and diplomatic relations were strengthened with the West. King Mongkut, Rama IV, who reigned between 1851 and 1868 and whose story was romantically told in *The King and I*, sent gifts of luxurious textiles, brocades and red and gold sarongs to Queen Victoria. King Mongkut began wearing a silk top hat and vest with his pleated pantaloons to encourage his people to be modern and combine Thai and Western fashions. He directed the women to wear European-style lacy blouses and camisole tops with their wrap-around *pha sing* skirts rather than a shawl, woven of local silk, worn diagonally over the bare breasts. Many women found Western Victorian dress uncomfortable and inappropriate in the hot climate and much preferred the cool sarong or *pha chong kaben* wrap with white silk stockings and shoes. Sir John Bowring, a British consul based in Bangkok during the reign of King Mongkut, wrote in one of his dispatches, that many high-ranking Thai officials kept skilled weavers in their homes to produce the exquisite silk garments because traditional dress was still worn for ceremonial and state occasions.

By now other countries had stepped up production and the flood of silk from China, Persia and Japan onto the world market had made it very difficult for Thailand to compete. In 1901, King Chulalongkorn, Rama V attempted to upgrade and reinvigorate the sericulture industry by inviting a team of Japanese experts to come and suggest improvements. In 1903, the Department of Silk Craftsmen was established and a School of Sericulture was set up to provide specialist research and training for Thai employees. Other sericulture schools were created in Pathum in 1904, and at the King's Dusit Palace. A School of Sericulture became the first specialist department of Kaset University, where it offered a two-year programme entirely in sericulture, and soon other educational facilities were established throughout the kingdom.

King Chulalongkorn, Rama V with one of his consorts, Queen Sukhumal. The Queen is wearing a European blouse under a wrapped sabai sash, with a crisply pleated Thai silk skirt. The king is wearing a European military jacket with his pha nung silk pantaloons, silk stockings and both are wearing European shoes.

Sericulture expanded and it went through a period of rapid growth. Mulberry trees were planted and local silkworms were cross-bred with Japanese varieties that had proven their resistance to the devastating disease pébrine. Modern spinning and hand-reeling machines were introduced and outdated looms replaced by newer and more efficient ones. By 1910, around 35 tons of silk was being exported every year, and between 40,000 and 60,000 people on the Khorat Plateau were engaged in sericulture. There were 23 merchants dealing with silk yarn, yet sericulture remained a cottage industry until the mid-twentieth century, especially in the northeastern regions around Khorat.

In the mountains and fertile valleys, people had for centuries been cultivating cotton, rice and indigo plants for making dyes. Local people who worked on primitive hand-looms or in small workshops were reluctant to make changes in their methods and equipment. When the Depression of the 1930s hit world trade, many silk-reeling filatures and weaving workshops, both large and small, failed. By contrast, a local businessman, Chiang Shinawatra, managed to keep his factory going by introducing some of the modern techniques he had seen being used for weaving silk in Burma. As a Buddhist, he was reluctant to use silk where the worm had been stifled, so he imported wild silk from Burma and had it woven and dyed in Chiang Mai.

Thailand was home to many ethnic groups from Burma, Laos, Vietnam, and parts of eastern India and southern China. Central and southern Thailand had fertile plains, a dependable water supply and a network of Buddhist villages along the *klongs*. Southern Thailand tended to be Muslim and after the border clashes in 1811, a number of Muslim silk weavers had been abducted and forcibly resettled around Nakhon Si Thammarat. They were skilled at *songket*, a handwoven brocaded fabric made of silk or cotton from Malaya, Brunei and Indonesia. It was intricately patterned with coloured silks, gold and silver threads and was made exclusively for the local rulers. Even today some weavers are probably descendants of those early weavers.

Jim Thompson

The Depression of the 1930s was followed by the tragedy of the Second World War, which left the silk industry in a state of collapse and it wasn't until the fortuitous arrival of Jim Thompson in 1945 that the industry gained new life, and worldwide fame. Jim Thompson was an American businessman, formerly with the US military. He was sent to Thailand and his curiosity was aroused when he found that the local silk industry was almost extinct.

Jim Thompson and Ban Krua weaver, enormous care is taken with design and quality control. The silks can be yarn or piece dyed depending on the design.

He found a few Lao-speaking villagers in the northeastern region that still produced limited amounts of raw silk for their own use, dyeing it using natural vegetable products. Their simple wood and bamboo looms were set up in the shaded area beneath their stilt houses. Jim Thompson began making enquiries and collecting all the samples of locally woven shot silk he could find. The knobbly texture of dupioni silk enchanted him with its vivid and unusual colour combinations, like magenta shot with lime green, or orange and purple, so different from the smooth, bland, machine-made silk generally available.

He was fired with enthusiasm, convinced that such unusual beauty must have market appeal, if only the local industry was organized properly and the silk brought to the attention of influential people. He tracked down the few remaining weaving families, and in one impoverished canal-side district known as Ban Krua, he found a community of Muslim weavers. Almost all had had to find other work, but he persuaded one weaver, who was working as a plumber at the time, to produce a number of sample lengths of silk in vibrant colours. The weavers had little faith in Jim Thompson's plans to

Silk in Thailand

regenerate their traditional livelihood, but he continued to visit and encourage them to keep weaving. His friends and advisers urged him to set up a proper manufacturing organization, but he refused, knowing that if he did, he would lose the unique quality that was Thai silk. He set up his Thai Silk Company in 1948 and took his samples to New York. He approached the editor of *Vanity Fair*, Frank Crowninshield, and obtained an introduction to the dynamic Edna Woolman Chase, then editor of *Vogue*. She was completely enchanted and arranged for the couturier Valentino to design beautiful garments using the stunning Thai silks, which were photographed and presented in *Vogue* magazine to instant acclaim. The rest, as they say, is history.

Jim Thompson returned to Thailand and encouraged the Ban Krua weavers to work independently from their own homes. He monitored their progress to ensure consistent quality and purchased their silk fabrics on consignment so he could control its worldwide promotion. The silk weavers of Ban Krua prospered, and some grew wealthy, as did Jim Thompson. With worldwide recognition of Thai silk, other silk businesses were set up, and many of them also prospered.

But mysteriously, while on holiday in the Cameroon Highlands in 1967, Jim Thompson disappeared. There was wide media speculation that he had been kidnapped, had a spell put on him by a local spirit woman, or had an accident, but to this day his fate remains unknown — he simply walked out of the cottage where he was staying, and never came back.

He left behind not only a revived and vibrant silk industry but also a gorgeous traditional teak house that he had had built. It would become the exquisite Museum of South-East Asian Arts. The business he started prospered and expanded. It included extensive lands in the northeast and their communities, where the company handled all aspects of sericulture, from hatching the silkworm eggs, mulberry plantations, reeling, dyeing and weaving, through to the finished product. Much of the industry has become mechanized and currently the factories employ over 20,000 people. But, in the narrow back alleys, the small community of the Ban Krua continues to thrive — a testimony both to the Muslim weaver's skill and to someone of vision who believed in them.

Village sericulture

After the rice has been planted, the women in the villages concentrate on their silkworms. The monsoon rains bring forth fresh leaf growth on the mulberry trees and the women buy or barter to attain silkworm eggs. With Thailand's favourable climate, sericulture is a year-round domestic activity. In the villages, the girls tend the domesticated silkworms and gather the wild cocoons from nearby forests. Other girls weave the silk for sale or into traditional garments for their trousseaux and for special occasions or funeral rites. These patterns are not written down. The mothers and aunts teach their girls the weaving skills and the intricacies and subtle meaning behind the patterns, unique to that village. It is her ability to weave the complex patterns that is a sign of her maturity and eligibility for marriage.

Sericulture can be an important source of additional income for some village families. In parts of northeastern Thailand, where land is poor and the monsoon rains unpredictable, unmarried women and girls can become part of the migratory workforce that

Thai silks, lengths of silk in a range of matmi patterns, woven in a village near Khon Kaen. Patterns include the hook, turtle, small diamond, python, squid, watermelon and diamond.

travels to the cities. The married women, children and the elderly remain in the villages, where most continue to weave textiles to supplement their income. Many girls no longer want to learn the art of weaving, preferring to get city jobs with higher pay and less restrictions. Weaving is exclusively women's work, although legend says it was a male guardian spirit, Khun Borom, who taught the skills of sericulture and weaving. Men continue to be involved, to work in the mulberry orchards, and to make the equipment, the looms and spindle wheels.

The end of the rice harvest is a time of celebration and traditionally an opportunity to relax and enjoy the fun of socializing and courtship. The girls gather together in the evening to spin, and the young men bring their musical instruments to play while they watch the girls. Silk spinning, weaving and dyeing are so much part of the lives of the people that their songs and poetry often compare the bride to the finest silken cloth. With a wedding planned, the house is decorated with flowers and incense, and candles and cushions are placed in front of the little altar. A Buddhist monk blesses the new home and after everything is sprinkled with holy water, special food and gifts are offered to the spirits and to the guests. The bride changes into a wedding *pha sing* and *pha sabai*, and the groom into clothes presented by the bride's parents. The more prosperous the family, the more silk and gold threads are incorporated into the clothes. A white cotton cord or a man's silk sash is passed around through the hands of the female attendants, then to the men, and finally the elders to signal the uniting of the families.

Traditionally, as each young man enters his teens, he spends three months in a monastery, or *wat*, during the Buddhist period of Lent. He discards his everyday clothes and, if he is very fortunate, puts on a *pha hang* of shot silk. These garments are later exchanged for a white cotton robe and he takes his vows of poverty, chastity and obedience. For some, this becomes a lifetime commitment. It brings great honour to the family when a son or male family member enters a monastery or is ordained, so weaving special textiles for the monks is an important task for the women. It is the custom to weave a silk blanket to be worn by the novice when he walks in procession to the monastery for his ordination. In the past, this blanket was hand woven but these days it is more likely to be machine made.

If a young man plans or needs to leave his village for an extended period, his mother might weave him a silk *pha sarong* as a parting gift, with Buddhist symbols for his protection from the evil spirits.

It is the tradition to wear silk during the many sacred festivals. In the early days both men and woman wore the *pha-nung*. It was a length of cloth between three and ten metres long that was wrapped around, and then pulled through to make knee-length pants. It was worn with a blouse, shirt or jacket, or a rectangular shawl for special occasions. By the turn of the century, the *pha chong kaben* had been replaced by the *pha-sarong* for men and the *pha sing* for women. Four woven bands are stitched together and it is gathered and folded into a pleat at the front and secured with a sash or decorative metal belt. The *jok*, or top band, is woven in silk or cotton in a variety of colours and features stylized plants, birds, flowers and abstract patterns that may include gold or silver threads. The Thai Yuan and Lao groups of northern Thailand favour flowing water patterns or warp stripes, sometimes enhanced by zig-zag tapestry bands of contrasting colours.

Textiles form an important part of the rhythm of life in the villages. The land is flat or undulating and much of the area is fairly isolated, with poor-quality soils. Despite its history of poverty and an intermittent rainfall, the Khorat Plateau is famous for its highly skilled weavers and top-quality woven silk. Some designs and patterns come from the Thai Buddhist and animist cosmology, and include natural items like running water, pine and bamboo, squirrels and snakes. The Thai-Lao people in northern Thailand weave a beautiful cotton and silk weft *ikat* called *mud-mee* and traditional silk brocades. *Ikat*-dyed silks in dark, rich colours are often the choice of the elderly. The Khorat Plateau weavers are also famous for weaving the highly complex narrow silk sashes and silk *ikat*-dyed *matami* with its rich variety of patterns and colours, featuring trees, flowers fruit, animals and birds. Complex geometric stripes, diamonds, zig-zags and circles add interest. The fabric lengths are wrapped into a simple sarong, short loincloth, ankle-length skirt or loose pantaloons that are gracefully pleated into waist belts. Bright-coloured shoulder sashes, elaborate headdresses, bracelets and other jewellery complete the outfit.

Commercial development

Central and southern Thailand is subtropical with predictable periods of monsoon weather, so Thai sericulture continues all year round using both yellow and white multi-voltine silkworm species that produce between eight and ten hatchings a year. The special lustre and brilliance of Thai silk comes from the indigenous silkworm, the *Bombyx mori linneus*. The slub effect results when two silkworms get tangled together when they are spinning their cocoons and the silk therefore has to be handspun. The warp is made from the commercially reeled smooth, fine white silk, and the slubby village hand-reeled silk is used for the weft. The two silks dye slightly differently giving Thai dupioni silk its special texture and brilliance.

In areas such as Phetchabun, large estates have been established to bring together under their control all the various aspect of sericulture. They also offer technical help and support to their suppliers and farmers in the surrounding villages. Some estates have over 2000 people working and living within the compound. In addition, there are the local farmers who bring their cocoons in to be weighed and graded and they are paid then and there for their cocoons. By overseeing all aspects of production, the estate can ensure that only disease-free eggs are distributed to the farmers. The very best of the 'green', meaning live cocoons, are set aside to allow the silkworm to develop, first into a pupa and then a moth so she can lay her eggs in sterile, controlled conditions. The extensive mulberry orchards have their own management and workers to ensure that a steady supply of the right mulberry leaves are available for the developing silkworms.

There is no waste and the pupae can be freeze-dried and sold as a tasty snack or pressed for their oil. The stripped mulberry branches are used for firewood to supply the hot water. In some villages and estates, the trays of silkworms are placed on open racks or mesh so the detritus and half-eaten leaves fall through and are collected and spread under the mulberry and other fruit trees as fertilizer. Some is fed to the cattle or carp in the large fishponds. These ponds can be both vast and ornamental and the fish provide welcome food.

Weighing and checking the silk cocoons, Phetchabun. There is no waiting, the cocoons are checked immediately for weight and quality.

Candling to check the cocoons, Phetchabun A local grower and her son bring in their cocoons to be checked for quality before she is paid.

In the fast moving world of commercial markets, the estates have had to respond to calls to improve the quality of the local product by using new species of imported hybrid silkworm eggs. This won't necessarily increase production immediately, or produce a higher yield, because the hybrids need to adapt to the humidity and high temperatures and to local pests and diseases. The new strains give a more uniform, international look but that could be a real loss as it would lessen the very particular and individual character of Thai silk.

Reeling and spooling the dyed silk, Jim Thompson's vast and impressive estate on the Khorat Peninsular.

In large complexes, the most modern and scientifically advanced reeling and throwing systems have been installed to guarantee complete quality control. A management team ensures that the business functions well and can supply all grades and styles of silk to the market. The company also provides quality housing, a substantial cooked lunch and medical and childcare. It offers training and technical support for all those involved including those people contracted to them working outside the complex.

Two estates have been put forward to receive the Global Organic Textile Standard (GOTS) certificate for their chemical-free silk yarn. This designation is defined and enforced by four member organizations from Germany, Japan, the United States and the United Kingdom. Requirements must be met, including internal control systems, the use of toxins and the treatment of wastewater. In addition, the harvesting of the raw materials, manufacturing of the textiles, the final labelling of the products, and all steps in the process need to be both environmentally and socially responsible. One of the most difficult parts of making organic silk is to ensure that the mulberry fields are free from harmful chemicals added to the land or absorbed through the air. Of the 985,000 mulberry growers that farm more than 108,000 *rai* across the country, very few adhere to organic standards. But with the certificate, these silk processors and manufacturers will be able to export their organic fabrics and garments to major markets in the United States, Europe and the United Kingdom. Silk fabric accounts for about half of the silk exported from Thailand. The rest is raw silk, yarn, cocoons and silk waste. Many of the silk districts are near the so-called Golden Triangle, and an ongoing problem has been piracy and the moving of silk products illegally across the borders.

Thailand contributes only a small amount to the global trade in silk, but since traditional Thai silk is hand woven, each length of silk fabric is unique and cannot be duplicated through commercial means. Thailand uses a peacock emblem to identify four grades or styles of silk. The gold peacock, premium-grade Royal Thai Silk, uses native silkworm breeds and traditional hand-made production methods. The silver peacock indicates Classic Thai Silk, developed from specific silkworm breeds and hand-made production. The blue peacock indicates a product of pure silk threads but with no specific production methods and chemical dyes can be used. The green peacock indicates a product of silk blended with other fibres and with no specific production method.

For over 60 years, Her Majesty Queen Sirikit has promoted the development and use of Thai silk far beyond Thailand. She has also assisted rural communities towards economic self-sufficiency. In 1976 she set up the SUPPORT Foundation to endorse silk, arts and handicrafts. She realiszed she had a unique opportunity to travel abroad and promote Thai silk. After some study and discussion with her advisers, she selected five Thai silk outfits for day and evening wear, woven using traditional techniques, to wear on her official trips to Europe. She is a beautiful and graceful woman and her stunning garments were widely admired and copied for their high fashion. She was presented with the Louis Pasteur Award by the International Sericulture Commission for her achievements in developing sericulture in Thailand. Today, Thai silk is distinctive and admired, sought after and exported for clothing and upholstery to all the major industrialized countries.

Ao tu Than, colourful Vietnamese 'Four Flapped dress' long skirt with tunic, split at centre front and sides, *vem* or top and long sash with distinctive straw hat.
Source: DUC Fashion

CHAPTER SIX

Silk in South-East Asia

It was believed that the thread of human history in South-East Asia went back over 1.83 million years, and this was confirmed by the thrilling discovery at Lenggong of a stone hand axe. Then in 1958, a 40,000 year old skull was found in the Niah Caves in Borneo and this was followed in 1991 by a complete 11,000-year-old skeleton, later named Perak Man. These ancient, indigenous people wore bark costumes decorated with beads, and wove checked and striped fabrics on a primitive backstrap loom. Later, travellers arrived from China and other lands traded textiles, including silk and cotton sarongs. The southward movement of people during the Han Dynasty, 220 BCE–206 CE, probably brought with them pottery, like the shards of first century Chinese pottery found in Borneo. Trade relations developed with India and gradually many people adopted the Indian religions of Hinduism and Buddhism and melded them with animism and other local tribal beliefs.

Vietnam

Vietnam has one of the longest continuous histories in the world, with archaeological findings of human settlement as far back as half a million years. Human teeth have been found in caves in northern

Vietnam from the Paleolithic and Pleistocene Ages. Vietnam was successively governed by a series of Chinese dynasties, beginning with the Han, and was repeatedly ravaged and divided by civil wars. The later Chinese dynasties, the Dutch, French and Americans, have each left their mark on its culture and textiles.

The Vietnamese were an advanced civilization, rich in exquisite treasures and detailed works of art, but over the years of Chinese domination and rule, especially between 1407 and 1427 during the Ming period, many cultural artefacts were destroyed. Sericulture was set up in some of the highland villages, but production was intermittent and most raw silk was imported from China. The Chinese governors put pressure on the local elite to wear Chinese-style clothing, insisting on a strict dress code, and ordinary people were limited to wearing undyed cloth in natural white, black or brown. Much later, in a decree from the court in 1826, skirts were banned altogether as they were deemed to be 'unseemly bottomless pants', but not all women followed the rules as many preferred skirts to pants.

Each region had its own traditional and recognizable style. The Kinh people were the ethnic majority and they usually wore the *ao tu than* or 'four-flapped dress'. It was made in plain, dark colours, except for special occasions such as festivals or weddings. It consisted of a flowing outer floor-length tunic, open at the front like a jacket and split at the sides. Under it was worn a long skirt with a *yem* or under-bodice, tied with a silk sash, as buttons did not appear until the eighteenth century. These days it is mostly worn at festivals and often very colourful, with different shades of the same colour for the skirt, jacket and bodice. In southern Vietnam, the simpler silk pyjamas, the *ao ba ba*, are preferred for day-to-day use, usually in brown or black.

The *ao dai* was originally worn by the royal and upper class but today it is the Vietnamese national costume. It is very graceful and consists of a long gown, made of silk or other specially beautiful fabric, slit on both sides, and must be worn over pants. It has some similarities to the Chinese *cheongsam* that is split to mid-thigh and worn as a dress. The Vietnamese national dress is compulsory in many high schools and sometimes in middle schools and colleges

Boiling yellow cocoons, still done in remote villages in a large pot of water over an open fire and hand wound onto a reel.

too. Women working in front offices as receptionists or tour guides are also required to wear *ao dai*. Some men wear the male form for special occasions like weddings, funerals or New Year, but in everyday life, Western fashions have replaced traditional Vietnamese styles.

Silk in South-East Asia

There are many silk districts, and the largest is in Lam Dong province at Bao Loc. It is in the highlands, and has a subtropical climate, ideal for sericulture. The total number of mulberry trees has been dropping and most of the trees that remain are old and no longer produce large quantities of good leaves. New species of mulberry have been offered but the hill-country people who have lived in these forests for generations do not always understand that the trees must be renewed, watered, pruned, weeded and fertilized regularly. Vietnam produces both white and yellow cocoons, but most of the available eggs are imported from China through private traders without strict quality control. Many of the eggs die through poor refrigeration and storage or they fail to thrive, leaving the farmers with little reward for all their hard work.

The Ministry of Agriculture and Rural Development is keen to improve the situation and has developed several silkworm egg producing centres, but the rearers are not accredited, so low quality silkworm eggs are still a problem. During the 1990s an international partnership was formed with Italy and the most modern reeling filatures were built. These companies supply the farmers with mulberry saplings, silkworm eggs and technical assistance. They tie them into contracts to buy back all the cocoons and arrange to spin, weave, sell or export the silk. The main export markets for Vietnamese silk are Thailand and China, followed by India and Bangladesh, although most is sold to Cambodia and Laos by the local people, using unofficial channels.

Weaving is still done in the villages as well as in large company workshops using locally produced and imported silk. With relatively low labour costs, Vietnam has a growth industry in making silk fabrics into garments and accessories such as long dresses, skirts, scarves, jackets, ties and shirts. Household items include cushions, pillows and bed covers, but there is still plenty of room to bring the quality up to international standards. Many areas in the country that are currently planted with coffee or tea could be used for sericulture where the income can be much higher. Sericulture is labour intensive, and as everybody works, Vietnam could have a bright future as an important international supplier of raw silk and silk yarn.

Cambodia

In Cambodia, weaving has been part of its history and culture since the eighth century. The Khymer Empire reached its peak between the tenth and thirteenth centuries and extended over much of South-East Asia, becoming part of the silk route between South India and China. Sericulture was an established craft of the northern Sukhothai people and raw silk was one of the main exports to China during this period. Silk was certainly being worn in the royal courts of Laos and Burma, now Myanmar, especially the sumptuous silk brocades glittering with gold and silver, incorporating many designs from India. The ancient temple complex at Angkor Wat, built in the early twelfth century, includes images carved in bas-relief of women wearing traditional garments similar to those worn today. There are only a few precious examples of Kymer silk left in museums and private collections, and they are mostly held outside Cambodia.

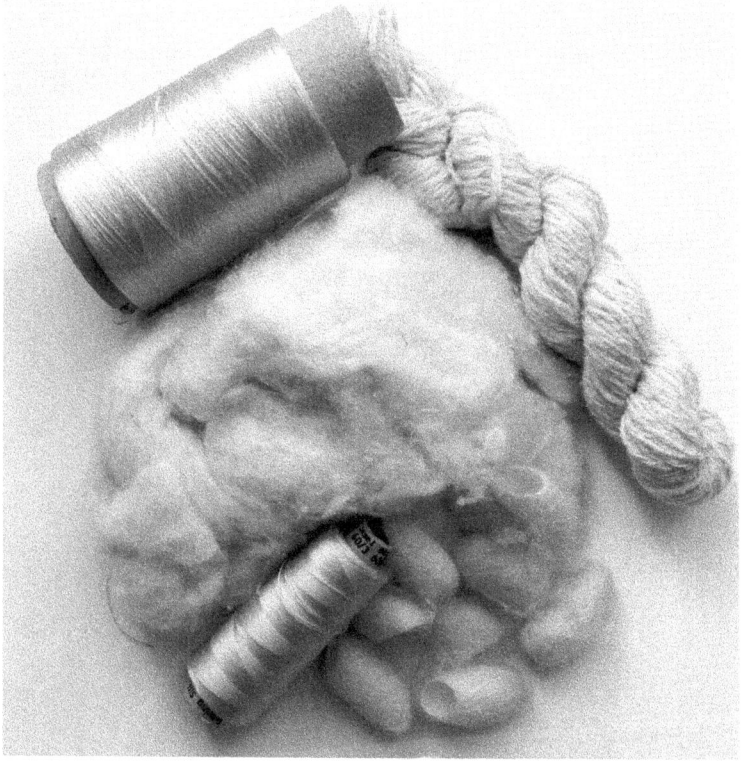

Yellow silk, including fine filament singles, plied handspun yellow cocoon strippings, unspun cocoon strippings, yellow cocoons and a spool of silk thread, especially spun for doing gold work embroidery.

Silks from the past 150 years were recently found in the basement of a museum in Phnom Penh. It was a wonderful discovery, because it was believed that they had long since been destroyed by war, flood and the years of neglect that had devastated the collection.

Cambodia has a tradition of making a fine silk ceremonial cloth called *samphot-hol* that was worn either as a sarong or pulled through to make trousers. It was similar to Indian *patola* cloth and coloured a reddish-brown with greens and yellow. The exquisite *ikat* or *hol* designs are woven from individually dyed threads using natural dyes from plants, insect resins, bark and herbs. The threads are wound on multiple spools and woven to produce intricate patterns that depict religious scenes and, in more recent times, aspects of village life and beliefs. The Khmer also weave the *pha chong kaben*, worn by both men and women, featuring tie-dyed patterns in the central area, with narrow patterned borders. Women in Pakse have a tradition of using imported silk mixed with cotton yarns to weave into tubular sarongs called *malong*, worn with colourful sashes and large head cloths. A beautiful fine, lightweight transparent silk organza is also made for sheer garments and window coverings. Complex brocade fabrics are hand woven, and often incorporate gold or silver thread, making them even more valuable. In the past, these gorgeous textiles

Freshly dyed cloth.

were only available to the royal family and the court, and they are still sought after for weddings and other religious ceremonies.

Cambodia has highlighted its 'golden' Khmer silk, named because of the natural yellow colour in the sericin gum that surrounds the silk fibre. The silkworm is multi-voltine and hatchings are almost continuous throughout the year. The most famous area for golden silk is *Phnom Srok*, in the hills above the Great Lake in northwest Cambodia. Sericulture is part of the mixed agriculture economy and mulberry trees are grown on small family blocks of land, along with their vegetables, fruit trees and rice that provide the rural family with its lifestyle and income. The knowledge of raising silkworms is passed down through the generations from mother to daughter. They learn to reel silk and throw it to make the desired quality yarn for weaving. Silkworms are called *neang* in the Khmer language, and it is also an endearing term for a pretty girl.

Before the civil war, 1967–75, all Cambodian silk textiles came from the golden Khmer cocoon, but 30 years of political strife and war have decimated the mulberry orchards. It has been very hard on the local people, making it almost impossible for them to feed their families and care for the mulberry trees and silkworms. Some subsistence farmers on the islands in the Mekong have continued to look after their silkworms and weave silk but many looms have been dismantled as the cost of silk yarn has increased and the market fallen away. Some weavers say they cannot imagine leaving a profession that has been in the family for so long, but many women feel they have no option but to look for other work. Garment factories provide one of the few sources of income for rural women. Although they provide a regular income, they also have a reputation for forced overtime, low pay and sweatshop conditions.

To assist the weavers and support local sericulture, the United Nations has helped to finance a project to create a silkworm production centre. The Cambodian government has also tried to keep down the spiralling costs to the village weavers by withdrawing all import taxes and value-added tax on imported and local silk yarn. It has encouraged the farmers to replant mulberry trees but the process is slow, and many Cambodian farmers prefer to plant more secure crops like cassava. Silk has always been at the mercy of fluctuating market conditions but there are signs of it becoming a significant export item offering work for women and households in rural areas.

Philippines

When Miguel Lopez de Legazpi conquered the Philippine Islands in 1564, he found the local leaders, the *datos* or *rajas*, were clothed in beautiful silks that clearly came on the silk ships, mostly from China. 'Silk in every stage of manufacture and of every variety of weave and pattern formed the most valuable part of their cargos'. These included the 'delicate gauzes and Cantonese crepes, the flowered silk of Canton called primavera or "springtime" by the Spaniards, velvets and taffetas and the *nobleza* or fine damask, rougher grosgrains and heavy brocades worked in fantastic designs with gold and silver thread. Of silken wearing apparel, there were many thousand pairs of stockings in each cargo, more than 50,000 in one galleon, skirts and velvet bodices, cloaks and robes and kimonos. Packed in the chests of the galleons were silken bed coverings and tapestries, handkerchiefs, tablecloths and napkins and rich vestments for the service of churches and convents from Sonora to Chile. Nearly all these were of Chinese workmanship.'

Since then, sericulture has developed in the Philippines, but it has been somewhat intermittent. In the 1930s the silk industry was revived using two Japanese species, Ichat White and Nismo Yellow, and although it was successful in Batac Ilocos Norte in 1936, it collapsed after the Second World War and the land was converted to rice, corn and tobacco, partly because those crops received government subsides. There was renewed interest with the arrival of overseas specialists. In 1948 an American entomologist, Charles S Banks, managed a 500-hectare mulberry plantation in Canlaon, Negros Occidental, and several Japanese sericulturalists under Charles Banks engaged in silkworm rearing and reeling cocoons for raw silk production, hand-loom weaving and silk fabric dyeing.

In the early 1950s, Upi Agricultural School in North Cotabato was understood to have extensive mulberry plantations and facilities to reel cocoons and weave silk on hand-looms. In 1969, the Bureau of Plant Industry (BPI) introduced imported silkworm eggs from Japan and

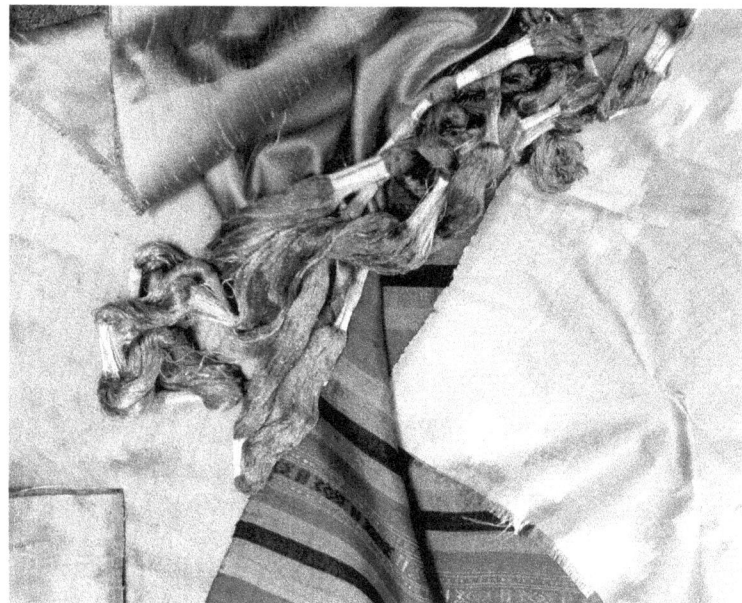

Silk fabrics, commercially woven shot silk, woven with a green warp and pink weft, two lengths of silk warp threads that have been tied tightly in a pattern before dyeing to control the position of the colour, a length of hand woven ikat dyed silk with typical dupioni texture, note the irregular selvedge edge compared to the commercially woven silk, and a vibrant silk shawl with stripes and inlaid pattern.

the Mountain Province Development Authority (MPDA) embarked on mulberry cultivation. It was abolished in the early 1970s, and now the facilities and most sericulture activities are under the management of the Philippine Textile Research Institute (PTRI).

Indonesia

Indonesia is made up of around 17,500 islands and of those, about 6000 are inhabited. Sericulture, being an ancient agricultural and village based industry, fits in well with the lifestyle and farming patterns. Sericulture was introduced to Java around 1720 by Hendrick Zwaardecroon, who was Governor General of the Dutch East Indies at the time. By 1735, Indonesia had exported 300 pounds of silk to the Netherlands but unfortunately this early silk production was deemed a failure. This was distressing for the Governor as he could be criticized for poor leadership, because silk represented wealth, power and status. Indonesia was a major source of gold and these textiles with their symbolic clan designs were intimately tied to the court, so sumptuary laws were introduced to limit the wearing of gold and silk textiles to just the elite. Men traditionally wore a loincloth and shawl, but many Indonesian tribes lack any differentiation between the clothes of men and women. The far more subtle messages are in the designs and symbols that reflected the person's status within the tribe.

Traditionally in the villages, many women spin using a spindle wheel, and weave on a backstrap loom. It produces a continuous circular fabric and so the ritual ceremonial cutting of the cloth has deep significance. The women wear the long and elaborate *tapis* skirt, in mysterious warp *ikat* designs that are embroidered with brilliant silk and gold bands. Their religious beliefs are integral to their lives and in some parts of Indonesia, Hindu gods, their weapons and other attributes are featured in their designs. Some of the Muslim patterns represent the cosmos with squares, circles and triangles. The complex double *ikat* and resist-dyeing techniques were copied from Indian textiles and include symbols that are locally significant. Java has some large and stunning designs, including elephants, peacocks, horses, griffins and ships.

Indonesian weaving is almost exclusively a woman's craft, and in earlier times the workshop was often situated near or within the court complex to ensure quality control and a continuous supply of the gorgeous textiles. The women and girls were trained from childhood to weave the complex patterns and to make the silk and gold brocades that are such supreme treasures and marriage gifts. These rich brocades, known as *songket,* and the various complex weft *ikat* designs were combined to produce the fabulous *kain songket limar.* The court did produce some silk yarn and recognized the value of having its own silk production, but most of the yarns and design ideas have filtered in from India via the travellers and trade routes, barter and exchange.

There was a new mood, drive and energy during the 1950s when a group of Indonesian and Japanese ex-war veterans, decided to explore and support sericulture as a home-based industry. As in many countries, sericulture in Indonesia is a sideline that offers an additional income and provides work for women to complement

Complex double ikat is being woven using a backstrap loom.

their other incomes. The pleasant climate is very suitable and cocoon production reached its highest level between 1962 and 1966, but collapsed again in the 1970s due to the spread of pébrine disease. This was devastating, yet the fragile industry rebuilt and from the 1990s, production increased, buoyed up by the rising cocoon prices. The number of farmers involved in sericulture rose, but it was a bit of a rollercoaster. The local silkworm eggs produced poor quality cocoons and silk of reduced value. The most urgent need was for controlled distribution of disease-free eggs so that each farmer could succeed and know that sericulture would be of value, expand and consolidate.

The government appointed the Forestry Department to oversee the mulberry plantations and establish sericulture at the borders of the forests. This had the added benefit of protecting the forest from people who were wilfully cutting down the trees for firewood, especially on the island of Java. This has become urgent as the number of mulberry trees has steadily decreased, and the *petani* farmers are moving into other crops or to the towns to find alternative work. Currently, sericulture is not a priority, but the government is attempting to pull together a plan for the future. Traditional methods are being upgraded and refined and gradually the disappointments and failures of the past are being overcome. There is a future for Indonesia, with proper leadership and management, enthusiasm and funding, to create a worthwhile sericulture industry.

Malay, Malaysia

In 1722, a high official and master weaver from the Bugis area called Tuk Tuan Keraing Aji came as a refugee to Pahang in the Malay Peninsula. He was a knowledgeable collector and connoisseur of fine fabrics and master weaver with a wealth of new ideas and patterns. He taught the women in his village and the surrounding area all the various processes associated with weaving silk. The designs in the sumptuous gold textiles included birds and serpents, parasols, flags and banners, all the symbols of prestige. His fame and that of the beautiful silks spread, and his students up to the present day continue the work, teaching his weaving techniques. The Pahang state government has been most supportive and the special loom used to weave *Tenum Pahang Diraja* or royal silk fabrics can still be found in most homes in the village where men and women, young and old, continue to weave when time allows.

Malaya was restructured in 1963 and the new confederation was called Malaysia. It is a melting pot of many ethnic groups and before the wide acceptance of Islam, many Malay women wore sarongs, known as *kemban*, tied tightly just above the bust. Indian-Malay women wear beautiful saris and Chinese-Malay women the *cheongsam*, a one-piece dress with a high collar, diagonally closed with small clips or toggles. It is usually made in a soft fabric such as silk with slits at the side. Older, well-respected women wear *samfoo*. They look like pyjamas, with a separate loose fitting top fastened by toggles and worn with cropped pants.

Batik dyed on silk or cotton fabric has a long history in South-East Asia and today it is often combined with contemporary fashion for formal occasions. The Malaysian government is keen to reinforce local traditions and directs civil servants to wear batik on the first and fifteenth day of the month. In Sabah in East Malaysia, teachers are encouraged to wear batik shirts or *baju kurung* to school on Thursdays. Usually the school will provide the fabric, printed with a particular design so that every teacher can have their shirts made up by a local tailor and their garments match.

Malaysia's small sericulture industry mainly produces cocoons for export to Japan. The United Nations Office for Project Services

(UNOPS) has been supportive of silkworm development projects to modernize and increase production through investment and project management. They want to improve working conditions and raise the women's income. They selected local cooperative farms and offered training to the people, and this has been a real boost and already brought benefits to around 1500 people and their communities.

Burma, Myanmar

Wars and pestilence have taken their toll on Myanmar's long and cultured history. These days it is home to more than a hundred ethnic groups, has a population of over 47 million, but nearly one quarter of the people live below the poverty line. Most people are Buddhists and would not take a life, even of a silkworm, but they are happy to wear silk from wild silk cocoons where the moth has escaped to fly free. While the women weave and wear silk, much of the yarn these days is imported. Like many of the surrounding countries, the national version of their *lon-gyi* or sarong is made from a length of hand-woven uncut cloth. One of the most beautiful designs is called *lun taya acheik*, which means 'one hundred shuttle wave'. It comes in many variations, with magical names like Emerald Palace, Princess's Curl or Ribbon of Orchids. It requires three girls to sit at each loom, and each one manages up to 35 tiny shuttles, full of brightly coloured silk yarns. The girls need both patience and concentration to weave together and it can take up to three months to make a length of two metres.

The Gangaw district in central Myanmar has traditionally been the home of the finest royal silks, woven in red and green exclusively for the king, with pink reserved for the royal women. Some tribal groups like the Shan a Thai people from eastern Myanmar specialize in weaving a fine silk weft-*ikat* fabric. The weft threads are tied and dyed before the fabric is woven so that gradually as the weaving progresses, intricate patterns emerge of flowers, butterflies or leaves. The town of Pyin Oo Lwin has a thriving Eurasian community of mostly Anglo-Burmese and Anglo-Indians who settled in Maymyo during the period of British rule. These days Pyin Oo Lwin is one of the four centres of sericulture designated as of national economic importance. It has a Research Centre near the Botanical Gardens that provide research into the intensive planting and harvesting of mulberry leaves, bark for hand-made paper and indigenous medicinal plants. It also includes a centre for rearing silkworms, and reeling the silk from the cocoons.

Laos

There is a rich oral tradition around silk in Laos. Some legends suggest that sericulture began around 1000 BCE but others maintain it was established around 700 CE when the Lao-Tai people brought their knowledge of sericulture with them when they migrated from Yunnan in Southwest China and settled near the great lake of Nong Sae. Ancient records tell of silkworms in the towns of Kouk Ching Chao and Thinh Si and both wild silk and dyed silk were exchanged in the market for valuable shells. The 8000 year old cave paintings at Kabi give enticing clues as to fabric, motifs and styles of garments. Unfortunately, as a result of climate change, migration, power struggles and war, there are almost no fabrics extant older than 200 years, so poems, legends, carvings and manuscripts are highly valued for their descriptions of these precious fabrics.

Laos is made up of many ethnic groups but the main one is the Mon-Khmer people who settled at least 3000–4000 years ago and who make up around two thirds of the population. All the tribes have different origins and experiences and their art and weaving styles reflect their legends and history. They raise silkworms and weave both silk and cotton on an upright loom, sometimes using silver and gold threads to stunning effect by adding red, orange, yellow, purple, indigo and black yarns, dyed from local plants.

Laos has both wild silkworms and the domesticated *Bombyx mori*, which is highly prized and called *fa* silk or 'magic silk'. There is a delightful story told of how Prince Nak got caught up in a fishing net made of *fa* silk. A lovely girl came and rescued him by singing a song to break the magic silk. The prince took her home to meet his parents and in thanks for her kindness they gave her two bags of ginger, one white which turned into silver and the other yellow which turned into gold, making her family rich. It is said that from this, the white and gold silk cocoons evolved. *Fa* silk is believed

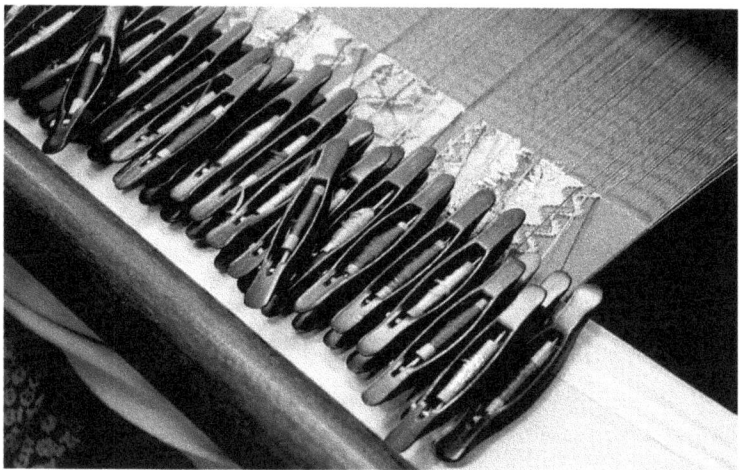

Myanma, speciality fabrics known as '100 Shuttles Wave' where three girls wove alongside one another and managed the multiple shuttles to produce the exquisite wave designs.

to have great protective qualities and many people would still not venture far without a little strip tied to their wrist.

Laos silkworms are multi-voltine, with six to eight hatchings a year. Each batch takes 28 days from newly hatched silkworm to the moth and because of the warm climate they are cultivated most of the year, beginning in February. The most common wild silkworms are the eri *Philosamia ricini* and the *Antheraea mylitta*, and both spin brown cocoons. The light-green *Aticas luna* moth is found in Khammouan province and gold coloured cocoons are found in Vientiane. They are usually collected for their pupae which form part of the diet, rather than for the silk thread, but experiments are progressing to reel and spin the wild tussah silks. The silkworm is protein rich and used in lots of ways as a food product, dried, powdered or fried, and in cosmetics, creams and powder.

A woman's weaving skills were highly valued and added to her status as a desirable bride. Weaving brought credit to her, her family and her prospective in-laws. The future of the family was dependent on the skills of both men and women, and an incompetent person had little value in the village. Part of the tradition, culture and duty of the women was to produce clothes for their family and keep the sacred traditions alive.

In the village there was an area where young men seeking a bride would bring their bamboo weaving or rope making and watch the girls, young widows and divorcees spin and chatter, and in the relaxed atmosphere get to know each other. Everyone carried a woven bag and a Tai Pouan girl could weave a love message into the red bag she gave to the young man of her choice. The richly symbolic designs, the fine colour combinations and ancient motifs showed her readiness for marriage. If his family approved of the girl they could respond by returning her bag with gifts of bracelets and coins, threads and herbs, showing that they would give their blessing to the marriage. Silk was used in the language of courtship: '. . . How ardent is my wish to have you weave on the landing of my stairs . . . Having you weave an *ikat sinh*, and feed silkworms at my house . . .' She replies modestly that her skills are limited, but in truth, she would need to be a good weaver to be considered ready for marriage.

In the Tai Deang group both the bride and groom prepare a dowry. She would offer lovely textiles including *sinh* skirts, which were worn with a pleated scarf across the chest. Later, the skirts would be returned to her so she could wear them after the wedding. She would also make mattress covers, drapes, cushions and mosquito nets. The nets were often exquisitely embroidered in brightly coloured silks. They were an important bridal item as they offered the young people a degree of privacy in the husband's family home.

The women sit on the floor to weave using a simple backstrap loom. It can be hard on the body as the threads are tensioned by leaning back or flexing the legs. The Hmong people's speciality was weaving cloth for batiks, dyed with indigo and embroidered with silk. The motifs were often copied from nature and include flowers and fish scales, fruit seeds and spiral designs, spider webs, tiger eyebrows, leaves and peacock eyes. The ethnic groups all have their own ancient symbolic motifs of both living and non-living subjects, including boats and small birds, the snake, lotus, clouds and water. All designs are woven in stripes in traditional combinations and colours. The Hindu and Buddhist communities both have special motifs, including the male and female river serpents to help and protect them. Some are composites like frog-people, the supernatural horse-deer, brilliant birds in flight representing a free spirit, flying horses and the elephant-lions of royal association.

A Buddhist sacred text, written on mulberry or palm leaf paper, then wrapped in a valuable handwoven cloth is a very precious item. It can take many years to write the manuscripts and weave the wrappers, so they are a valued gift to the temples, as they help to ensure the continuation of the sacred truths. The donor also gains merit and some manuscripts are given in memory of parents. When a child dies, some parents donate their child's beautiful *sinh* and wrap it around a sacred text or manuscript, in the hope that in the next life their child will be a refined and educated person.

The women of the family are the weavers, but in times of war or distress it can be almost impossible to settle down to the time consuming tasks of preparing, threading up the loom and weaving cloth. The men rarely weave or assist with any aspect of women's work, but they do collect the dye plants and mordants, harvest the mulberry leaves and carry the heavy baskets of washed and dyed cloth. They also take the surplus and sell it in the markets. The various governments have attempted to support the weavers, drawing them into a cooperative, supplying the silk or cotton and distributing the woven skirts throughout the country. Until the Second World War, the materials, weaving patterns, motifs and dyes could date and place any textile to one of the many tribal groups. In 1975, a reform that came to be known as the New Economic Mechanism allowed many weavers to establish their own businesses and sell the finished woven articles.

These days the women who work in the upmarket shops and hotels are encouraged to wear the expensive handmade sinhs but usually Western clothes are worn and few people wear traditional costume even for special festival occasions. Sericulture does provide gainful employment and can improve the quality of life for the people in the rural areas. It is therefore important in lifting the standard of living and reducing the migration of people to urban areas in search of employment.

Fine, pure silk Persian carpet featuring animal and traditional floral motifs.

CHAPTER SEVEN

Silk in the Balkan and post-Soviet States

Turkey

The ancient silk route from China to the west passed through parts of the Byzantine Empire, bringing trade and wealth, luxurious silks and an aura of the exotic East. When it became the Ottoman Empire in the fifteenth century, the powerful Ottoman Sultan, Mehmet II, 1432–1481, recognized silk's value as a domestic industry and special privileges were granted to silk workers to ensure its continuation. By the sixteenth century, planting mulberry trees for sericulture was recorded in Bursa, and almost half of the empire's silk fibre and fabric was produced there. However, its quality was variable and the European merchants and agents bought it reluctantly, preferring finer silk from Russia, India or China.

The two big importers of silk fibre in the seventeenth century were France and England and both had tightly controlled standards and sophisticated weaving facilities. The European importers preferred to buy silk yarn rather than fabrics, to have greater control over how they were woven and finished, but this left very little yarn for the Turkish domestic industry. The court became increasingly dependent on importing Lyon's speciality, their flamboyant 'bizarre' silks that had been specifically woven for a foreign market and taste. Some high-quality silk fabrics were still produced in Turkey, but by then, the demand for extravagant furnishings and textiles had diminished.

Then in 1860, a crisis hit the industry with an outbreak of pébrine disease. In Turkey, egg production was not centralized but managed by local egg hatchers who had little concern for the care or hygiene required to raise healthy eggs. Turkey was not alone, and throughout Europe the silkworm industry was disintegrating. Identification of the disease was urgently needed and new methods required to develop strains of disease-resistant eggs, preferably in controlled hatcheries. It was many years before the stellar work of Louis Pasteur, 1822–1895, identified the disease and new solutions and practices were found.

Gradually, the industry recovered using disease-free eggs imported from Japan. By the early 1870s, over 400,000 people were employed in the silk industry and exports of cocoons and reeled silk grew, but another major change occurred when the Turkish court adopted European dress, with its radically different fabrics and styles. Western clothes and values were all the rage and people preferred imported cotton cloth and ready-made garments to locally woven silk. Girls continued to embroider their trousseaux with gilt thread, floral sprays and foliage, and still included a set of exquisite silk bed hangings inspired by French designs, but the quality of the local silk fabric was poor, the selvedges split and some of the new chemical dyes were unstable.

The quality did improve and the local strain of *Bombyx mori*, known as Bursa White, was considered the best in Europe, until new Japanese breeds were introduced. Bursa White was a 'soft' yarn, woven 'in the gum', with the sericin still in it. This made it a strong but heavy yarn, perfect for soft, easily draped fabrics like crepe de Chine, but it was not really suitable for producing the fine, smooth, hard twist organzine thread used by the new machines. After the opening of the Suez Canal, a flood of raw silk from China and

Harem, the sultana's maid brings her the latest beautiful silks for her to choose. She is surrounded by silk in the cushions, curtains and divans.
Painting by Amadee van Loo, 1719-95, Louvre Museum, Paris.

Japan hit the market, so although domestic production increased, the price declined. French experts were brought in to modernize all aspects of sericulture, and this led to the establishment of the Sericulture Research Institute in Bursa in 1888. This new industry was quite different. Foreigners now owned the new mills, making it difficult for local people to become involved or to own their own business. The factories produced only raw goods that were sent to Europe for further processing before being imported back into Turkey for sale as cloth and clothing.

Local guildsmen and master weavers had traditionally held status

A 18th century Turkish woman and her maid at the Hamman, pastel by Swiss artist Jean-Etienne Liotard 1702-89 who visited Turkey with the British ambassador in 1738. The high wooden pattens worn by the woman would not have been unusual as Western women wore similar overshoes. The full trousers would have been much more scandalous.

in their community. They trained their apprentices, established the quality of goods, performed guild and civic rituals and collected taxes. Work in the new foreign-owned mills was hard and unpleasant. It was low-paid and required little skill and many guildsmen refused to enter the new mills. Unskilled rural workers seized the opportunity and flooded in from the countryside, looking for work, any work. Some of the women and girls came from Greece or Armenia. They

Girls at a Greek wedding wearing all their jewels and embroidered garments.
Source: NHK.

lived in dormitories, contributed little to their new community and left after a short time, usually to marry. For them, working in a silk mill was merely an interlude, a brief brush with city life.

Greeks and Armenians continued to build mills and weaving workshops and manage the industry. Wars and skirmishes between 1895 and the end of the First World War contributed towards the demise of the Ottoman Empire and the establishment of the Turkish Republic, but war also decimated the population and dislocated the silk industry. In the countryside in the early 1920s, the government supported the industry and many farmers still raised silkworms. The government infrastructure continued, including the Sericulture Institute, but the silk industry did little to revive the Turkish economy. Sericulture never returned to pre-war levels, and although the output improved during the 1930s, the Second World War disrupted both production and marketing once again.

In 1940, the *Kozabirlik*, the Silkgrowers Union, was founded in Bursa to market silk. It aimed to inspire and encourage the local growers and it presented sericulture as an easy cash crop, with few up-front expenses and high profit. Making silk for parachutes appealed to the patriotic, but after the Second World War, despite the government's efforts, silk could not compete with synthetics and other fibres. By the 1970s, the Arab states were the main market for both silkworm eggs and the beautiful carpets. The Turkish government supported prices until 1995, but sericulture was still unsustainable, and many villagers chopped down their mulberry trees to make way for more profitable crops. Those families still in production went back to reeling the silk at home rather than selling it to the mills and cooperatives.

Sericulture in Turkey is now mostly a thing of the past, but silkworms are still cultivated in a handful of villages around Bursa, and several small manufacturing plants still make and sell Bursa silk. The most visible reminder of the time when silk was king is the imposing Koza Han, or Cocoon Inn, built in 1490. For over 500 years it served as a world centre for silk trading, but these days much of the silk used in the workshops and mills is Chinese, because it is cheaper, finer and of a more consistent quality than Turkish silk.

Greece

Even in classical times there were indigenous varieties of wild silkworms and local varieties of mulberry. In Aristophanes' *Lysistrate*, a comedy produced in Ancient Greece in 411 BCE, the women hope to stop the men fighting by withholding their sexual favours and yet enticing them by coming forward 'almost naked in their Amorgian chitons'. Amorgos is an island on the trade route between Turkey, Cos and Greece. Cos had wild silkworms, and the luxurious, sheer and costly garments the women wore were probably silk, either traded from the East or made from local wild silk. Pliny the Elder, 23–79 CE, certainly mentions wild Coan silk being produced on Cos and dyed purple for the court.

Many Greek cities had a fine reputation for their silk, including Athens, Thebes, Thessalonica and Corinth. In 947 CE, Roger I of Sicily invaded Greece and captured a number of silk weavers, who were forced to settle in Palermo. They were a real prize and valued for their skills. For centuries, cocoon production and silk processing had been familiar activities in the Greek territories and by the

Miniature painted on mulberry paper, of the young sultan being advised by his ministers.

eighteenth century had reached a high level of production. From then on there were many parallels with Turkey. Initially, sericulture flourished but declined after the pébrine infestation of the 1860s, and mulberry trees in many regions were grubbed out and replaced with crops that would provide a more predictable income.

Soufli, or Thrace, however, was a real success story. This area is in the far eastern region of Greece and was once a significant silk town and centre of trade, with connections throughout Europe. The highlight of the year occurred during the two months of May and June when the town really came alive. There was an air of excitement and everyone was involved — farmers, merchants and craftsmen — and silk products were exchanged, bartered, sold and distributed. Soufli flourished from the eighteenth century until the early 1980s when new technology and economic changes put paid to a once-thriving industry.

Today it is just a memory. The Bouroulitis silk mill in the centre of town still gets some of its cocoons from the surrounding villages or the few families that still breed silkworms in their homes, but barely three or four tonnes of cocoons a year are produced. This is hardly enough for the needs of the existing silk mills, so they import the valuable thread from China. The impressive 'cocoon houses' once devoted to breeding silkworms still stand, but most have been abandoned. The Kourtidis mansion (1883), now the Museum of Silk, is elegant proof of Soufli's once glorious success and displays the pre-industrial techniques of breeding silkworms and how silk was woven. The renovated Brika mansion is now the town's Folk Museum and the Kalesis cocoon house has been turned into a guesthouse. The latest development is the Art of Silk Museum belonging to the Tsiakiris Family Silk Mills. The renovated neoclassic building, built in 1886, has a wonderful display of sericulture, especially the industrial aspects and the social effect of the rise and fall of the silk industry in Soufli.

The European Union will subsidize silkworm rearing and mulberry cultivation in its member countries, and additional national funds can be available for silk reeling and processing. There is increasing interest among Greek farmers to become involved and expand their cocoon production using modern technology. Greece imports its silk from China and other countries as it still cannot produce sufficient for all its needs, but manufacturing, processing and distribution still create opportunities for jobs and export.

Ancient Persia and modern Iran

Ancient Persia was another civilization that prized silk and both Herodotus and Xenophon mention Persians wearing the precious and luxurious 'Medic dress'. Procopius wrote: 'This is the silk of which they are accustomed to make the garments which of old the Greeks called Medic but which at the present time they call seric.' Alexander the Great recognized the value of silk and demanded huge amounts as the spoils of war after he defeated Darius III, the King of Persia, around 330 BCE.

Six hundred years later, the Sassanid Shah, Shapur II, 309–379, hired skilful weavers from Mesopotamia and Syria to manufacture silk. Locally made silk fabrics have been found in Northern Bactria, dated to between the second and third centuries, so manufacturing could have begun even earlier. Silk mills are well documented during the

Sassanian Dynasty, 226–641 CE, and by the late thirteenth century, with relative peace across Asia under Mongol rule, supplies of Chinese silk to the West were substantial, especially the finest woven silks desired by both the Christian Church and the various royal courts.

Silk was extremely valuable and a horse could cost as much as ten lengths of silk. Silk could be used to pay for having work done, for the upkeep of the army, as a bribe or even to avoid punishment for a crime. Silk was enticing and could be used to cajole governors of other countries, start wars or end them or be given to ambassadors and military commanders as official gifts. Silk became a symbol of power and riches, and if you had silk, you were in a strong position to get allies, mercenaries, slaves or anything you fancied.

Long caravans of camels carried silk from the heart of Asia to Damascus in Syria, the marketplace where East and West met. One important route developed under the Mongol Ilkhanids in the early fourteenth century, and it ran between Anatolia and Tabriz, near the Caspian silk-producing region. The collapse of the Mongol Empire in the fourteenth century had a major effect on trade and the ready supply of Chinese silk across the Silk Road. Persia seized the opportunity to control all the routes across its territory demanding taxes and bribes, which by the early 1580s led to a substantial increase in the price of raw silk.

Shah Abbas I 'the Great' of Persia, 1571–1629, was the fifth king of the Safavid Dynasty. He brought the Persian Empire to the zenith of power and influence politically, economically and culturally and centralized all its activities under his royal control. Dyeing was subcontracted by the state at fixed rates, informal trading of silk was discouraged and all silk was transferred to Isphahan to be weighed and taxed before being on-sold. Sericulture was centred on Yadz, Kashan and Isphahan but it was the shiny, soft silk of Guilan that was most highly sought after in the European markets. A former British foreign secretary, Lord Curzon, confirmed that Guilan alone produced around 1300 tonnes of silk in the seventeenth century.

Although Shah Abbas was very accommodating of foreign traders, later shahs discouraged Muslims from trading with the Christian infidels. With all the additional state controls, the English, Dutch,

French and Italian merchants had difficulty buying dried cocoons or silk fabric and they found it simpler to go straight to India for the products they needed. The fabrics were similar, as many designs were based on the Koran. The human form was to be avoided and Muslim men were forbidden to wear silk as it could be seen as feminine, extravagant or luxurious, but it still remained popular. By the eighteenth century, the most sought after were the lovely brocades, satins and stripes, some mixed with flowers, and elaborate silver and gold arabesques. Gradually, tastes changed and by the nineteenth century the designs had become smaller and featured buds rather than full-blown flowers.

Persia and India both had long traditions of weaving velvet and it was sometimes difficult to tell them apart. Persian velvets had diagonal lines on the back, compared with Indian Mughal velvets with their plain weave. Persian court workshops were set up earlier than those in India and were highly regulated. Only certain nobles could purchase these exquisite expensive silk velvets, most of which had large-scale repeats and striking patterns and were made into fabulous court robes. Some glittered with gold and silver and were used as wall hangings for maximum effect. These velvets required highly skilled weavers, but by the eighteenth and nineteenth centuries, Persian velvets had begun to decline in quality as poorer silk was used or mixed with cotton and dyed with chemical dyes. Many were cut up and ended their days as prayer mats.

Throughout Persia, carpet weaving has played a major part in the silk industry and monopolized the available raw silk. The city of Qum was an important weaving and religious centre and its prayer rugs were beautiful. Exquisite Judaic silk carpets depicting ancient biblical stories were also made. The early weavers were mostly rural women who had acquired their skills over generations and each village had their own special designs, sometimes with deep symbolic meaning. People also made other silk-related handicrafts such as special fabrics, embroideries, hand-woven scarves, traditional *babouche*, or heel-less slippers, and souvenirs.

The number of villages where silk was made has declined, despite the worthwhile contribution sericulture can make to the income of rural families. As elsewhere, there are all the usual obstacles —

increasing costs of production, an unstable international silk market, competition from other agricultural or industrial products — along with an increase in smuggling cocoons and raw silk and other nefarious activities. Recently, the Iran Silkworm Rearing Company (ISRC) and the Iran Sericulture Research Center have been working with the University of Guilan in all areas, from technical guidance and assistance to biotechnology, genetics and molecular markers, in their zeal to expand sericulture and involve more people and make it once again a great success.

Post-Soviet states

Before the break-up of the Soviet Union in 1991, sericulture played an important part in the life of rural people in many of the southern Russian states. Each country has its own culture, strengths and weaknesses but decades of state control have left them with similar problems. Since independence, most are working towards making sericulture a viable and positive contributor towards the health and welfare of their people and the national economy. Most have a favourable climate, existing networks for the distribution of silkworm eggs and larvae, and facilities for purchasing, drying and storage of cocoons, but most need serious upgrading.

The main areas of concern are the lack of quality control, the slow introduction of hybrid disease-free silkworm eggs and improved mulberry trees, as well as the need to replace old, out-of-date silk reeling and throwing machines. Other problems include lack of fuel, intermittent gas and electricity supply, breakdown in communications between growers and distributors, irregular payments, unreasonable quota demands and heavy taxation. Sometimes management is unskilled and there is a backlog of practices that, although acceptable in Soviet times, are no longer appropriate if their silk is to be sold on the international market.

Working with silk and making silk handcrafts is still valued but as farmers' incomes are comparatively low and unemployment high, there is a need for alternative opportunities, as in some cases the government has not been able to assist the farmers with reconstruction and renewal.

Although sericulture offers both seasonal and permanent jobs to thousands of family members, it can be demanding and unpredictable and many farmers have changed to other crops. There is a real need to raise incomes and the belief that agriculture, including sericulture, has an important part to play in the renewal of their country. All recognize the need for scientific development and have included sericulture in at least one of their universities and research centres. There is new energy to revive sericulture, but the difficulties of being a post-Soviet state are legion, especially the loss of the traditional silk markets in Russia and the Baltic countries.

Georgia

In Georgia, sericulture was one of the oldest branches of agriculture and legends give credit to King Vakhtang Gorgasali in the fifth century CE for establishing silk in the country. There is a rich history of Georgian silk cocoons, fabric, grain and other products being exported along the old Silk Road. Georgia's high-quality silk won medals at Torino in Italy in 1850 and at the International Exposition in London in 1862.

The Caucasian Sericulture Station was established in Tbilisi in 1887 as a scientific institute, unique in the Russian Empire. The substantial museum was a hive of activity, leading the research into all aspects of sericulture. It had on display a most impressive collection of items and textiles from all the Soviet states. The fine library held the records of the latest scientific developments and techniques associated with sericulture. Regrettably, the First World War followed by the Great Depression meant that funds were no longer available, and by the 1930s this famous museum, with its fine reputation for scholarship and research, had descended into a state of abject decay.

Sericulture continued in the country areas, but unfortunately the mulberry mycoplasma disease, 'leaf curl' or 'dwarf leaf', was endemic, and in the 1950s it led to the destruction of more than 15 million mulberry trees, the loss of thousands of jobs and the collapse of the industry. The state once again supported sericulture and gradually mulberry trees were replanted. Cocoons were raised

Tbilisi Silk Museum in Georgia. The static displays of cocoons and all aspect of sericulture and a most impressive archive and library are frozen in the 1930s when this building was virtually abandoned.

within families and cooperatives, but the world's requirements for silk products had changed. Competition has been brutal since Georgia's separation from the Soviet Union and by 1995 nearly all the silk reeling and weaving factories had closed. Yet, in 1998 the Platinum Star, one of the highest quality awards in Europe, was given for silk fabric made from Georgian breeds of silkworms, the Mziuri 1 and Mziuri 2. For many years the Agrarian University of Georgia had a department of sericulture and led the research, but the university is now in private ownership and is no longer supported by the state. There are plans to reintroduce sericulture to study genotype and phenotype properties of silkworm breeds of Georgian origin, but so far there has been little progress.

Albania

Although Albania was one of the earliest European countries to cultivate silk, most of its development was between the sixteenth and nineteenth centuries when it was traditional for young women to look after silkworms, weave and make handcrafted garments. The country traded with its neighbours but this dramatically declined during the twentieth century due to the pébrine epidemic, the disruption of the First and Second World Wars, and the increasing availability of synthetic fibres.

From 1950 to 1990, the Albanian economy was centralized and everything, including sericulture, was owned by the state. They concentrated on local needs and did not look to neighbouring countries to either expand or trade. The Albanian climate was ideal for many varieties of mulberry and the pupae were used as protein food, for fertilizer and to feed the birds and animals. Cocoons were collected at the silk factory in Shkoder, where dyed fabrics, medical and surgery thread and silk for the military were made. The fabrics fitted in with tradition and local taste and some, like the men's *fustanella*, or Albanian kilt, were made from silk for special occasions, as was the jacket with its striking, dull red sleeves with a white stripe. The women of each district had their own identifiable costumes with blouses, vests and full skirts, rich with embroidery and strings of gold coins and chains.

The withdrawal of the Soviet Union from Albania in 1991 left sericulture unprepared and in disarray. Since then, there have been many attempts to reinvigorate the industry by working with neighbouring countries, but as funds are limited, there has been only minimal success. More promising has been help from the FAO and opportunities to get together with sericulturalists in the Black and Caspian Seas and Central Asian (BCSCA) region. The silk industry and silk handcrafts are part of the cultural tradition in Albania and provide a valuable asset that is worth supporting.

Armenia

Local tradition says that a royal clan from central China immigrated into Armenia during the fifth and sixth centuries CE, bringing soldiers and workers, with skills and experience in sericulture. Arab historians reported on trade and sericulture in ancient and medieval Armenia, writing about silk being used in lieu of cash and to pay taxes. The cities of Dvin and Artashat in the shadow of Mt Ararat produced the expensive Armenian Red cochineal dye made from crushing a ground-dwelling scale insect and Kermes Red made from an insect that lived on oak trees. This was used to dye wool and silk and these textiles were exported to Europe under the name 'Kirmiz'. Silk printing was an ancient art and a feature of the national costume. Some designs were hand painted while others used molten wax to cover the cloth and then print it in brilliant colours, a technique similar to batik. Many new designs incorporated national symbols and motifs, and new fabrics were introduced including silk crepe, plush and velvet.

The Amenian silk industry has had its problems over the centuries and during the Soviet period mechanization was introduced to assist with cocoon reeling. The viability of the industry was threatened as production of cocoons declined, locally produced raw silk was of variable quality and imported silk was needed to make fabrics for domestic use. Since 1990, however, the Armenian government has gradually started to restore sericulture, beginning with an 800 hectare mulberry plantation to enable cocoon production to begin again in earnest. An electric device for rooting mulberry cuttings has been developed to increase the production of saplings, and the Faculty of Sericulture at the Armenia Agriculture University is currently concentrating on the genetic selection of silkworms. There is still much to do to regenerate the industry but the signs are encouraging.

Azerbaijan

Azerbaijan has traded its silk along the old Silk Road to the countries of Asia and Europe since the twelfth century, but it was not until the seventeenth century that it became one of the premier regions for silk production. Many different species of silkworms have been raised, including some local breeds. The main silk districts are Shirvan, Shamakhi, Basqal, Ganja and Sheki, where a substantial caravanserai is still operating. The village of Lanbaran became famous for its silk and wool carpets, and various kinds of silk fabric were made in Shusha. These include a colourful cloth to make headscarves, bedspreads and covers, a thick pure silk fabric called *alisha* used for clothing, and a striped fabric called *jamb*. They were all made from waste silk, from damaged cocoons or from raw spun silk, mixed with silk floss. Shusha was also famous for the silver and gold embroidery done by girls as part of their dowry.

Sheki caravanserai has all its rooms facing inward to the central courtyard. It was built in the 17thc, and is still offering accommodation in the 21st century.

Women wore brocaded jackets, fastened at the waist over a red silk chemise top, with wide trousers rather than a skirt. The *chrypy* was a traditional, embroidered silk coat worn by nomadic Tekke women from Central Asia. They had block-printed linings and long, false floating sleeves and some were embroidered in a hook-and-tulip motif, using a variant of buttonhole stitch called *kesdi*. There was a colour code: yellow for married women, dark blue or green for unmarried women, and white for the matriarchs. The Tekke people were also famous for their silk carpets.

The first vocational training school for the development of sericulture was opened in Nukha, now Sheki, in 1843. A Sericulture Experimental Station was established in the city of Ganja in 1925 and in 1958 was renamed the Azerbaijan Sericulture Research Institute (ASERI). By 1989, over 150,000 families were involved in sericulture and in a national Soviet competition, Azerbaijan took second place for the manufacture of fresh cocoons and first place for the quality of its cocoons and raw silk. Central organization up until then had been very good, but after independence in 1992, production fell dramatically and by 1996 had practically stopped. Without a strong infrastructure, the whole system was in turmoil. There was high inflation, delayed payments to farmers for their

Chrypy coat from Turkmenistan with its long floating false sleeves hanging down the back and embroidered with the hook and tulip design.

cocoons and a lack of a reliable supply of electricity or natural gas. As a result, many families cut down their mulberry trees and abandoned sericulture to search for more regular work and income.

As in other post-Soviet states, every branch of sericulture needs attention but there are rays of hope. The government is supportive, and substantial funds have been allocated from the state budget to restore Sheki Ipak JSC, formerly the Sheki Silk Factory. This has the capacity to process vast quantities of cocoons, although so far the local production has been insufficient and most of the cocoons have been imported. There has also been significant progress with the reopening of an egg station that produces high quality eggs for local use, and the surplus is now being exported. The country has an excellent climate for sericulture and as some mulberry orchards remain, it is hoped that at least some of the infrastructure can be revitalized and modernized.

The Ukraine

Sericulture in the Ukraine dates back to the eleventh century when a large mulberry garden was planted near the Clovskiy Monastery in Kiev and a filature and manufactory was built to weave silk into fabric. Commercial cultivation only began seriously in 1929–30.

Until that time, only village families were producing silk and making silk goods. After the Second World War, production improved using imported eggs and over 2000 collective and state farms were involved, the silk being used to make parachutes, surgical sutures and fabrics.

Since independence there have been difficulties. While labour is cheap and available, poor infrastructure, untrained personnel and dilapidated premises have held sericulture back. In an effort to meet world standards, the government has offered some scientific and practical support. A team of skilled professionals is now based at the university and all the prerequisites are there for the revival and further development of the industry. Foreign private investors from Italy, France and Germany are interested in joint ventures, and it is hoped that funds could be available through the European Commission.

Tajikistan

In recent years, the Tajikistan government has been keen to revitalize the historic silk industry and maximize its economic potential. It started with improving the quality of both mulberry and cocoon processing, right through to weaving the fabric and making its products available on the world market. The accomplishments of the Pilla association are impressive. Coming under the care of the Ministry of Industry, 58 enterprises engaged in the growing and processing of cocoons have been set up. There are three regional associations, 42 cocoon-drying enterprises, two silkworm egg factories, one parental silkworm egg production station, three facilities for mulberry sapling production, two silk-reeling factories, two joint ventures, a sericulture experimental station, and two silk-weaving factories. Tajikistan already produces pure-line silk seed and mulberry seedlings, and although the total production of all branches of sericulture and yarn is still far short of its potential, Tajikistan is serious about solving its problems and restoring and developing its sericulture industry.

Uzbekistan

Sericulture is part of Uzbekistan's long history, and silk is grown in many areas from Khorezm in the west to the Ferghana Valley in the east. In the ninth century, Margilan was a major Silk Road stop in the fertile Ferghana Valley. Marco Polo rested there and local legend maintains that Alexander the Great, on his arrival in the town, was given a chicken (*murgh*) and bread (*nan*), from which the town Margilan acquired its name, and the Uzbek word for 'cocoon' gives Kokand its name also. Almost everywhere in Uzbekistan, women can be seen wearing the distinctive, wave-patterned *abr-ikat* dresses. Legends say that the pattern was inspired by an artist sitting by the side of a fast-moving stream and seeing the reflection of clouds and a rainbow in the water. Although these days many of the fabrics are neither silk nor dyed with natural dyes, their history and vibrant glowing colours make them truly distinctive.

Uzbekistan is still a major supplier of silk to the world markets. The state has a monopoly and supervises all aspects of the industry, and modern machinery has made Margilan the heart of silk production. The local authorities have a quota system based on farm size. Although collective farms were disbanded after Uzbekistan became

Girls wearing abr-ikat dresses in the old Samarkand Silk Market, now a shadow of its old vitality and centrality in the trading of silk.

independent in 1991, land was never privatized and so ownership can be insecure. Every year in early May, farmers and rural householders are given one or two 30-gram (one-ounce) boxes of silkworm eggs to be hatched, fed, nurtured and kept warm and safe from predators. The farmers are encouraged to do their very best for their country but some farmers come under pressure with threats of fines or loss of their land leases if they do not fulfil their quotas.

In the cities, many schools continue the tradition of sericulture and raise silkworms as part of their class activities. For generations, rural children have been taken out of school for the month of May to help the family with the silkworms. Unfortunately, May is traditionally the time when children sit their most important exams. The government insists that it has banned child labour but families are often totally dependent on their children's help. In can be very difficult to balance educational needs against the demands of caring for the silkworms. The days are very long, from around 4 a.m. until midnight, as the silkworms need to be fed every two hours when they are tiny, although less often as they go through the other stages but with much larger quantities of leaves. Silkworms are voracious feeders and while some countries have switched to planting dwarf mulberry trees or using machines to make it easier to harvest the leaves, in Uzbekistan old methods are only gradually being changed.

In Tashkent, a techno-park has been built to specialize in *Vodiy Ipagi*, or Valley Silk. This is a large-scale project designed to cover all aspects of sericulture from growing mulberries to weaving fabric, and especially to advance science and new technologies. It has created new jobs to replace those lost when the former Atlas Silk Company collapsed. Another project in Namangan will create another 700 jobs and Uzbekistan has several shared international schemes. Silver Silk is a British-Uzbek joint venture but Western investment is limited, and the companies keep a low profile. The Khanatlas Silk Factory and the Margilan Silk Factory are the largest filatures in the region and are state-run giants, with thousands of factory workers involved in the various processes of silk production. Uzbek Ipagi, the state-run monopoly, exports Uzbek silk to China, India, South Korea and Western Europe.

Four men sit and tie the silk fibres for the warp to make the abr-ikat woven designs. They are following a specific pattern designed by the man obscured to the far left. It will be tied and dyed, untied, re tied and dyed repeatedly for each new colour.

Weaving silk abr-ikat on a modern industrial handloom. The silk is held under tension and it requires great experience and skill to weave the complex designs. While the rooms are kept light and clean, the noise is terrific.

Suzanni hand embroidery, used as an all over decoration on table and bed covers, cushions and runners, in a pleasing range of colors, tans, red, greens, a little blue and yellow.

Once export orders have been met, the remainder of the silk is used locally to weave scarves or rugs in small factories like the Yodgorlik factory. This was opened in 1983 by a group of Margilan silk workers who aimed to make the plant capable of mass-producing silk while still using traditional methods. The factory employs around 2000 people, with the men unwinding the silk from the cocoons and dyeing it, increasingly with natural dyes, and the women weaving the carpets and *khanatlas* silk fabrics in the vibrant local *abr-ikat* designs. Most of these items are sold to tourists, but the local people value their national silks and have a tradition of wearing silk for festive occasions.

The world-famous *suzanni* embroideries are made for bridal hangings, shawls, cushions, bed and table covers. A diagonal stitch called Bokhara couching, chain stitch or tambour-work is used to fill in the designs of fruit and flowers, especially pomegranates and carnations, in wonderful deep reds and greens, creams and blues. The traditional art of making paper from mulberry is still practised in Samarkand. The thin mulberry branches are stripped of their bark and soaked and pounded into a mush using a heavy wooden water-hammer mill. It is then spread in a frame, drained, pressed and dried to make wonderful, grainy art paper for painting and calligraphy.

The annual revenue collected by the state from sericulture is tiny compared with the one billion dollar cotton industry, but silk has status, especially with its connection to the golden days of the Silk Road. Artificial fibres have lessened the demand for real silk but it still has the aura of luxury and style. It is also used for beauty creams, food products, medicines and in the military. Uzbekistan's silk production is third in the world after China and India. Although it accounts for less than 5 per cent of the world's production of silk, it still represents the highest amount per capita, at almost a kilogram per head of the population of 27 million. Recently, thanks to the government's initiative, there has been a renewal of energy and drive to revive the industry and strengthen the export potential. All areas of production are on the increase and ways are being found to solve the problems and make it a worthwhile contributor in the twenty-first century.

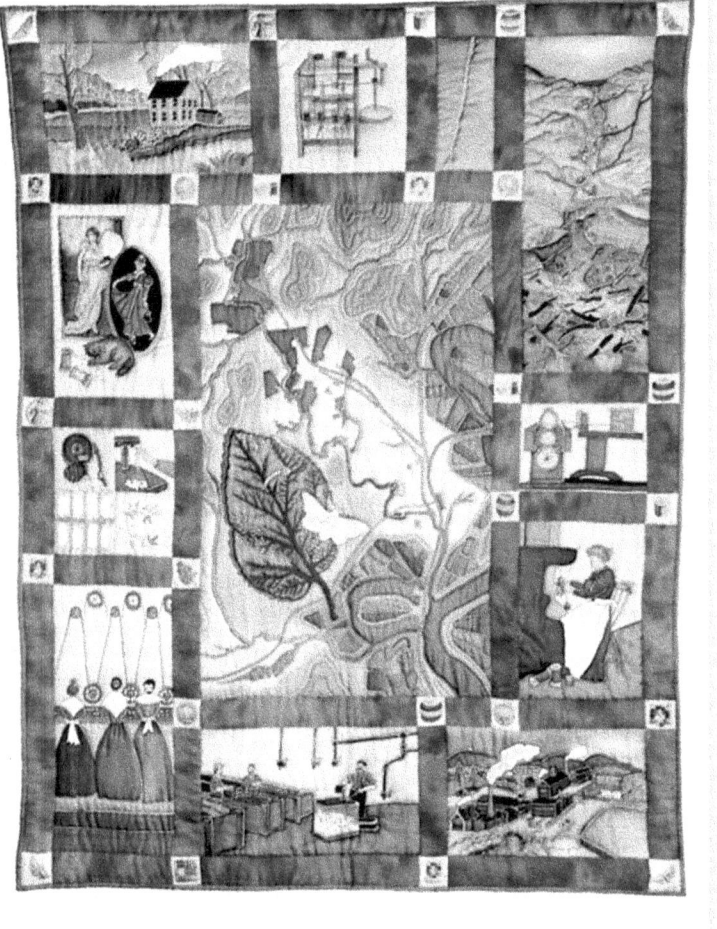

Northampton Silk Industries Quilt, showing the Northampton Silk Route, and the silk mills that made Northampton a prime and thriving industrial center for domestic silk production for one hundred years.

Source: Handpainted silk by Sally Dillon, hand quilted by Janet Hale 2002, on display in the Neilson Library at Smith College.

CHAPTER EIGHT
Silk in the United States

The new colonies

The story of the silk industry in America began in 1622 when James I of England, 1566–1625, heard that silkworms had been imported into Virginia in 1613 and he immediately saw an opportunity. He was envious of France's highly developed sericulture industry and felt that England was at a disadvantage, as it had to rely on Italian and Chinese silk. He believed that the native red mulberry would be suitable for sericulture and saw the new colonies as the best chance for England to have its own prestigious industry. He wanted the colonies to be a supplier of raw silk, not a manufacturer or competitor to English factories, so he urged the Virginia Company to promote the cultivation of mulberry trees and breeding silkworms.

The plans were put into action and there was extensive promotion of the benefits of sericulture. In 1623 the Virginia Assembly required each man to plant six mulberry trees annually for seven years and a landowner was fined £10 if he did not cultivate at least ten mulberry trees for every 100 acres of his plantation. In spite of this, there was little interest in sericulture. Between 1656 and 1667, bounties

Benjamin Franklin's, three piece silk suit, 1775 was originally a claret colour now faded to brown. He wore it in Paris when negotiating an alliance with France. Franklin's plain style stood out at the flamboyant court of Louis XVI.
Source: Smithsonian's National Museum of American History.

and levies were tried, extended, dropped, extended again and finally abandoned. In Georgia, South Carolina and Pennsylvania there was no royal or government support for the industry. Farmers found sericulture difficult due to the high labour costs, although initially there was slave labour. There were some attempts to mechanize the system but they were not successful. No one wanted to 'farm' silk. It was too labour-intensive and although the climate was excellent, tobacco and cotton were much more profitable.

Sericulture was tried again in Georgia in 1732 when land belonging to the government was gifted to any settlers who would plant ten white mulberry trees on every acre of cleared land. The widely read *Farmer and Garden* promoted sericulture, saying: 'We wish the farmer in moderate circumstances to bear in mind that a single acre in mulberries will feed and clothe and educate his children, and that five (acres) will enable him to live sumptuously and lay by enough in ten years to leave his family independent.'

The government again offered a premium for planting trees and producing raw silk, but sericulture was seasonal. The eggs needed to

Gown of American grown silk, incorporating sprigs of flowers on a checked ground with a trim of silk fringing. c1850s.

be free of disease, the leaves perfect, the timing exactly right and the farmer free of pressure from other crops. Looking after silkworms was not a hobby for the 'little woman' but required skills, perseverance and commitment from all members of the family and community.

In the first half of the eighteenth century, the Connecticut General Assembly, the London Society, the Administration in Georgia, Pennsylvania and North Carolina all offered bounties, financial incentives and awards of various kinds, and for a while sericulture became fashionable. Mrs Pinckney from South Carolina travelled to England in 1755 with enough of her own silk to weave three dresses, including one she presented to the Dowager Princess of Wales, 1719–72. Small quantities of some excellent silk were produced, but very little raw silk was exported.

Dr Nathan Aspinwall developed his mulberry nurseries in New Haven and Long Island, and by 1762 he was also raising and distributing silkworm eggs in Pennsylvania and at Mansfield in Connecticut. His friend the Reverend Dr Stiles, a Puritan minister and early president of Yale College, kept a diary between 1763 and 1790 of his silk-raising activities. Stiles was obsessed with the concept of silk production and found it 'a kind of El Dorado to lure the prudent and industrious as surely as others were lured by a fast horse or a legend of gold in the hills'. He experimented and even gave some of his silkworms names like 'General Wolfe' and 'Oliver Cromwell'. He formed a company in the 1780s to promote silk production through the churches. He shipped seeds and plants to fellow ministers in Connecticut parishes with directions that after three years, each minister was to distribute one quarter of his trees free to local families, while continuing to cultivate the rest. White mulberry trees grew quickly, up to 30 or 40 feet high in the rocky Connecticut soil. They were planted in orchards as well as along roadways or in hedges, so as not to use valuable agricultural land.

Silk production in Mansfield was a success, and in 1789 the town produced almost 200 pounds of raw silk, valued at five dollars a pound. While the quantity was high, quality was a problem with the threads often uneven and gummy. Some women dedicated their spare bedroom to raising silkworms and several people built special rearing houses or cocooneries. Usually it was the daughters of the family who reeled the silk from the cocoons and spun it into thread for sewing or embroidery. Silk was used to barter and was traded for goods at the local store, and the storekeeper sold it on to agents in New York or Providence. The Mansfield Historical Society Account Book records that 'the widow Abiah Harvey bought five yards of gingham and quarter pound of tea and gave in exchange 75 skeins of silk' and in 1825 a shoemaker called Christopher Spencer made three pairs of boots and mended two shoes in exchange for 494 skeins of silk.

Benjamin Franklin, 1706–90, one of the Founding Fathers of America, was multi-talented, a social activist, scientist, inventor and diplomat and from the age of 23 in 1729, enthusiastically promoted sericulture, telling his friends in Philadelphia:

> *There is no doubt with me, but that it (sericulture) might succeed in our country. It is the happiest of all inventions for clothing. Wool gives good deal of land to produce it, which if employed raising corn, would afford much more subsistence for man, than the mutton amounts to. Flax and hemp require good land, impoverish it, and at the same time permit it to produce no food*

at all: but mulberry trees may be planted in hedgerows, in walks or avenues or for shade near a house where nothing else is wanted to grow. The food for the worms who produce the silk is in the air, and the ground under the trees may still produce grass or some other vegetable, good for man or beast.

He set up a filature in Philadelphia around 1770 and consistently encouraged silk in Pennsylvania and New Jersey until the American Revolution in 1775.

Benjamin Franklin's three-piece silk suit that he wore in 1778 while serving as America's first ambassador to France is one of the treasures owned by the Smithsonian National Museum of American History. It is modest and restrained and was originally a plum or claret colour, but has faded. Alice Roosevelt's wedding gown and the inaugural gowns worn by Mrs Woodrow Wilson and her three daughters were all made from new American silk.

Early manufacturing

Essential to the success of sericulture was a strong infrastructure of filatures with experienced operators, good transport, investment and markets. In 1788, a group of Mansfield men petitioned the government to be allowed to form a corporation called The Director, Inspectors and Company of Connecticut Silk Manufacturers. The corporation, the first of its kind, was designed to regulate and standardize the quality of production, not as a single factory but as a collective of producers owning contiguous plots.

Previously, the best cocoons had been shipped to England for processing, leaving the remainder available for local use. There was great enthusiasm, and sericulture attracted investment. The first American silk mill to manufacture sewing thread was set up in Mansfield in 1810 by Rodney and Horatio Hanks. It was housed in a tiny building, 12 feet x 12 feet, and the machine was run by water power. Unfortunately, in 1828 it had to close because the machinery proved to be too rough to handle the delicate silk and to produce commercial-grade sewing thread. Nine years later, William H Horstmann built a mill in Philadelphia for weaving trimmings and ribbons and he later imported a Jacquard loom. The Cheney brothers, Ward, Frank, Ralph, and Rush set up their first mill, the Mt Nebo Silk Mill, in 1838 at South Manchester. This was the only mill that was intermittently but finally successful.

The demand for finished silk products was rising and so the government commissioned a manual to promote silk. By 1830, John D'Homergue and Peter Duponceau reported to the US Department of Agriculture that 'suddenly and by a simultaneous and spontaneous impulse, the people of the United States have directed their attention to this source of national riches . . . Everywhere, from north to south, mulberry trees have been planted and silkworms raised.'

Morus multicaulis mania

The search was now on to replace both the indigenous red mulberry and the imported white mulberry, the *Morus alba*, with a mulberry tree with large tender leaves, hardy and quick growing and more suitable for the production of top-quality silk. A new variety, the *Morus multicaulis*, hit the market. Apparently, it had been imported from China by way of the Philippines, then France to Baltimore, and was first planted by a Mr Gideon B Smith in 1826. *Morus multicaulis* was widely promoted in the newspapers as the long awaited hope. It had large leaves, 'almost as large as cabbage leaves', and branches that drooped close to the ground making it easier to pick. Promoters such as Edward P Roberts, who wrote a mulberry tree manual in 1839, suggested this could cut costs by up to 90 per cent. The rapid-growing, bushy plant could be easily propagated from cuttings and was a labour-saving import that would finally, it was believed, launch sericulture as a successful industry.

Silkworms were reputed to love it, although it is not clear how many silkworms ever fed on *Morus multicaulis* because mulberry leaves cannot usually be harvested for five to eight years. Everyone understood that providing enough of the right mulberry leaves was key to successful sericulture. The local paper reported that not only agriculturalists but doctors of divinity, law and medicine, scholars, farmers and landowners who had nothing to do with raising silkworms caught the excitement and planted out seedlings they hoped to sell for a huge profit.

Publications featured numerous stories promoting silk production. They saw the day coming when each farm would be a nursery for young trees, and every house have its silkworms yielding two or more crops of cocoons every year. Farmers' wives and daughters, when not feeding the silkworms, were to reel the silk that would become as cheap as cotton, but hardly anyone mentioned the real difficulties of sericulture.

When news spread, nurserymen were inundated, and the demand soon exceeded supply. A wild rush took place. Records show that *Morus multicaulis* seedlings sold for $4 a hundred in 1834, rose to $10 in 1835 and to $30 in 1836. Prices for the trees soared, as did profits for those selling them. In 1837, a Hartford nursery sold 300,000 trees in one year, and the *Silk Culturist* listed two million white mulberry trees and 320,000 *Morus multicaulis* trees for sale. Meanwhile, the *Farmers' Register*, a newspaper published in Petersburg, Virginia, reported in its January 1837 issue that one farmer invested $17.50 in mulberry trees and made a $2,500 profit,

Multicaulis mulberry tree, believed to have the advantage of being quick growing, with large leaves and low growing branches, but regrettably not the choice of the silkworms.

while a sale of 260,050 trees in Germantown, Pennsylvania sold for $81,218. The *New England Farmer* reported: 'We hear daily reports of individuals who have made thousands and tens of thousands of dollars and the storekeeper, farmer and mechanic rush from their useful employment into the grand speculation.'

Fraud followed speculation and some dealers who promised *Morus multicaulis* seeds substituted turnip or other seeds instead. Others sold silkworm eggs that were really fish eggs or were made of beeswax. One of the strongest charges of fraud was levelled against one of the biggest promoters of domestic silk production, Samuel Whitmarsh of Northampton, Massachusetts. He had a large nursery and had written a sericulture manual. He was accused of selling *Morus multicaulis* seed for $480 a pound when the product was actually white mulberry seed worth $15 at the most.

There were so many mulberry trees that a futures market developed, with owners renting out their orchards or selling notes of agreement to later purchase trees. The thrill of possible riches swept everyone along and cuttings were selling for $500 per hundred. Then suddenly, in New York in 1837, the banks failed and this meant that finance was no longer readily available and optimism turned to panic. A reporter sounded a note of warning: 'The product increases too fast — we grow rich too rapidly.'

In addition to the financial concerns, some farmers were becoming disappointed with their silkworms' poor acceptance of the *Morus multicaulis*. In truth, there had been little scientific research or testing and the silkworms much preferred the *Morus alba*. The crash finally came in the autumn of 1839. Trees that at the beginning of the year could fetch $1 to $1.25, by the end of the year sold for between two and four cents. At one auction, 30,000 *Morus multicaulis* trees that would have sold for $20,000 just a year before now had no takers. The selling price fell to 50 cents a hundred. The farmers were angry and in despair, and many uprooted and burned their *Morus multicaulis* trees. The unusually cold winter in 1844, followed by a severe blight, killed off most of the remaining trees.

This had been a delusion of riches, an exercise in promotion and hope over reality and the crash took the whole industry with it.

According to Brockett's 1876 history, one group of investors on the East Coast loaded their entire inventory of *Morus multicaulis* onto a dilapidated, unseaworthy ship, bought full insurance on the cargo, and sent it to New Orleans and up the river to Indiana and were appalled when the worthless trees reached their destination safely.

Samuel Whitmarsh, who had been in trouble for fraud, put up a 'feeble defense' against the charges, but it was too late. By then his stockpile of trees was worthless, wiped out by the crash in mulberry sales. In 1842, his Silk Company was reborn as the main enterprise of an abolitionist utopian community, the Northampton Association for Education and Industry. The community collapsed in 1846 as did growing silk in Northampton, but not the manufacture of products from imported raw silk from China. Some of its members remained in the area and continued their efforts to create a humane industrial society.

The religious communities

From the early 1800s, the religious communal societies, the Quakers and Harmonists in Pennsylvania, the Shakers in Kentucky and the Mormons in Utah, raised silkworms and reeled silk both for themselves and for the market. They all produced to a very high standard and had the advantage of being deeply committed to their community. The children helped the Sisters to feed the silkworms, the Brothers planted and cultivated the mulberry trees and the more experienced Sisters reeled the silk off the cocoons and did the weaving.

Quakers were also dedicated abolitionists and women like Susannah Wright, 1697–1784, made her family home at Wright's Ferry on the Susquehanna River one of the 'stations' on the secretive 'underground railway'. Oral history tells of the way the women would hang their hand-worked quilts on the fences along the route the slaves took when escaping from the South. Various quilt patterns — the star which gave directions, the log cabin indicating shelter and the bear's paw which showed the mountain route — were a code 'hidden in full display' that the illiterate slaves and their guides could 'read'. The beautiful quilts used both their own silk and old silk garments and were art treasures, practical and beautiful. Elizabeth Buffum

Chase, 1806–99, was also the daughter of an abolitionist and kept a diary of her Quaker childhood. She was only one of many women whose skills with sericulture and quilting combined silk scraps and old garments to provide practical help.

The Shakers were also a strict community, hardworking, celibate and clearly focused on Christ's imminent return. Their founder, Jane Wardly, had a vision of the second coming. She had been a Quaker in Lancashire in England when she married James who was not, and they were expelled from the Quaker community. They gathered a group around them, and after much persecution, sailed to New England in 1774 where they became known as the Shakers. They took the utmost care in everything they did and are credited with many innovations and improvements for working with silk. Other practical inventions include the flat broom, a wood-burning stove, various types of machinery and an improved washing machine.

The German Harmonists were another group who took sericulture very seriously. They based their silk programme on research into the best French and German practices. They built a separate two-storey building to house the silkworms, the reeling machinery and looms, including a Jacquard loom to weave the brocades. Gertrude Rapp, 1808–89, the grand-daughter of the founder of the Harmony Society at Economy in Pennsylvania, was a pioneer in the American silk industry. Between 1827 and 1852, the Silk Mill at Economy made silk handkerchiefs that they distributed to everyone to encourage them to work hard for this new enterprise. They manufactured everything, including silk ribbons, velvet and satin fabrics and dyed them with natural dyes, obtained from indigo, logwood and cochineal. Gertrude was praised in the *Journal of the American Silk Society* in 1839 as 'the enterprising, intelligent and ingenious Miss Rapp'. She was placed in charge of the society's silk industry when she was just 22 and based their work on research and carried it out with such scientific efficiency that she was recognized as an authority throughout the country. Despite such dedication, it became increasingly difficult to function without protective tariffs, and sericulture was discontinued in the community in 1852.

Although the Shakers and Harmonists had by the 1850s discontinued sericulture in their communities, in 1855 Brigham Young, the founder

Quilting Bee, a pleasant sociable way to get together with friends, note the scissors on a chain and the elderly coloured maid. Henry Mosler, 1841-1920.

of the Mormons, imported mulberry seeds from France and planted them on his Forest Dale Farm, where he had established a large colony of the faithful. He thought sericulture would be a suitable occupation for women to make beautiful fabrics, to be self-sufficient and even make money. In 1875, he arranged for Zina DH Jacobs Smith Young, 1821–1901, the thrice-married General President of the Relief Society, to set up the Deseret Silk Association. She travelled widely between the various communities promoting sericulture, despite her obvious dislike, even fear, of the silkworms. Later, in 1880, she acted as a liaison between the Mormons and the Utah government's Silk Association. Under her influence, the legislature funded the purchase of reeling machinery for a factory at the mouth of City Creek canyon and six years later passed an act providing a 25 cents per pound bonus for new growers of cocoons.

Utah silk scarves, dresses, shawls and a United States flag were displayed at the World Fair in Chicago in 1892. Elise Forsgren of Brigham City spent four months at the fair demonstrating the art of silk-making and in 1895, Emmeline Wells, editor of the *Woman's Exponent*, read a paper on silk at the National Council of Women. There are lots of silk stories from this period. One concerns a woman who spun and wove her own silk to make two dresses for herself and a wedding dress for both of her twin daughters. Another woman had to make a hasty exit from church because the silkworms had started to hatch in the little bag she had tucked in her bosom to keep them warm. Although silk was successful, Brigham Young's dream of silk providing a substantial income never materialized. Some Utah silk was sold in the eastern markets and in California but the new railroads made new commodities readily available. More importantly, silk from Japan and China undercut Utah silk. The enthusiasm of the community waned and the people developed other interests, so when the Utah state legislature ceased funding silk in 1905, few women carried on the project.

All the groups, the Quakers, Harmonists, Shakers and Mormons, lived and worked together for common goals and a purpose beyond this world. They undertook the whole process of silk culture, and had a strong work ethic and desire for quality and efficiency. Yet all gave it up because they found the costs too high and the difficulty of coordinating the mulberry leaves, silk moths, reelers and weavers, made domestic sericulture unprofitable.

Manufacturing

It was unfortunate that the *Morus multicaulis* crash came just as silk manufacturing was beginning to create a market that might have repaid the labour of rearing silkworms. Before 1810 there was no commercial manufacturing; although some manufacturers operated filatures for reeling silk, most did not want cocoons, preferring top-quality filament silk that had already been reeled. Too often the local cocoons were of mixed quality, and were used to make spun silk. Many attempts had been made to spin this waste silk, until finally in 1855 the Cheney brothers pioneered a new branch of the industry when they found a way to deal with the short sticky fibres by adapting woollen and cotton spinning machines.

In the mid-1840s, Samuel Lapham Hill, 1806–86, had assumed the debts and ownership of the silk mill belonging to the Northampton Association of Education and Industry. With the invention of the sewing machine, he believed there would be a huge demand for sewing silk. A number of people, including Elias Howe, Isaac Singer and Allen Watson, were working to perfect the sewing machine, but it was still plagued with problems, made worse by the uneven quality of the available thread. Samuel Hill seized the challenge and by 1852 had perfected his 'machine twist'. Mr Singer tried it, was delighted with the new thread and said he would take all Hill could make. For 30 years, between 1846 and 1876, Samuel Hill worked tirelessly for his community, and the silk industry grew into a major contributor to the local economy. In 1854, he established

Singer Sewing Machine advertisement, the development of the sewing machine revolutionized sewing, but needed a fine and even thread to work well.
Source: Singer archives.

the Nonotuck Silk Company with Samuel L Hinckley and his silk businesses increased until he became Northampton's largest employer, processing 'machine twist,' sewing silk, embroidery thread, and other silk thread products. The business continued to expand even after his death and was later renamed the Corticelli Company, of world renown.

The Civil War in the 1860s intervened, and silk manufacturing slowed to a trickle. However, the tariff put on all imported silk goods during the war served to encourage the development of locally woven silk fabrics and haberdashery. The Cheney brothers wove ribbons and grosgrains using multi-looms that produced between 20 and 30 ribbons at the same time and in 1880 they found a new way to make velvet. In the past, velvets had been woven over wires and hand-cut to make the pile. The Cheney brothers invented a double cloth. After dyeing, the velvets were sent to the shearing room,

Cheney Brothers advertisement for their new season's style using their fine silk crepe.
Source: *Good Housekeeping* Magazine, 1913.

then to the brushing machines, where the pile was evened up and the cloth finished. Later it was sized and stretched on a tentering machine, ironed and finished. During the various processes, a piece of velvet could go through the machines up to a hundred times. By 1900, there were over 500 silk mills making ribbons, sewing silk, laces, braids, military items, upholstery and dress trimmings, buttons, veiling, millinery silks, ties, scarves, brocades, satins and velvets.

Paterson, New Jersey

During the late nineteenth century, Paterson in New Jersey developed into an important centre for all the various divisions of silk manufacture, becoming known as 'Silk City'. It had a major river to power the machinery and was close to New York City with its steady stream of immigrant labour. Unfortunately, the raw silk was imported, mostly from China, Japan and Italy, rather than using the locally produced silk that could have really helped the struggling silk industry.

Paterson had a history of difficult industrial relations and between 1881 and 1900 there were over 130 strikes and some of the mill owners moved their operations to Pennsylvania where there were no labour unions. Many of the master weavers and dyers were male immigrants from traditional silk centres in England, Germany, France or Italy and they had a reputation for being political radicals. Nearly half the workers were women, but men had the best-paying jobs, and wages for both the skilled and unskilled were well below the average for the industry. Children began work around the age of 14 and might spend the rest of their working lives 'in the silk'. By 1913 the working day was 10 hours long with a half day on Saturday. Workers could sometimes move up to skilled jobs like weaver or loom fixer and in very rare cases they might be able to rent space in an old mill and set up on their own. Because silk was so valuable, the mills were generally clean, with good natural lighting so necessary to produce a faultless product. But good conditions were not sufficient to compensate for the long hours, noise, managerial controls, petty indignities and poor wages.

With so many mills trying to claim a piece of the market, owners

Silk Mill, in Buffalo, upstate New York, before the First World War, where the sea of women are standing in front of their looms.

tried to save money by changing the rules. They used differences of gender, ethnicity, skill and ideology to keep workers divided. Violence, discrimination against recent immigrants and repression of radicals increased, and the police became involved. By 1911, there were some gains. Organized labour in Paterson had helped achieve a 55-hour working week and delayed the introduction of a system where one person looked after four looms, already common in new mills elsewhere in the country. By now, practically every broadloom and silk ribbon mill had one or more labour organizations. In 1913, Paterson was the site of a major strike, lasting over six months, led by the Industrial Workers of the World, or the 'Wobblies'. They focused on child labour legislation and demanded an eight-hour day and better working conditions, but were defeated by the employers who forced them to return to work under pre-strike conditions.

Local sericulture

Demand for imported silk remained strong, so efforts were made to revive the domestic silkworm crop but without success. Several American silkworms, like *Antheraea polyphemus*, can produce a strand of silk capable of being made into textiles, although not of the quality demanded by modern machinery. In 1868, a visiting French astronomer named Trouvelot imported gypsy moths, *Lymantria dispar*, from Europe. He had hoped to use them in a crossbreeding programme with native silk-producing moths in order to control flacheria, a wilt disease, but the experiment had gone terribly wrong after some of the gypsy moths escaped from the laboratory in Medford, Massachusetts, and they are now one of North America's most serious forest pests, defoliating and destroying the hardwood trees.

In another venture to promote sericulture, an entomologist from Missouri, CV Riley, experimented with a strain of silkworms that could feed on the leaves of Osage orange trees and many were planted across the Midwest as hedges for use as windbreaks, living fences and posts. In 1881, Riley produced a manual for raising silkworms and began a government programme to support the industry. The plan involved purchasing silkworm eggs from an Italian dealer and distributing them free to anyone who wanted to raise cocoons. A small reeling establishment was set up in Washington to buy the cocoons at standard European prices. The raw silk was to be sold to American manufacturers, but unfortunately silk could not be produced for the price the government was prepared to pay and the venture failed.

Concurrently around 1880 in California, Piedmont was but one of the many centres for sericulture on the West Coast. Along with over 6000 mulberry trees, it had a two-storeyed building which housed the Ladies Silk Culture Society where over 100 women worked, spinning thread from local cocoons. Initially it was very successful but by 1895 it could no longer be sustained. The area around San Diego also developed sericulture, including the commercial rearing of the native ceanothus silk moth, *Hyalophara euryalus*, until Felix Gillet in 1879 showed that the cocoons could not be reeled satisfactorily or compete with fine reeled silk being imported from Japan, China and Italy.

Silk trains and ships from Japan

In 1859, Japan opened its ports to foreign trade and the demand for silk was so high that between the 1890s and the late 1930s, special ships and trains were commissioned to bring top-quality raw silk at record speed from Japan to the docks of Vancouver and San Francisco. The sealed 90 kg bales of silk streamed off the ships down the conveyor belts under armed guard and were reloaded onto dedicated silk trains. The stevedores became so skilled they could unload a ship and reload the silk onto the train in just one hour 39 minutes. The trains had up to 15 wood-panelled, windowless, steel wagons, and were pulled by a series of powerful locomotives. They carried armed guards and speed was of the essence because the silk cargo carried an insurance premium for each hour it was in the railroad's possession. The silk trains had priority, and even the train carrying Prince Albert, later King George VI, had to pull into a siding and wait until the silk train flashed past on its way across the continent to the markets in New York and the East Coast. On arrival, the silk was speedily transported in convoys of trucks with armed and bonded drivers, and distributed to the waiting industrialists. The silk on each train could be worth two million dollars, and was as valuable as gold bullion. Imports of silk from Japan reached $400 million, 20 per cent of all imported goods.

Japan was the greatest supplier of silk to the US until the market dropped from $7.50 per pound to only $1.25 in the unsettled period after Japan invaded China in 1938, triggering a boycott of Japanese products. Some anti-Japan students at US universities promoted local cotton over silk by chanting 'Make lisle the style, wear lisle for a while', and others at the 1938 convention of the American Student

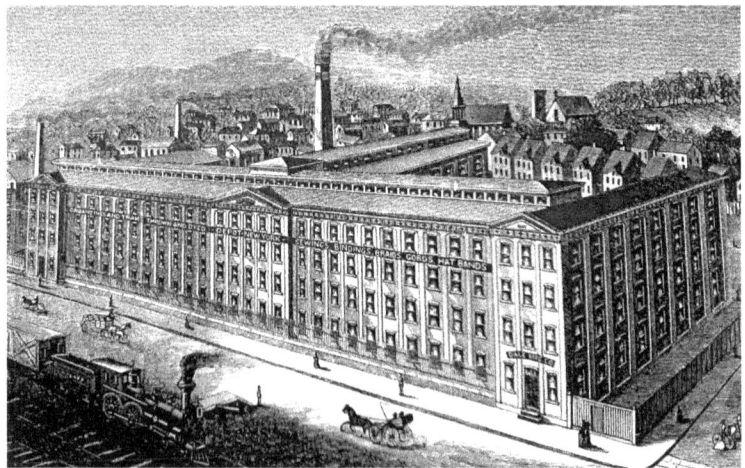

Dales Silk Manufactory in Paterson New Jersey, carefully positioned alongside the railway. This enormous factory of five floors above ground was only one of many built during period, when silk was king.

Unloading silk from a silk ship, and loading it onto the waiting silk train
The Empress line was famous for their speed and reliability and first choice for bringing the silk at speed from Japan to the West Coast of Canada and America.

Union tore off their silk stockings and ties and flung them into bonfires as a protest. The argument continued until the bombing of Pearl Harbor in December 1941 when the US government placed an embargo on all Japanese silk and requisitioned the entire US supply for the manufacture of parachutes and gunpowder bags. This ended the use of silk for sutures, umbrellas, dental floss, fishing lines, camping tents and beautiful clothes. Everyone had to become resourceful and innovative and canvas was used for tents, stocking seams were painted up the back of the leg using an eyebrow pencil, and cotton was used for fishing lines.

The Second World War did stimulate and accelerate the development of many new artificial fibres, including rayon and nylon, which gradually replaced real silk in most areas. The United States had been the largest manufacturer of silk goods in the world but eventually the emergence of artificial fabrics completely destroyed US silk production. Today, 'real silk' has made a comeback, although no one suggests that every household turn over a shed or bedroom to cultivate silkworms. Today, most silk in the US, in all its many forms — raw, reeled or woven — is imported from China.

The *Needlewoman*, December 1926, price 4d, a monthly magazine produced by a thread company, Coats-Clark. It included paper patterns and embroidery charts and focused on fashionable clothes and accessories that could be handmade, shawls, dance dresses and embroidery.

CHAPTER NINE
Silk in England

The rise and fall of the silk industry

When the British Empire expanded and became a world leader in the heady atmosphere of the Industrial Revolution, it saw itself challenging Lyon in the production of silk. England gained a real advantage with the influx of experienced Huguenot silk weavers after France revoked the Edict of Nantes in 1685. Many of the most skilled weavers left France and were welcomed in England, and the silk-weaving industry blossomed, spreading from Canterbury to Spitalfields in London, and later to many English counties. But, after flaring briefly like a bright flame, silk manufacturing almost disappeared, swamped by the production of cotton and other products, lack of innovation and style, and repeated punitive legislation by the English government in the nineteenth century.

England had a tradition of individual craftsmen who worked from home. In Spitalfields, rows of three-storeyed terrace houses with banks of windows to let in maximum light were built to accommodate the looms on the top floor. Everyone worked, even children from the age of six or seven. They learnt all the weaving

Woman weaver in her garret, working on a 'Little Rocking Loom'.
Source: Bigelow-Sandford Inc.

skills from their parents while they wound silk onto trimmed swans' quills or paper tubes that slotted into the shuttles. Weavers typically worked for 14 to 16 hours each day, yet many could still not make ends meet. Often the work stopped while they waited for the next order of silk to arrive. Everything was controlled by the guilds, by legislation or the manufacturers. At times there were bitter disputes within the craft, between master weavers and their journeymen over conditions, quality of work, materials and wages. This resulted in the Spitalfields Acts of 1773, 1792 and 1811 and a ban was put on all imported silk. These acts should have protected all sides, but in fact they paralyzed the industry because they set fines for working outside the stipulated rates, but did not recognize the weavers' different skills and experience, or the quality of the work.

In London, it was the powerful silk manufacturers who organized several hundred weavers under contract. They imported processed silk from Persia and Italy through the Levant Trading Company and later, during the 1800s, the East India Company. The manufacturers had an office, not a factory, and increasingly they controlled the industry. They distributed silk to the throwsters, warpers, spreaders, dyers and other associated crafts and stipulated the exact type and quality of the fine satins, damasks and velvets to be woven. It was a Golden Age, but the weavers were vulnerable, because they were only paid after the fabric had been returned to the manufacturer and closely checked. If the fabric was rejected, not only were the weavers not paid, they would be charged for the silk they had used. Their payments could be slow, and in some instances, the weaver could be paid by the unsatisfactory and illegal 'truck system', with goods in kind, not cash. The weavers were frequently short of money or in debt to the manufacturer who had advanced payment against the next lot of fabric to be woven. While many manufacturers made dazzling profits, they could be very hard-nosed and brutal, leaving the weaver and his family in a downward spiral of debt and despair.

After years of poor harvests, a sharp rise in food prices and a steady stream of soldiers returning after the battle of Waterloo in 1815, Spitalfields was inundated with unemployed weavers willing to accept lower wages. Many weavers were die-hard traditionalists in their attitude and methods, trying to hold on to what they saw as their standards and values by opposing innovation and change within the industry. A 'List' was finally agreed upon. It stipulated the pay for each type of cloth or weaver's skill, but it was violently opposed by the manufacturers who promptly took their business out of London into Essex, the Midlands and Macclesfield to escape the restrictions of the List. Many country weavers were happy to do the work, but in general they were not as skilled as the Spitalfield weavers and the quality of their work was often poor.

The eighteenth century saw many exciting new developments in the silk industry. Industrial espionage had enabled Thomas Lombe to construct his water-powered throwing mill in Derby in 1721 and Charles Roe had built a new water-powered silk mill in Macclesfield in 1743. There had been a flood of other new developments and technologies in the textile industry, including a multi-loom for weaving ribbons, the flying shuttle invented by John Kay in 1733 and the spinning jenny by James Hargreaves in 1767. Richard Arkwright patented Samuel Compton's spinning mule in 1781 and around 1804, the Jacquard loom, using a string of punched cards, was developed in France. By 1824, at the height of the silk industry in England, there were 70 mills in Macclesfield alone. Concurrently, by 1826, steam-powered looms were being used to weave plain silks, although perfecting fancy silks took a little longer.

The English silk industry lurched between wealth and despair, fashion and failure. In 1826, Parliament allowed all foreign silk goods to be imported, but, in an attempt to protect the local industry, added a 30 per cent duty onto imported silk. Twenty years later, they voted to reduce those duties, then repealed them altogether. Parliament saw silk as a 'minor handicraft' and passed the Cobden Free Trade Treaty in 1860 and the French added their 30 per cent tax against English silk. The English silk industry was now at a debilitating disadvantage and could not compete on style, quality or price. The French designs had an extra flair and style. Their silks were fashionable and imaginative, making English silk look dowdy and poor in comparison and the result was disastrous. Hardship in the silk community became widespread, sales dried up and warehouses groaned under the weight of unsold silk.

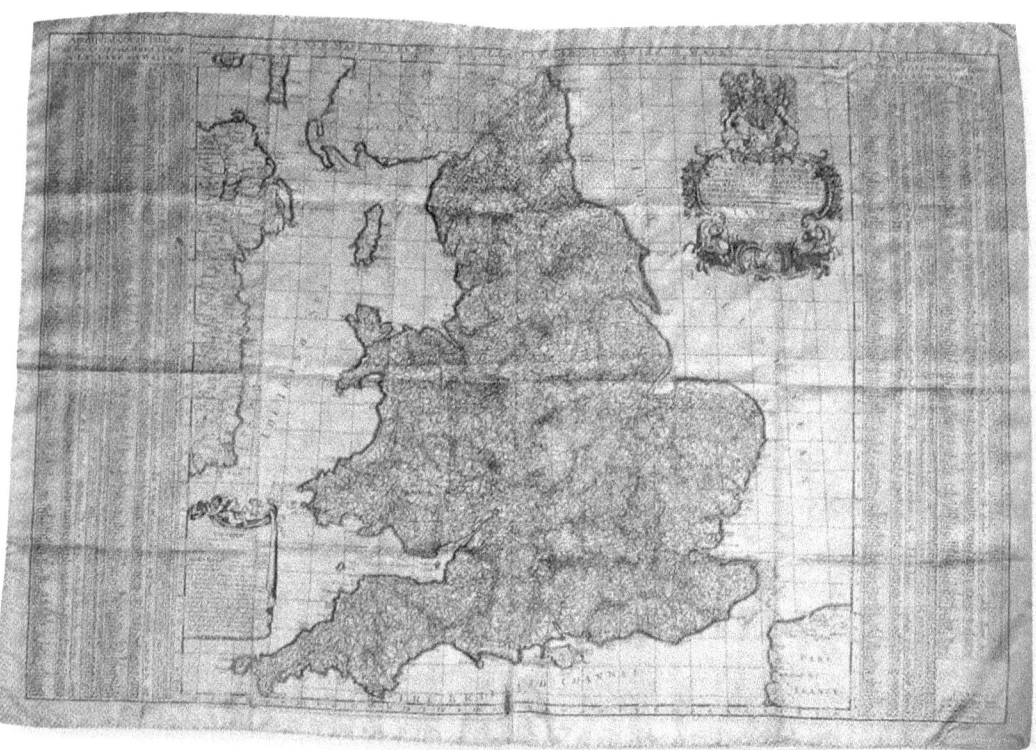

Map of England, printed silk handkerchief, 17thc a early version of the secret maps printed on silk. They were hidden in the airmen's jackets in case they were shot down during the war.

Eastern England

Textiles, especially wool, had brought wealth to eastern England, leaving a legacy of fine churches and elaborate timber-framed merchants' houses. Common phrases like 'on tenterhooks' and 'a web of lies' came from the cloth trade. With the movement away from London in the 1770s, over half the population of Coggeshall in Essex was involved in producing silk and velvet. By the mid 1860s, John Hall, who owned the biggest silk mill in Coggeshall, was employing over 700 people. The situation was similar in Suffolk where Sudbury, Haverhill and Glemsford also became important silk-manufacturing centres with over 600 hand-looms in the district. They did not have power but later, when the looms were mechanized, a steam engine was built in the yard outside the last cottage in the row to supply steam power to all the looms. Some of the weavers' cottages still remain in Sudbury.

Nineteenth-century documents refer to silk 'manufactories' but most were just modest houses used as warehouses, and the weavers only went there to collect their raw material or return the finished roll of cloth. Manufacturers sometimes had trouble getting skilled people, so to control the quality of the finished fabric, they built factories and installed the large, complex Jacquard looms. Here they could provide training and supervise the work of throwing, warping, dyeing and weaving, all under the one roof. In Sudbury, William Hill's factory had a connecting door into his house in Gainsborough Street, and by 1851 he was employing 200 men, 400 women and 200 girls, and had installed a factory bell to summon them to work each day.

By the 1870s, many silk manufacturers were established in Sudbury including Stephen Walters, and over time his property in Acton Square was occupied by a number of silk weavers, all specializing in high-quality fabrics and furnishings. Stephen Walters and Company was the oldest and had begun in 1720 with Benjamin Walters, a master weaver from Paternoster Row in Spitalfields. Each generation of the family introduced new technology to weave the fine silk fabrics, including brocatelles and damasks for clothes and furnishing. With the company's growing prosperity, they moved premises a number of times between Braintree in 1822 and Sudbury in 1860 where they began weaving the stiff mourning silk called crape, and fine umbrella and parasol silks. Power looms were first installed in Kettering, in Northamptonshire, and the firm prospered as each generation joined the company. They made parachute silk and secret silk war maps during the Second World War and later wove silk for the wedding dresses of both the Princess Royal and Princess Diana. Today the company continues to prosper into the ninth generation of silk weavers.

The expansion of the railways and the Great Exhibition in London in 1851 had been a terrific boost to British manufacturing and many firms like Vanners Silk expanded and moved from Spitalfields to Suffolk in the 1870s. Vanners opened additional warehouses and, after a merger with Fennell Brothers, settled into premises in Gregory Street in Sudbury and more recently have been weaving

Great Exhibition 1851 set up in the Crystal Palace in Hyde Park by Prince Albert and enthusiastically supported by Queen Victoria and court as it highlighted Britain's place as a world leader.
Source: British Library.

silk for ties on the latest computerized looms. The Gainsborough Silk Weaving Company, founded over a hundred years ago, has been reproducing historical designs for the restoration of Windsor Castle after the fire. They also hold a Royal Warrant as an Official Supplier of Furnishing Fabric to HM Queen Elizabeth II.

The Warner family have been involved in the silk industry since the seventeenth century and after William Warner's death in 1712, his sons and grandsons continued his business in Spitalfields. In 1857, Benjamin Warner, 1828–1908, bought Alphonse Burnier's business, cutting pattern cards and assembling Jacquard machines. He paid £175 10s for the entire stock, along with thousands of designs and in 1895 the company moved to Braintree in Essex. Benjamin Warner was particularly interested in contemporary design, especially that of Owen Jones, 1809–74, and these designs stood the test of time and had great appeal for companies like Liberty and Co and Debenham & Freebody in London. Warners also wove silks and velvets, supplied fabrics for King George VI and for Queen Elizabeth's coronation in 1953. Although the company ceased weaving in Braintree in 1971, their Silk Museum continued until recently, with a display of the history of silk from the district. The Humphries Weaving Company moved back to Sudbury in 2004, after 30 years at Castle Hedingham.

Weaving figured velvet at Warners, New Mills, Braintree, Essex.
Source: Sir Frank Warner.

Silk in England

They specialized in exclusive furnishing fabrics for royal palaces and National Trust properties and used evidence from 1699 bills and inventories to accurately weave and replace the furnishings lost during the disastrous fire at Hampton Palace in the 1980s.

Central England

The area around Manchester and Cheshire became a mecca for the silk industry. Each town had their speciality. During the seventeenth century, Stockport, Congleton, Leek and Buxton were famous for their lace, while people in the area around Macclesfield made embroidered buttons and wove narrow silk tapes, bindings and ribbons. Later, John Prout in his 1829 record of the silk trade, states that broad-silk weaving began in 1756 and Macclesfield became one of the largest producers of finished silk. Over the years, horsepower, water and steam were used to power the many machines and by 1832 there were 71 silk mills operating in the district. Today, Paradise Mill in Macclesfield is a working museum featuring the

Leodian, Specialists in Macclesfiled Silk, publicity advertisement.

history and all the various aspects of silk in the area. HT Gaddum & Co have been importing and trading in silk fibres and fabrics for both the weaving and knitting industries since 1826, a service still valued by both domestic and commercial spinners.

By 1752, Congolton had an established silk mill with valuable water rights to run the machinery, secured for 300 years. The mill was over 240 feet long with 390 windows, a sign of a very modern and superior mill, and was capable of processing between 15 and 20 large bales of Chinese silk into a range of yarns, including fine organzine and loosely spun tram. Silk spinning was done at Stonehouse Green and Brooks Mill, Forge Mill and Bath Vale and offered employment to many of the town's workers. George Reade and Sons of Congolton began spinning waste silk in 1829 and by 1846 there were 27 silk-throwing mills, including those at Knutsford, Derby and Mobberley, but by 1905, once again the industrial turmoil of the Silk Acts and Free Trade Agreements took their toll and only two remained.

Leek in Staffordshire

The parish of Leek had collected generous funds of £6 5s 0d to welcome the Huguenot refugees in 1685 and they were greatly valued for their skills. A ditty was sung: 'For silken fabrics soft and rare, What citie can with Leek compare?' Silk manufacturing expanded and by 1800 companies like James Horton had begun making figured ribbons, sewing twist and embroidery floss, industries that made Leek prosperous. Samuel Bamford, 1788–1872, noticed the neat, clean weaving girls in Leek, and observed that with their fancy combs and earrings, they were probably well paid for their work. With the introduction of steam weaving, the number of silk mills increased, as did the number of men and boys employed to manage them. The mills included Brough, Nicholson and Hall who began in 1815 and had a silk spinning mill, two dye houses and a workforce of over 2000 in their factories. They specialized in sewing and embroidery twist, braid, cords, woven labels and bindings. They later diversified and advertised their 'New Artificial Silk, rayon ties, motoring scarves and ladies coats'.

William Morris designs printed by Thomas Wardle on Indian tussah silk in 1878.
Source: Whitworth Art Gallery

The firm of Wardle and Davenport began in 1831 as a silk printing and dye works but the drive, energy and leadership of Thomas Wardle, 1831–1909, grandson of the founder Joshua Wardle, made Thomas an international figure. He was primarily a silk printer and dyer, and in 1877 when William Morris, 1834–96, came to Leek, their artistic collaboration was a turning point for both men. Both wanted to obtain a greater depth of colour and colour-fastness and experimented with Indian natural dyeing methods and block printing. Their personalities sometimes clashed as these talented, artistic men struggled to get the results they needed. By 1876, Wardle was printing a range of 14 distinctive patterns for Morris, incorporating fruit, flowers and meander designs, so in keeping with the Arts and Crafts Movement of the time. After William Morris left Leek, he set up his own print works at Merton Abbey and an embroidery studio, with his daughter May and others.

Wardle continued experimenting at his silk mills and his breakthrough came when he found ways to bleach and dye Indian tussah silk from Bengal and Kashmir to make them more desirable and marketable in England. He visited India to report on sericulture

Thomas Wardle during one of his visits to the silk station in Kashmir.

and was enchanted with everything Indian, especially its wild silks and natural dyes, and enthusiastically promoted them. In India, there had been many problems with quality control and he was invited by the Indian government to return in 1896 to suggest changes to improve silk quality and sustainability. He journeyed via France and Italy, obtaining quality disease-free eggs and new machinery on the way.

In 1899, Wardle & Co became a public company and greatly extended their range of sewing twist, dyed embroidery threads and mercerized cotton thread. At the time, Thomas Wardle was chairman of the Silk Association of Great Britain and Ireland and after years of dedicated work as a Fellow of the Geological Society, the Society of Chemists, Society of Arts and the South Kensington Museum, numerous writings and public duties, he was offered many honours, including a knighthood.

His wife Elizabeth, was not only a full partner with her husband, sharing all his interests, but also a significant and public-spirited woman in her own right. She was highly artistic, a superb organizer and imaginative embroiderer. She established the Leek School of

Elizabeth Wardle with some of her pupils at the Leek School of Embroidery she had established in 1879. Her work was very highly regarded and widely exhibited. The embroidery kits she designed and supplied used her husband's tussah silk and dyed silk embroidery threads.

Embroiderers in 1879 and taught 30 local ladies all the different stitches and techniques. They revived the art of embroidery, using and promoting many local textiles, manufactured, printed or dyed in Leek. The designs often showed the influence of Indian textiles and the Wardles' friendship with William Morris. The fame of the Leek Embroiderers spread when they put together embroidery kits and made them available by mail order. Their needlework was displayed at many international exhibitions to great acclaim and they produced many exquisite articles for churches and other public buildings, including a very fine copy of the Bayeux tapestry, now at Reading.

Courtaulds of Essex

Another name that became synonymous with British silk was George Courtauld, 1761–1823. He was from a Huguenot family and entered the silk industry at the age of 14 in 1775. After a seven-year apprenticeship with Peter Merzeau, he set up his own business as a throwster in Spitalfields. On one of several trips to America between 1785 and 1794 he married Ruth Minton, and after returning to England with his family, joined Peter Nouaille who owned a silk mill at Sevenoaks in Kent. The two men argued over Courtauld's support for the French Revolution and after the partnership ended in 1797, he managed a silk mill in Pebmarch in Essex with his cousin Peter Taylor, 1790–1850. In 1809, he opened his own silk mill in Braintree.

Like most other mills he employed children, mostly girls between 10 and 13 from the workhouses in St Pancras and Islington, and insisted that each child arrive 'with a complete change of common clothing'. The workhouse paid Courtauld £5 for each child with another £5 after a year. The children also signed a contract that bound them to the mill until they were 21. He paid them between six and eight shillings a week and promised to teach them the skills needed in the silk industry. He believed this was honourable, and he was doing a public service, claiming in a letter written in 1813 that his 'mill will prove a nursery of respectable young women fitted for any of the humble walks of life'.

In 1814, several of the girls ran away from Courtaulds saying they were being badly beaten by the woman supervisor at the mill. Two men claiming to be relatives of one of the girls arrived at Braintree threatening revenge, and a nasty scene developed. Although Courtauld denied all knowledge of violence, he agreed to sack the woman accused of beating the girls, and got his daughters Louisa, Catherine, Eliza and Sophia to supervise the mill girls, using a system of marks on a chalkboard that reflected their work and behaviour. Talking was forbidden, but they could sing hymns because Courtauld believed that singing hymns could be 'a help to industry, attention and orderly conduct'.

By 1818, the company was in financial trouble following the end of the Napoleonic Wars, and George Courtauld chose to retire to America where he died in 1823. His ambitious son Samuel, 1793–1881, turned the company around by centralizing production in the factories and introducing two 12-hour shifts so that his spinning and weaving mills were working all day and night. He built two more mills and installed power looms at Bocking in Essex and within ten years he had 106 steam looms at Halstead, gradually ending the tradition of weavers working on hand-looms at home. He was still heavily dependent on women and children to keep labour costs down and believed they needed to be firmly supervised to protect their morals. In 1838, the men at Courtauld's mills earned 7s 2d per week, women 5s, and girls under eleven, 1s 5d a week. By the 1850s, Samuel Courtauld employed over 2000 people in his three silk mills.

Samuel Courtauld was a Unitarian and like many of the industrialists of his time, he was paternalistic in the way he ran his factories, a benign despot, yet he still could not support the Factory Act of 1833, maintaining there were 'no exploited children at his mills'. By the 1870s, he was an extremely wealthy man, but all attempts by the workers to improve their wages failed, and they went on strike. He refused to allow any trade union activity in his factories but offered his own system of rewards and punishments, building cottages for the workers, schools, reading rooms and a hospital in Braintree. The mills produced a variety of different silks, especially the mourning silks that were very successful and lucrative, but the company's masterstroke was to diversify into the production of artificial fibres like rayon, to survive and to become one of the leading textile companies in Great Britain.

The Whitchurch Mill is another survivor. In 1817, the mill was powered by water from the river Test and owned by a silk weaver called William Maddick, originally from Spitalfields. In 1830, he advertised for girls aged between 10 and 14 years to be apprenticed for silk winding and weaving. They were expected to pay a large premium of £8 to secure their apprenticeship and by 1838 the mill employed 108 people, including 39 children under the age of thirteen. Later, a schoolroom was built on site, probably as a result of the Factories Act of 1844 that limited the hours children could work and required them to attend school, but for many mill children, the only schooling they had was in their own time at a Sunday School.

The Whitchurch Mill spun silk and wove dress fabrics including taffeta, bombazine, ottoman, faille and organza, as well as black ottoman and satin for lining legal gowns. It also produced fine furnishings, ribbons, serge, silk linings in 22 colours for Burberry and, during the Second World War, silk for insulating cables and even, it was said, cream silk for a scarf, tie and handkerchief for the notorious Kray brothers. Today the Mill functions under a trust, and costume departments in both television and the film industry call upon it to make authentic materials for their period dramas.

English fashion

The silk manufacturers of Victorian England were well equipped to produce plain silks, ideal for the full, gathered skirts of the gowns. They were draped over stiffened slips, wire or wicker crinolines, and the height of fashion between the 1850s and 1870s. The large fringed paisley shawls, locally made or from Kashmir, worked perfectly, balancing the wide skirts. The death of Prince Albert in 1861 had the most profound effect on English fashion, when overnight, Queen Victoria adopted widows' weeds and black silk crape became *de rigueur* for all those in mourning. It proved to be a bonanza for many English manufacturers.

Two women, one in mourning dress 1878. Mourning crape was a black silk that had been stiffened with metallic salts to make it rustle, but unfortunately it caused the silk to decay.
Source: Elliot and Fry

Magazines highlighted the glamorous film stars, latest trends, beauty products and the joy many women had in making fashionable garments for themselves.

From the 1880s, it became the fashion for full skirts to be drawn back to provide a short train and bustle, leading to the excruciating S-bend shape controlled by the corset. The leaders of fashion looked to the Lyon silk mills and the Paris salons, not the English mills, so rather than producing a larger selection of fabrics, the more resourceful English mills sought to expand the range of embellishments, ribbons, roses, lace, gauzes, fringe and cords that were in constant demand by fashionable women.

During the London Season the dressmakers and seamstresses worked under unrelenting pressure to make the elaborate, flounced and embellished gowns ordered by the rich. These fashionable English women looked to the many women's magazines like *The Lady* and the *Gazette Du Bon Ton* to keep abreast of the latest styles and colours, hats and accessories. Fashion could be fickle, and overnight, what had been highly desirable could be abandoned without warning, and something else take its place, often leaving piles of unsold stock in shops and warehouses.

The First World War put silk on hold until the exuberant 1920s flapper era. That was followed by the exquisitely fluid, bias-cut silk dresses of the 1930s, with hand-stitched gossamer silk lingerie, cami-knickers, nightwear and pure silk stockings.

Printed silks

England did produce very beautiful printed silks. London had been the home of many small printing, bleaching and dye works since the 1680s. The Thames River between Crayford and Southwark provided the motive power for the washing stocks, squeezers and calenders to grind the madder, alum and indigo for dyeing. The apprentice prepared the dye on the blocks and the master dyer carefully laid the screens in the exact position to transfer the pattern. It was found that silk needed a mordant so that the dye did not run and could stand repeated washing. From 1843 onwards, the firm of David Evans & Co pioneered unusual dyes and techniques, including a laborious process using blacks, reds and lilacs with varying strengths of alum, followed by madder. Yellow was obtained by using the same mordant at the printing stage, followed by a weld dye, while indigo was overpainted to produce variants based on blue. The invention of synthetic dyes in 1856 by William Perkins, 1838–1907, revolutionized dyeing with its strident purples and range of vibrant colours.

For most of the second half of the nineteenth century, the Crayford Mill continued making silk bandanas and handkerchiefs for the navy, cravats, scarves, trimmings and upholstery. They diversified into crepe de Chine and other silks, chiffons, muslins and gauzes. The factories block-printed silks and paisley scarves, long before the original design from Kashmir became all the rage. David Evans was an avid collector of printing blocks and bought from bankrupt firms and independent tradesmen, and accumulated an enormous stock of over 20,000 patterns. Silk fabric continued to be imported from China and Japan, and the company had close connections with the Aylsbury Silk Company and Norwich Crape Company who had extended credit and supplies, and later he supplied beautiful finished items to large firms like Debenhams and a small group of wealthy clients. The company continued until 2003 when sadly, it was the last of the Crayford Silk companies to close.

Lullingstone, Kent

In the twentieth century, Lady Zoe Hart Dyke's passion for sericulture began as a hobby in a garage at Lullingstone Castle in Kent during the 1930s. She was a superb organizer and her childhood passion for silk became a flourishing business. She was invited to produce silk for the Queen Mother's coronation robes in 1937 and during the Second World War her silk was used for parachutes, although she stressed that the silkworms were imported from China, not Italy as that would have been unpatriotic. Her son, Guy Hart Dyke, recalled how 'the army took over the house and we were booted out to one of the gardeners' cottages, but mother still got the soldiers organized to feed the silkworms whilst they were there.'

Before Queen Victoria and Prince Albert married in 1840, royal brides usually wore coloured wedding dresses that were practical and could be worn later, so perhaps Victoria started a trend when she chose to wear a cream silk satin gown woven in Spitalfields. It was trimmed with 'Honiton' lace that apparently took 200 people from the Devon village of Beer eight months to make. For Queen Elizabeth II's wedding dress in 1947, Lady Zoe was asked to supply the silk and everyone near and far was called in to help. Guy remembered rearing silkworms at school and sending them home to Lullingstone so there would be sufficient silk to make the robes. The silkworms were fed and cared for at Lullingstone Castle, the cocoons rushed to Macclesfield to be reeled and 'thrown' and then to Braintree to be woven and finished. The ivory silk gown had been designed by Sir Norman Hartnell, the Queen's favourite couturier, and decorated with 10,000 American seed pearls and thousands of fine white crystal beads. It took Hartnell three months to make the Queen's dress, working in his Mayfair workshop behind whitewashed windows, hung with thick white muslin to keep the details secret until the wedding. The Queen, like all brides, was offered 200 extra clothing coupons to put towards her trousseau. Since then, the silk in the wedding dress has deteriorated. It had been treated with a tin weighting solution to stiffen the material to give it the distinctive rustle effect, and this has caused the material to decay. In the 1970s, the dress was given an internal silk support to hold the weight of the crystals and pearls without further stressing the fabric.

Sericulture took over Lady Zoe's life and home. Thirty rooms of the house were used for caring for the silkworms and more than 20 acres of the estate planted with *Morus alba* mulberry bushes to feed them. Everyone was involved and when reeling machines were required, her husband Sir Oliver, an engineer, came up with the appropriate design and later many more reeling machines were made and exported. In 1947 she was asked to provide silk for an altar frontal at St Botolph's Church in the village, where the traditional silkworm blessing ceremony took place at the beginning of each season, and in 1953 she supplied silk for the Queen's coronation robes. After her death in 1975, the silk farm was sold to Robert Goodden and moved to Compton House in Dorset where he had a world-class collection of butterflies and silk moths. Compton House had been the home of the Goodden family for over 270 years, but unfortunately it too has recently been sold.

The story of silk in England has been a mixed one, with some stunning successes, but too often England has run second to France. The austerities put in place during the Second World War continued for many years and since then the range of man-made fibres has increased enormously, with their ease of care fitting well into people's busy lifestyles. A few special silks are still woven in England using imported silk, and silk fabric can be bought for special occasions, but sadly, most of the hopes and dreams for a vibrant English silk industry have not been realized.

Georges Barbier 1882–1932. La Dance 1914. Barbier was a costume designer and illustrator extrordinaire, much influenced by the Ballet Russes and Eastern exotica. The languid pose gives an intimate yet erotic feeling, emphasizing the dramatic break with the old world and its style.

CHAPTER TEN
Old World, New World

France, pébrine and fashion

The invention of the Jacquard loom at the turn of the nineteenth century sent ripples of excitement and apprehension through the silk industry. This loom used a series of punched pattern cards and was based on earlier looms, first developed by Basile Bouchon in 1725, followed by Jacques Vaucanson in 1740 and was finally perfected by Joseph Marie Jacquard, 1752–1834. Despite its cost, the Jacquard loom had superior speed and accuracy and enabled greater complexity in the designs, making it vital to the fast moving fashion industry. The loom was declared public property in 1806, and Jacquard was rewarded with a pension and royalty payments for each loom sold.

For the Canut silk weavers of Lyon, change was coming too fast. They denounced the Jacquard loom, as they feared it would devalue their hand-weaving skills, cause their unemployment and end their traditional way of life. The weavers were especially upset when their wages were steadily reduced and so in 1831 they tried to set minimum prices for weaving silk. When this failed, they revolted in a violent and bloody battle. A National Guard of 20,000 men was sent in under

Wooden Jacquard loom with the punched pattern cards that automatically select the pattern.
Source: Museum of Science and Industry, Manchester

Marshall Soult, who managed to defuse the situation, but the weavers had gained little. By 1834 there were already 2885 Jacquard looms in use in Lyon alone. Frustrated and angry, the weavers protested again in 1836 and 1848 but to no avail — the advantages of the loom were too great and the manufacturers held firm.

Then in 1856, there was another catastrophe. This time it was worldwide, and resulted in the almost total collapse of the silk industry. The infectious pébrine disease had been observed in silkworms in France as early as the 1820s. It started to spread, slowly at first, and in 1851 was discovered in Italy. From there it spread rapidly to every country except Japan, whose silkworms were more disease resistant. *Nosema bombycis* is described as 'a type of spore-forming, parasitic, single-celled organism that undergoes repeated asexual divisions'. Rogue cells were called 'corpuscles' and the disease caused the silkworm to become weak, stop eating and its body to be covered in small brown spots. The silkworm either dies or spins loose, flimsy cocoons and rarely pupates or develops into a moth to lay eggs to continue the life cycle. After some years of experimentation, the famous French biologist Louis Pasteur, 1822–95, found that it was not one disease but two, and could be either flacherie or pébrine. The disease was hereditary and could be identified through a simple microscopic examination of adult moths, and overcome through stringent hygiene by destroying all the contaminated moths and using only healthy, disease-resistant Japanese breeds and eggs.

The collapse was devastating and caused silk countries around the world to reassess their industry. Before the mid-nineteenth century, Europe generally relied on its own home-grown raw silk, with limited imports from Syria, Turkey, India and China. Although raw silk from outside Europe was cheaper, the cost of transportation and the variable, unpredictable quality of the imported silk caused difficulties and problems. For the millions of peasant farmers around the world, the pébrine infestation left them without an income and their way of life in ruins.

Despite this, some countries, especially France and Italy, chose not to support their silk farmers by revitalizing sericulture locally but to import raw silk and concentrate on weaving, manufacturing and finishing. This made sense from the government's point of view, as the tax income from peasant farmers was infinitesimal compared with tax returns from the manufacturing industry. Designers and technicians concentrated on adapting their machinery to use imported raw silk, and they experimented with mixing expensive silk with local cotton and wool. Silk was sold by weight, so they increased that by adding mordants and chemicals that also enhanced the lustre and 'handle', or feel, of the silk. They improved their dyeing and printing techniques, based on the vivid colours, now possible with the new aniline dyes. Quinine was synthesized to make indigo dye and Perkins mauveine was a sensation that took the fashion world by storm. Then in 1884, Count Hilaire de Chardonnet, 1839–1924, developed the first artificial silk, which cost far less and threatened to totally replace natural silk.

The fashion industry

By the end of the nineteenth century, Paris had become the fashion centre of the Western world, and in France, factory numbers increased as manufacturers threw themselves into the task of supplying the fashion industry with a constant flow of new designs, florals, stripes, meanders and new colour combinations, pushing the boundaries of what the weavers, designers and technicians could produce.

The major area where money could be made or lost overnight was not in yardage but in haberdashery. Only the very rich could afford to visit a Paris salon to order a gown, but as standards of living rose after the 'Long Depression' of 1873–79, more and more women found they could dress fashionably by changing their silk trims and accesssories. Paris designers led the trends with their exquisite ribbons, enhanced with flowers, medallions and fancy purl edges that for a season were all the rage.

The earliest fashion designers were not courturiers but high-class dressmakers who made garments to order, sourcing beautiful fabrics, following the latest trends. They subscribed to magazines

Dressmakers shop in Arles by Antoine Respal, 18thc.

Madame Paquin, in her fashionable Paris Salon at 5pm, painting by Gervex in 1906 shows Madame and her assistants talking to clients and demonstrating the lovely clothes with both men and little pet dogs in attendance.

with fashion plates, or dressed little dolls, called *poupee*, in the latest fashion. The *poupee* were sent to clients, and usually the dressmakers went to the lady's home for private consultations and fittings. One of the first couturiers to make a name for himself by establishing a salon in Paris, where the client came to him, was the Englishman Charles Frederick Worth, 1825–95. He concentrated on impeccable cut and fit, using the most luxurious silks rather than the over-fussy fashions of the day. He dressed his beautiful wife, Marie Vernet, in his sumptuous gowns and as they were seen at all the most fashionable events — the races, soirées and theatre — his client list blossomed, especially after Empress Eugenie, 1826–1920, ordered some beautiful gowns.

Worth was followed by many talented designers including Paul Poirot, 1879–1944. By 1910 Poirot had captured the exotic, free spirit of the Ballets Russes' performance of *Scheherazade* and transformed his clients into harem girls in vibrant silk pantaloons, brief jackets and turbans, or geishas wearing exotic kimono. Jeanne Paquin, 1869–1936, was one of the first successful women designers. She was the first to organize and stage fashion shows and to open branches of her salon in London, Buenos Aires and Madrid. The signature gowns of Jacques Doucet, 1853–1929, captured the prevailing interest in Impressionism with their shimmery pastel shades and hues. Silk absorbed the new dyes in a unique way to produce delightful and fascinating effects. The fluid Delphos designs of Mariano Fortuny y Madrazo, 1871–1949, were made from a single piece of the finest hand-pleated silk. Among his long list of inventions, he had perfected a special pleating process and new dyeing techniques. His long clinging dresses displayed the body to perfection and the iridescent colours were reminiscent of the lagoons of Venice where he lived.

The First World War not only put high fashion on hold, but garments now had to be practical so that women could dress without the help of a maid. By the 1920s, the practical bob superseded the pre-war bouffant hairstyles, long trains were abandoned and dresses shortened to the knee. Tight, boned corsets were now a thing of the past and women adopted the androgynous, boyish style of the *garçonne*. Uncluttered, skimpy little dresses of the flapper age, portrayed in the fashion magazines and exquisite designs and drawings of Erté and Paul Iribe and many others, fitted the mood exactly.

Jeanne Lavin, 1867–1946, had started out as a milliner, but the clothes she made for her daughter Marguerite were so fresh and delightful that she was asked to make copies and was soon making exquisite garments for little girls and their mothers too. Her distinctive style and skilful use of complex trims made the dazzling embroideries and beaded decorations sparkle on the floral silks. By 1925 she had expanded into many different products, including sportswear, furs, lingerie, men's fashion and interior design, a forerunner of today's designer houses.

Coco Chanel, 1883–1971, also had a finely honed instinct for the times and her relaxed sportswear, 'little black dress' made in silk crepe de Chine and smart, boxy suits became the look of the decade, a sensation that has stood the test of time. Elsa Schiaparelli, 1890–1973, showed her first collection in 1929 and her witty and innovative designs had great originality that ignored

Elsa Schiaparelli 1890–1973 Italian designer, Surrealist jacket designed with avant guard artist Cocteau, superb embroidery by Lesage for her 1937 show.
Source: Philadelphia Museum of Art.

conventional boundaries. She designed a black jersey with the white *trompe-l'oeil* bow knitted in, had a hat made in the shape of a shoe and featured shocking pink, a colour she made her own. In complete contrast, Madeleine Vionnet, 1876–1975, made timeless Greek-inspired, bias-cut silk gowns that slipped over the body and became the essence of the 1930s. Her reputation for perfect draping created a sensual effect that became her trademark beyond her retirement in 1939.

After the Second World War, Paris still held its unique place in the fashion world, despite the Swinging Sixties and Carnaby Street in London, and the expansion of significant fashion designers in the United States, Japan, Italy and around the world. Traditionally, in France more than 70 per cent of silk fabrics were used for clothing, but silk has become increasingly fashionable for drapes, wall covering, bedspreads and upholstery.

Italy

During the Middle Ages and Renaissance, the Italian city-states, especially Venice, Florence and Genoa, produced most of

Europe's luxurious, expensive and prestigious woven silks. Many incorporated gold and silver threads with large floral patterns, based on the pomegranate motif. By the seventeenth century, Genoa was producing superb polychrome, floral velvets. They remained the top choice for formal interiors, wall covering and furniture, even as fashion in dress looked for lighter fabrics. The San Leucio region of southern Italy had a history of silk production dating back to the eighteenth century when Charles VII of Naples and his son Ferdinand I built a silk factory in the region. They believed that high-quality products would result when workers were well educated, so schools were established for the weavers' children, educating them in silk production and land cultivation.

Como was an ideal area for silk production as it had crystal-clear mountain water for washing and dyeing, and was relatively near the vast silk-growing districts of Piedmont and the Po Valley. By the 1850s and 1860s, silk factories had sprung up in many rural areas and Como had grown into the second largest manufacturer of high-class silks after France. It became famous for black taffeta mourning fabric and bolting cloths for sifting flour. At this time, there were around 800 companies engaged in the silk textile trade, manufacturing, printing, dyeing, designing and selling, involving more than 23,000 local people.

During the Great Depression of the 1930s, many silk companies failed and by the 1950s, almost no silk was being grown in Italy, so the few remaining companies began importing silk from China and South-East Asia. Como became the world's largest importer of different styles and qualities of waste silk, used in the production of silk knitwear, and a major importer of *greige*, or raw silk yarn. Italian expertise is in finishing raw silk, dyeing and printing it, then designing and making ties, scarves and other high-priced apparel displayed in elegant shops around the world.

It also concentrated on finishing silk to supply the top fashion houses like Chanel, who require a fast turnaround of short runs for their two or three collections a year. Como filled a niche because unfortunately China was too slow and far away and not geared up to supply such small quantities of specialized fabrics. Change was inevitable for many fashion houses, and they diversified and made cheaper *prêt-à-porter* ready-to-wear lines. Today, Como concentrates on supplying high-end designer stores with their cutting edge fashion, rather than *haute couture.*

Italian companies produce over 90 per cent of Europe's silk exports, but there is conflict with the United States over the introduction of legislation that would require manufactured Italian silk to be labelled 'Made in China'. Under this legislation, at least four steps in the processing of fabrics, including dyeing, printing or weighting, must be done locally for a product to qualify as being made in Italy and not China. The uncertainty has caused anger and discouraged growth in the silk industry, and discussions are continuing, to find agreement between the United States and the Europeans.

Germany

The German city of Krefeld in the Rhineland welcomed French Mennonite silk brocade weavers and velvet makers after the Revocation of the Edit of Nantes in 1685. By 1846, the Krefeld district had 8000 hand-looms weaving silk. The silk industry was largely in the hands of the Van der Leyen family, who dominated production in the district. The weavers rolled their silk fabrics on polished tree trunks to deliver them to their customers and this practice was honoured in a statue of Master Ponzelar carrying a roll of woven silk on his shoulder. Many of the modest weavers' houses that doubled as workshops and living space remain, protected by preservation orders. Textiles still play an important part in the city and every September, the top art museums, including the German Textile Museum and the Museum of Silk Culture, put on special silk displays. The skill of the Krefeld silk weavers is reflected in the city's official motto: '*Stadt wie Samt und Seide*', the City of Velvet and Silk. Even today, the vast majority of ties worn in Germany are manufactured in Krefeld.

Spain

In the seventh century, the Arabs conquered the Persians, claimed their magnificent silks and spread the knowledge of both Islam and sericulture as they swept through Africa and Sicily. They conquered the Iberian Peninsula in 711 and ruled there for almost 800 years until 1492. Sericulture thrived and by the tenth century, Andalusia was one of Europe's main silk-producing areas. A twelfth century text mentions thousands of silk looms in Almeria and the industry continued to expand in many regions, including Valencia, Murcia, Castile, Aragon and Catalonia.

Beautiful silk textiles and tiles decorate the Alhambra palace, first built in Granada in 889. Arabic kufic inscriptions and mottos were incorporated into the tiles, silk drapes and divan cushions, including 'There is no conqueror but God'. Sayings and blessings heighten both the pictorial and emotional depth of the palace. Silk was very much a part of the glory that was Spain.

Spain had an unusual speciality that legend attributes to Don Quixote. In the story, published in 1605, he was on the road to La Mancha when he met some merchants of Toledo on their way to purchase silk thread in Murcia. Apparently, some rag-pickers had come across silkworms that had split open and the silk glands were exposed. The two long gelatinous threads of tough, translucent silk could be withdrawn and stretched to between eight and eighteen inches. Murcia became the centre of this new industry and supplied the world with gut for fishing lines. It became women's work and the farmers' wives collected silkworm eggs in autumn and kept them chilled until the first Friday in March when the eggs were taken to church to be blessed. Some women kept the eggs in a little bag around their necks to keep them warm until they hatched, although incubators have now been introduced. These days, the silkworms are fed until they are about eight centimetres long. Each family has its own secret formula for pickling the silkworms, using a combination of beer, water, vinegar and salt. The silkworm is then opened up and the gut carefully removed, washed and pulled to its full length. They are then collected into bundles and dried in the hot sun and the discarded silkworms fed to the chickens as a tasty snack. The stretched gut is then pulled through a pierced diamond die to ensure its consistency. In truth, nylon leading lines are cheaper but many anglers still prefer gut as it remains supple in icy water, and some surgeons still use natural gut for suturing wounds because the body rarely rejects it.

Spain was not immune, and in the nineteenth century, the worldwide pébrine epidemic saw the Spanish silk industry collapse and only Murcia survived. Stringent hygiene regulations were put in place and a new Technology and Research Centre was established in Murcia. Sericulture recovered and continued until the 1930s when the Great Depression, followed by Civil War and the Second World War saw silk prices collapse. By the 1950s and 60s, there had been some recovery, but Spain could not compete with Asian silk on price and by 1975, sericulture was in terminal decline. Since then, Spain has concentrated on scientific research into many alternative aspects of sericulture, other than textiles.

Portugal

Portugal benefited from an influx of Spanish silk workers after the expulsion of the Moors from Spain during the reign of Dom Filipe II, 1556–98. Many silk workers went to the province of Trás-os-Montes in northeastern Portugal where their expertise was welcomed and the Portuguese silk industry experienced a period of expansion and renewal that lasted a hundred years. Silk was grown in local towns and villages, especially Chacim, and Bragança was described as 'an opulent city, filled with numerous silk merchants'. Velvet and taffeta fabrics were exported to Porto and Lisbon and in return the Royal Silk Factory in Lisbon ordered silk to be dyed in Bragança, despite the cost of transport. Unfortunately, once the Rato Silk Factory was established in Lisbon, demand for silk fabrics from Trás-os-Montes began to fall.

The period between 1640 and 1763 was not particularly tranquil and many conflicts continued with Spain. The upheavals of war, the Portuguese Inquisition, 1536–1821, and ongoing persecutions made consistent production in some areas almost impossible. Hundreds of people were arrested or persecuted, especially anyone designated as Jewish, *Marrano* or *Conversos* or suspected of still having a secret adherence to Judaism. Many people involved in trade or industry felt threatened and insecure and they also abandoned their homes, farms and businesses in their desire to escape the conflicts.

Gradually, life became more settled and sericulture flourished.

Records show that in 1724, Bragança had 30 registered spinning wheels and 350 looms, while the town of Freixo de Espada à Cinta had more than 100 looms. António José Lopes Fernandes, a remarkable businessman, installed 200 silk looms in Bragança and experts were invited from Toledo to teach the latest techniques and methods. At this time, Rodrigo de Sousa Coutinho was the Portuguese ambassador to the silk district of Piedmont in Italy and his influence was invaluable in advancing the Piedmontese method and technique of commercially reeling silk in the Trás-os-Montes region. The Arnaud family from Piedmont settled in Chacim between 1770 and 1834, determined to build a successful silk industry using the new organzine mill and spinning jenny. Mulberry plantations expanded and a spinning school, filature and silk-twisting mill were established in Chacim. By 1794, nearly 20 per cent of the total population of Bragança was working in the silk industry. It could still be a battle, as the local people were very wary of change and resisted the Piedmontese method and many clung to their traditional and outdated hand-reeling techniques.

Portugal had to mobilize all its resources during the French invasions between 1807 and 1810. This paralyzed the economy, and once again skilled people took flight to avoid military recruitment. The Arnaud family was no longer involved, and without their leadership, promoting and reinforcing the Piedmontese regulations, there were no further technological advances, no capital investment and no entrepreneurial initiatives. By 1817, the Trás-os-Montes silk industry was in serious decline. The Chacim factory continued to manufacture fine silk but it could not compete with other districts. Porto was better equipped technically, and the commercial attitude of the progressive, entrepreneurial businessmen who owned the factories dominated the industry, both nationally and internationally. The nineteenth century saw Portugal decline with the loss of her colonies. Chinese and English products were of a higher quality and also cheaper than silk produced in Portugal.

Sericulture in South America

Portugal's main export market was Brazil until its independence in 1822 after which time trade decreased significantly. By the 1850s

Silkworm bed, with 4th stage silkworms where whole stems of mulberry are placed for them to eat, but already the bed needs to be cleaned and fresh leaves given to the silkworms who at this stage do not stop eating for 10 days, before spinning their cocoons.

Brazil had tentatively begun to develop its own sericulture industry near Rio de Janeiro, encouraged by Emperor Dom Pedro II, 1825–91. Sericulture was given new life in the 1920s, when there was an influx of Japanese and Italian immigrant silk farmers, with their high standards and meticulous training, attention to detail and efficiency.

Sao Paulo and Paraná are the main silk-growing districts, followed by Mato Grosso, Minas Gerais, Goias Island and other smaller areas along the Tropic of Capricorn. Brazil's climate ranges from subtropical monsoon to humid and tropical savanna and so sericulture begins in September through to the end of June the following year, with seven to eight hatchings each year. Brazil is very fussy about the choice of both silkworms and mulberry trees, and their care and selection play an important part in the industry.

Brazil has its own traditions and methods of sericulture. The silkworms are bred in huts where 'beds' are covered with mulberry leaves and changed regularly. The carers supply a type of cubby-hole or 'apartment block' called a 'forest' in which the silkworms spin their cocoons. After the cocoons have been collected they are soaked and boiled for two hours at 94°C to soften the sericin and release the silk. To provide consistency, firmness and resistance, the yarn is then twisted up to 500 twists per metre. Natural dyes, made from Brazilian flora, seeds, leaves, bark and roots, are boiled for up to eight hours to extract the maximum dye from the plants. The yarn or fabric is held in the concentrated dye for 40 minutes and the colour is set using vinegar and salt. The silk is then washed under running water to remove excess colour, then dried and packaged.

Bratac is now the sole silk-reeling company in Brazil. It began in 1992 with six filatures and by 2012 it was processing nearly 20,000 tons of cocoons and has become the second-largest exporter of raw silk in the world after China. Its silk is of an exceptional standard but unfortunately the cocoon price is still not really sufficient to sustain the farmers, despite the rise from US$3.51 per kg in 1989 to US$5.83 per kg in 2012. The silk filatures are still not working to capacity despite Bratac continuing to look for international partnerships. Sericulture was a reasonably secure industry for many farmers, but with other crops now available and soil exhaustion, profitability and production have declined. The Brazilian government takes pride in its culture and organization and is sympathetic to sericulture, having faith that the quality of their silk will ensure it survives, even when other countries have faltered.

Since the 1980s, many other areas in South America have promoted sericulture. Both Colombia and Bolivia have had joint ventures with Korea and by 2004 Cuba had a small experimental station producing high-quality cocoons, mostly for the tourist industry. In Ecuador, sericulture flourishes all year because of its favourable climate and top-quality leaves. In 2004, 110 hectares of mulberry were planted and 500 farmers were trained and by 2010, ten of those farmers had produced over 500 kg of cocoons. In Peru in 2005, a national law was enacted to support sericulture as an alternative to coca, an alkaloid of cocaine. Ten hectares of mulberry were planted and 50 sericulture farmers and ten artisans trained. In 2008, there was a joint agreement between Peru and China to plant another 14,000 hectares of mulberry. In Paraguay between 1988 and 2003, sericulture was promoted as an alternative crop for small farms and a partnership was formed with the State University of Brazil to develop parent races and hybrid silkworms.

Mexico

A number of Spanish explorers claim to have brought the *criollo* silkworms to Mexico and by 1531, friar Juan de Zumárraga reported that sericulture had become an important cash crop, and *graine* or silkworm eggs were being imported from Granada. As the missionaries converted the Indians, they also taught sericulture and the silk industry spread into much of the conquered land, from Pánuco to Yucatán and from New Galicia to Oaxaca. Initially, the Spanish overlords allowed the native Indians to weave and produce silk without restriction and did not make unreasonable demands, but by the 1540s, many Indians had been forced to work as slaves. Weaving had deep meaning for the Aztecs and was linked to fertility and the need for rain.

Mexican wild silks have been used by the Aztecs since the time of Moctezuma II, who reigned from 1502 to 1519. The two main species make large bag-like communal nests, over a metre long. They leave the nest at night to feed on the leaves of the oak, madrone and magnolia trees, leaving long trails of silk hanging from the bag to guide them back to the nest, where they will eventually lay their eggs. These silken bags, called *capullos de Encino* or 'live-oak cocoons', are common in the temperate coastal regions of Veracruz, Puebla, and the Huaxteca Potosina. The fine, pale tussah silk was spun like cotton and woven into sashes and shawls to trade with other areas. The industry was reasonably stable until 1580, when it began to decline, and by 1801 had virtually ceased. Later attempts by the Spanish government to revive sericulture in Mexico might have worked except that the Mexican War of Independence, 1810–21, wiped out fields and mulberry orchards and forced peasants into the military.

In spite of the failure of sericulture as a commercial undertaking, it did survive as a cottage industry for more than 150 years. During 1955, the Mexican government began spraying for malaria and continued into the 1960s, killing the silkworms, chickens, birds and other small animals. It was very distressing for rural communities, but many stories relate how one woman escaped to the mountains and hid her rescued silkworm *graine* and then sold it to others to restart silk production. The local mulberry trees, *Morus celtidifolia* or *Morus acuminate bonplandi*, are acceptable to the silkworms and thankfully, they survived.

To reinvigorate the industry, weaving cooperatives were set up in Teotitlán de Valle between 1960 and 1990 to assist with marketing silk, but many of the members found that they could sell their products themselves for a better price in Oaxaca, rather than through the cooperative. Until 1985, the girls used to walk from the village, over the mountains to the coast to sell their silk yarn, net bags, rope or purses. It was a journey of eight days over rough tracks. They returned in large groups, because they were carrying money and afraid of being robbed, and these days they travel by truck.

In Teotitlán de Valle in 1986, Aurora Contreras Lazo set up a cooperative called Women Who Weave. This has thrived and many women and girls formed new groups to work together to sell their silk. Women's cooperatives have helped them gain some standing in their community and the right to apply officially for government grants. As the girls became more independent, there has been an unexpected outcome, as many now feel strong enough to defy their family, refuse to marry and stay independent as businesswomen.

The Mexican government continued to offer grants and loans to assist the community, hire teachers and supply mulberry trees in the spring and silkworms twice a year. Most people prefer the traditional yellow multi-voltine *criollo* silkworms. The government promotes the larger, white Japanese hybrid, the *mejorado*, and although the people have little faith in it, many work with both. Electric spinners are available in some centres, but often there is no electricity in the silk sheds, and many older women still prefer to hand spin using a *malacate*. Some use a bicycle spinning wheel, believed to be the invention of Victor Aquino. All the family members are involved in spinning, weaving or dyeing silk, using natural dyes whenever possible, to reinvigorate the ancient art. It takes around a week to weave a *rebozos*, the long narrow shawl, on a backstrap loom.

Most communities have at least one family or community silk group, some with up to 100 members, but many function poorly, grants are sometimes taken away or diverted, and not everyone wants to work that hard. There are also traditional taboos around

African silk fabrics, Top: Madagascar, Left the Asante people of Ghana, Right: Ethiopia, from an embroidered tunic, Below: a ceremonial cloth from Nigeria.
Source: British Museum.

sharing information and techniques. Wild silk is still gathered by native Zapotecans in the mountains beyond Oaxaca and some native tribes eat the larvae and pupae rather than collect the silk to spin. There have been times when silk production has almost disappeared in Mexico, and then revived, but sericulture still does not always provide enough to support the families.

Silk in Africa

Silk, both locally grown and imported as yarn, is part of African history and until the early twentieth century, hand-woven textiles often included silk yarn unravelled from imported silk fabrics. Waves of immigrants brought their skills and designs and were adapted and absorbed into the local culture. Both men and women could weave but domestic embroidery was the domain of women. The textiles vibrate with glorious colours, dyed with indigo, natural or chemical dyes, and some designs include fertility symbols and protection against the evil eye. Silk and sericulture can be found in many areas including Morocco, Algeria and Tunisia, Libya, Egypt, Ethiopia, Ghana, Nigeria and Madagascar.

The kingdom of Aksum in Ethiopia was converted to Christianity in the fourth century. Under King Ezana, c320–360, the kingdom attained its greatest wealth and power. Vast amounts of silk were imported from India, Arabia and China and stored in deep caves in the central highlands. 'The Keeper of the Caves' had special status and at the king's command would distribute the gorgeous textiles to other Christian churches. Locally woven silk was used for regalia, parasols, book covers, garments and spectacular hangings. Status was displayed in the colours and patterns woven into the long *shamma* shawl worn by both men and women. The women and the guilds of craftsmen were responsible for the rich silk embroidery and gold filigree work.

Some of the earliest written records of wild silk come from tenth-century Tunisia. The trans-Saharan trade routes regularly carried silk from China and Asia, and up to 400 camel loads of silk were traded from Ghadamis in Libya to Kano annually. By the fifteenth century, waste silk from Tunisian silk filatures and French and Italian mills was being transported, and inns were available for merchants and tiraz factories, with 20,000 artisans, were producing luxurious garments for the Muslim elite.

Over the centuries, many people of Jewish ancestry fled to Ghana from Spain or Tripoli in Libya. They brought their weaving skills and made stunning silk curtains, rich with complex patterns within the stripes. The main Ghanaian tribes who worked with silk were the Asante and Ewe who lived near Kumasi. The king commissioned special silk textiles, and retained a monopoly over specific patterns. The complex patterns often incorporated proverbs or sayings, like 'Money attracts many relatives.' In the tiraz factories, the men wove luxurious silks for garments, as gifts or tribute to rulers and Muslim diplomats. These included the red outer wedding garments worn by brides and sleeveless outer robes worn by the men. They used hand-operated treadle looms, but for the most spectacular textiles, a large draw-loom was used, with a boy pulling the threads and calling the pattern.

Mulberry trees were noted in Madagascar during the time of Radama I, 1817–25, suggesting that both *Bombyx mori* and wild silks were grown there. The indigenous *Borocera madagascariensi* is found in the highlands of Madagascar and this wild silkworm produces a dull, tough greyish-brown silk that was hard to dye, but still so precious it was used for weaving prestigious shrouds. Madagascan silk textiles are associated with royalty, immortality and the deity. The women of Merina and Betsileo are the main silk weavers, especially of the shawls known as *lamba*. The elaborately patterned strips are sewn together, and often incorporate the colour green to indicate mourning or status, both here and in the afterlife, although these days white has acquired a special significance and prestige.

Northern Nigeria has two wild silks, *Anaphe infracta* and *A. moloneyi*, which feed on tamarind trees. They form a cluster of cocoons and cannot be separated and reeled, so the silk is boiled, dried and handspun. The light-beige silk from the *A. moloneyi* is coarse and lacks lustre and is used mostly for embroidery. An embroidered gown, especially if it displays the 'guinea fowl' pattern, was an especially treasured gift. It indicated political and religious affiliation and was often a reward for loyalty and service. Muslim scholars usually drew the design to be embroidered on the cloth, and sometimes incorporated the 'two knives' or 'eight knives' pattern of swords and daggers that were symbolic of protection.

In recent years, African countries keen to increase their sericulture have imported the hardy eri silkworm. They eat castor oil leaves, and farmers and households are being trained to care for them. The castor oil trees grow quickly and easily, even on marginal land, and can be inter-cropped with coffee. Eri also have the advantage of completing their life cycle within 45 days so the household can receive a regular income. The silk thread is easily spun on a drop spindle and women can earn extra income from their silk if they spin and sell the thread rather than selling the cocoons. But the African farmers are used to larger animals and fairly rough conditions with sketchy hygiene, so there has been limited development of *Bombyx mori*. They are much more fragile and require light handling and totally hygienic conditions, not always available in remote villages. Nevertheless, there is a bright future for sericulture in Africa.

Empress Cao, Consort of Song Renzong, scroll on silk c 1040-60 CE The two attendants, being less important are smaller and wearing matching silk robes over a red pleated under-robe and smaller headdresses and hold a 'towel' and ewer for purification rituals. The Empress's polychrome silk robe has richly embroidered silver dragon bands and she is sitting on a small throne on a valuable woven cover. Song Dynasty 960–1127.

CHAPTER ELEVEN
Silk in China

The magic of silk really begins in China. Traditionally, sericulture was dated to 2640 BCE when the beautiful but mythical Lady of the Silkworms is said to have discovered how to unwind silk by soaking the cocoons in hot water. In fact, much older silk fragments have been found in many areas along the old silk routes, through eastern China, in caves and tombs and at outposts in the desert. Silk items have survived from the Neolithic period, c5000-1700 BCE, including dyed silk threads and parts of a braided belt dated c2570 BCE, found at Wuxing Qianshanyang on the eastern coast of China, not far from modern Shanghai.

Silk has always been part of Chinese culture and was not only used for clothes, bedcovers and cushions but stiffened silk was perfect for manuscripts and scrolls. Calligraphy was an art form and a precious silk manuscript from the Warring States period, 475 BCE–221 CE, has columns of script surrounded by illustrations of fantastic deities. It offers advice on religion and when to go to war, take a concubine or allow a daughter to marry.

Silk paper was used for recording the Emperor's decrees, and scrolls from the late Zhou period, c1046–256 BCE, are known to include delicate paintings, songs and poems praising silk. One special poem suggests that 'mulberry orchards are the perfect place for birds to sing sweetly and lovers to meet'. Silk maps were found in the tombs at Mawangdui in Changsha Province, dated to the second century BCE, giving directions to both the physical and the nether world. Many practical books were written about silk, indicating the importance of agriculture and sericulture. One of the most complete is the *Can Shu*, 'Book on Sericulture', dated 1090 CE, and printed 400 years before Gutenberg perfected printing in Europe.

Bombyx mandarina Moore and wild silks

The most ancient silkworm, the forerunner of the domesticated *Bombyx mori*, is the semi-wild *Bombyx mandarina* Moore, officially identified in 1872. This silkworm can be found in many areas of China. It spins a skinny, wispy yellow cocoon and differs from the *Bombyx mori* in that the male moth can fly. There are wild silkworms of the Saturniidae species that are native to China. Many have been semi-domesticated or farmed for their silk, and the oak silkworm, *Antheraea pernyi*, is the most common. Although wild silks contribute very little to the total production of silk in China, in remote areas the income they generate has always been important.

Many ancient Chinese documents tell the history of the wild silkworm. Cui Bao wrote:

> *At the fourth year of Emperor Yongguang during the Han Dynasty, around 40 BCE, wild silkworms were emerging in Dongmou Mountain [in Shandong Peninsula].... The cocoons gave birth to moths that produced eggs and about 10,000 dan [135,000 kg] cocoons were collected to make use of raw silk as floss.*

Between the Jin Dynasty and the early Ming Dynasty, 265–1443 CE, numerous other documents from the provinces of An Hui, Hebei, Henan, Hunan, Jiangxi, Liaoning, Shandong and Shanxi also record wild silkworms. Seeing a wild silkworm spin its cocoon was considered a very good omen because the silkworms were very illusive and were seldom actually observed.

Historic records from the Ming Dynasty, 1368–1644, note that artificial rearing of Chinese oak silkworms was practised, including selecting the best stock for breeding. Each of the wild silk species produced its own unique cocoons, and each had to be handled differently. The local people were skilled in identifying which native plants could be boiled up to dissolve the hard outer coating on the cocoon to unreel the precious thread.

Education was seen as important and in 1739 Chen Yuxi, the Mayor of Zunyi City, sent his subordinate to buy cocoons of oak silkworms and enlist a sericulture master to teach the local people how to raise them. His first batch failed because the moths emerged on the way home and flew away, but in 1741 he succeeded. The provincial government recorded in June 1762 that: 'There are lots of oak trees on the mountains . . . Now many refugees from Shandong Province come here to put up shanty for residing and raise oak silkworm for a living. They raise silkworms twice a year. After harvest, they produce pongee [a plain tussah silk fabric] for a living.' Nevertheless, it was still the *Bombyx mori*, or white mulberry silkworm, that was the most widely produced all over China.

Treasures from the tombs

Although silk is really fragile and ancient fragments are rare, the tools for weaving are often hardier, and loom weights, combs and spindles have been found. Those from Hebei Province date from around 5000 BCE and bone needles and battening blades, used to pack down the weft threads when weaving, have been found at Banpo and Jiangzai in Shaanxi. A fragment of purple silk from a mirror case, dated around 1100 BCE, was found fused onto a bronze mirror, and another from a tomb at Anyang showed fine chain-stitch embroidery. One of the richest early finds came from the tomb of Marquis Yi of Zeng, dated 433 BCE. It contained a stunning collection of musical instruments, an enormous rack of musical bells, human sacrifices and ritual vessels as well as 234 silk fragments, clothing, shrouds and quilts. An even greater collection of exquisite silks came from the tomb of a woman at Masham in Jiangling Province, from around the same time. She was found buried in a relatively small tomb, clothed and wrapped

Mawangdui 168 BCE dolls, dressed in wrap-over gowns like the actual silk gowns found in the tomb with their embroidered bands and long sleeves covering the hands.
Source: Hunan Provincial Museum.

in embroidered silk quilts. In all, she had 13 layers of clothing, lined and unlined skirts, jackets, quilted trousers, shoes and belts. In her hands were more rolls of dyed silk, brocades, damasks, gauzes and embroideries, along with her mirrors, bamboo cosmetic boxes, pottery, bronze and lacquerware. Carefully wrapped beside her and placed within the coffin was another bundle of clothing, tied with nine braid ribbons. It all indicated that she was a woman who loved beautiful, precious things and planned to be comfortable and well equipped in the afterlife.

But of all the finds, the discovery in 1973 of Xin Zhui's tomb at Mawangdui near Changsha was one of the most spectacular, partly because it had not been robbed and damaged. She was known as Lady Dai and had overseen the construction of the tombs of her husband, the Marquis of Dai, and of her son, but over the centuries they had both been breached, although some treasures remained. Her own tomb, dated 168 BCE, was packed around with thick layers of charcoal and kaolin to ensure that microbes were totally excluded and her body and the contents of the tomb were in perfect condition. Her skin remained soft and pliable, and scientists have determined that she was around 50 years old, had blood type A, had previously had a child, broken her elbow and that heart disease had probably caused her death. She was placed in the innermost of the three nesting lacquered and painted coffins and covered with an extraordinary T-shaped, painted silk banner that seemed to give pictorial directions to the next world. She also was tightly wrapped in nine silk quilts, tied with nine silk ribbons. There were 22 silk gowns, and a gauze dress 'as light as a cicada's wing' weighing under 50 grams. There were also embroidered brocades and quilted wrap-over dresses, rich with embroidery, 40 small bolts of woven fabrics and figured silks, many embroidered and dyed in sumptuous colours. With her were her painted wooden attendants wearing gowns just like those found in the tomb, lacquered cosmetic boxes with combs, gloves and hairpieces, and an array of different foods including meat, fruit, spices and preserved eggs — everything she could possibly need for her journey to the nether world. It was indeed a treasure trove.

Woven silks

The earliest silks were woven on a backstrap loom in plain, twill and gauze weaves in narrow widths. The designs included patterns of checks, diamonds, zig-zags and coins. The development of large draw-looms, where a boy sat high up on the loom pulling the cords to control the complicated patterns, enabled multi-coloured polychrome weaves with designs of clouds, dragons, lions, horses, flowers, birds and fish. The secret knowledge of these designs and techniques was handed down from mother to daughter over many generations. The most important weaving workshop was within the Emperor's palace and the women could spend their whole lives there, privileged and valued, but trapped.

During the T'ang Dynasty, 618–907 CE, silk was manufactured in most places, especially in the provinces of Shandong, Henan and south of the Yangzi River around Lake Taihu. Weavers were employed full time producing exquisite brocades, highlighted with gold thread. Both government and private workshops produced for the state, the court and for those who could afford such luxury

Sui 581–618 tapestry woven silk fabric with complex animal motifs, one of the extraordinary items found in the caves at Astana near Gaochang in Xinjiang Province, NW China.

goods. The inhabitants of Lu and Xiangyi, now modern Suixian in Henan Province, were famous for their woven polychrome brocade *jin* silks. These were all exceptional fabrics. In contrast, most households produced plain silk in the home for domestic use, to sell or, more frequently, to pay their taxes.

Silk velvet was produced in China from the fourteenth century, and these superb fabrics in glowing colours often featured dragon or peony designs. In the eighteenth century, velvets were designed as floor spreads or fragile carpets or as part of a suite of furnishings, including chair covers, and by the late nineteenth century, velvet was fashionable for court robes.

Trade and 'gifts in reply'

Beautiful woven silks were some of the most highly valued trade items. Traders ventured far and wide, and silk was also carried across the South China Sea, to the Indian Ocean, Arabian Sea and as far as the Mediterranean. Silk could also be a diplomatic gift or political bargaining tool. Tribute was required by the Emperor from various states on its borders, and in return, the court offered 'gifts in reply'. In theory, the Emperor showed his compassion and generosity by providing presents in return for foreign tribute offerings. The rate fluctuated throughout the dynasties, but as both parties came to an agreement before engaging in tribute transactions, it was really trade by another name.

Every item had its value and the court could offer extremely lavish 'gifts in reply'. In 33 BCE Princess Wang Zhaojun, one of the Imperial concubines, was given in marriage to the Sanyu Huhanxie to ensure his continued loyalty. She is known to have sobbed pitifully at being separated from her family, without, she said, even the comfort of silk. By the fourth century, the price of a woman in Central Asia was 41 bolts of silk and a Western horse was worth five lined garments of coloured silk satin. As late as 1490, each newborn colt was valued at three bolts of coarse silk and the court even offered to pay the same amount for a horse or a camel that had died during the long journey to China.

During the time of Kublai Khan, 1260–94, the first banknote was issued. It was made from silk and mulberry bark that had been pulped and pressed into paper, then imprinted in red ink with the chop or seal of the most senior official. The paper money was called the *sichao* and was officially backed by silk and could be exchanged for silver. The court insisted that all goods be brought to the border to be exchanged for paper money and since foreigners could only spend the paper money in China, the court lost nothing in the transaction.

There were few complaints about the system of 'gifts in reply' as it usually benefited both parties. In 1406, Emperor Yung-lo offered a typical gift to Togto, the prince of Hami, when he sent an envoy with 60 bolts of fine silk and 214 of coarse silk and similar amounts to Togto's extended family, but unfortunately these good relations deteriorated after Togto's death. There were accusations of offering inferior goods and of expecting higher rates of exchange and some of the states began to demand prohibited goods, like silk dragon robes. To bolster its image, the Chinese court also started awarding the rank of Regional Commissioner to each important visiting commander

Bactrian camel & driver, earthernware, Tang Dynasty 618-907 CE, 80cm high.
Source: Royal Ontario Museum.

or envoy. They gave the appropriate gifts of two lined garments of pure satin, the value in paper money of one bolt of coarse silk, and one robe of gold-brocaded fine silk. A mission composed of several thousand men could return home with thousands of lined garments of coloured satin and bolts of coarse silk along with other items, all of which put a severe strain on China's economy.

Archeological treasures.

The Han period, 206 BCE – 220 CE, was a time of both military and trade expansion in the far western mountain and desert regions of China, and it was the remains of these settlements that were discovered by foreign explorers of the Silk Road between 1880 and

1920. This was the period of the Great Game, when many countries were interested in the vast, unsurveyed areas of Central Asia. Some foreigners were surveyors or spies sent by their government, others were archaeologists, adventurers or just plain treasure seekers. Excitement mounted when ancient artefacts, manuscripts, paintings and textiles were discovered in remote middens, watchtowers, tombs and fortresses. Initially, China showed no interest in these finds and made no attempt to stop foreign exploration, but then everything changed. The Sinologist Paul Pelliot, 1878–1945, shipped to France precious manuscripts he had found at Dunhuang in 1909 and then mentioned them to some of his Chinese colleagues. They reported it to the authorities and China immediately forbade any further exploration or export of these treasures. By this time, many cases of priceless artefacts had already been trans-shipped out of China into museums and collections around the world.

The explorations and discoveries produced new evidence of silk from the Han period. Although there were very few complete garments found, there were parts of collars, sleeves, bows, sashes and footwear. One item was a woman's hood made of two pieces of red silk fastened at the collar by a silken cord, and another fascinating find was a needle case containing two iron needles, probably made at Edsen-gol. The case was carefully embroidered in five silks in different colours, including wine red, deep blue and several shades of soft blue and green. A small roll of undyed silk was found, still with both selvedges. It was 2.2 Han feet wide and 40 Han feet (9.2 metres) long, and weighed only 25 liang (380 grams). This was a real discovery because up until then, no accurate measurements had been known. The inscription suggests that it was made in eastern China, probably Shantung, and was worth 618 coins. There were also fragments of taffetas, gauzes and crepes, some with patterns similar to damasks. The fabrics were probably trade goods or the stipend of one of the soldiers or officials who were often paid in a combination of coins and textiles. An officer serving on the northwest frontier could receive two rolls of silk to the value of 900 coins as his month's pay. He then had to on-trade or exchange the silk for cash.

Servicemen's outer garments were made of good-quality silk in plain colours, lined with an undyed silk. Sometimes a layer of floss silk

Kasaya patchwork Cave 285 Western Wei Dynasty 535–556. The monk, surrounded by female spirits called flying apsaras, wears his painted patchwork robe. It was customary for travellers to offer a gift, and a piece of precious silk was considered appropriate. The fragments were made into robes, banners, hangings and coverings for precious items.
Source: Dunhuang Research Academy, Cave of One Thousand Buddha's, Dunhuang.

or vegetable fibre was added between the layers for warmth and the jackets were fastened with loops and buttons. It was believed that silk would protect a soldier because if he was shot with an arrow, the silk would allow the arrow to be removed relatively easily, although the prognosis may still not be very good.

Soldiers were at times based at Dunhuang, at the Caves of the Thousand Buddhas on the edge of the Gobi and Taklamakan deserts. This remote oasis grew into a Buddhist religious centre between 366 CE and around 1000 CE when it was effectively abandoned, but not before a priceless cache of books, manuscripts, silk banners and textiles had been sealed into Cave 17. The silk banners were painted or embroidered and long enough to hang from the top of the cliffs above the caves. There were fragments of bright silks with complex weaves and an altar valence made up of narrow strips in many colours, probably each a gift from a grateful pilgrim. Even the sculptured deities had patchworked kasaya robes of silk.

The Southern Route of the Taklamakan desert, and especially around Niya, Bezklik, Astana and Loulan where mummies have been found, have yielded wonderful textiles and most are dated between the third and the sixth century CE. There are warp-faced silks in a simple tabby or twill weave, some brocades with geometric or auspicious designs and some with cloud forms or mythical beasts. Other designs incorporate Taoist and Buddhist motifs and colour schemes that relate to the universe, the five elements, yin and yang, happiness and longevity. Many were important ritual items, rich in meaning and exquisitely embroidered.

Silk embroidery

Embroidery in China has a very long history. Satin stitch appears to date from as early as the Shang Dynasty, 1523–1027 BCE, and examples of appliqué and silver and gold work from the Chou Dynasty, sixth century BCE, have been found in tombs in Mongolia. Gold and silver leaf or glittery painted papers were sliced into narrow ribbons and rolled around silk yarn. They were couched onto the surface of the textiles, as the threads were too fragile to draw repeatedly through the fabric.

Textiles from Han Dynasty tombs show the painstaking, minute Pekin knot, or forbidden stitch, as well as couching, stem and running stitch. Buttonhole stitch was used to appliqué and finish the edges, and during the Ming Dynasty, 1368–1644 CE, some new quilting stitches were added. Embroidery needles were quite short, around 2 cm long with a round eye, and made of bone, ivory, copper or bronze, depending on the technical developments of the time. Embroidery frames were made to accommodate fabric of any size and the design for a court robe was often traced onto a length of silk attached to a frame, and not cut out until the embroidery was complete. Some designs were transferred using a paste dusted with powdered oyster-shell, while others used a cut-out stencil or the design was outlined with running stitches in preparation for the embroidery work.

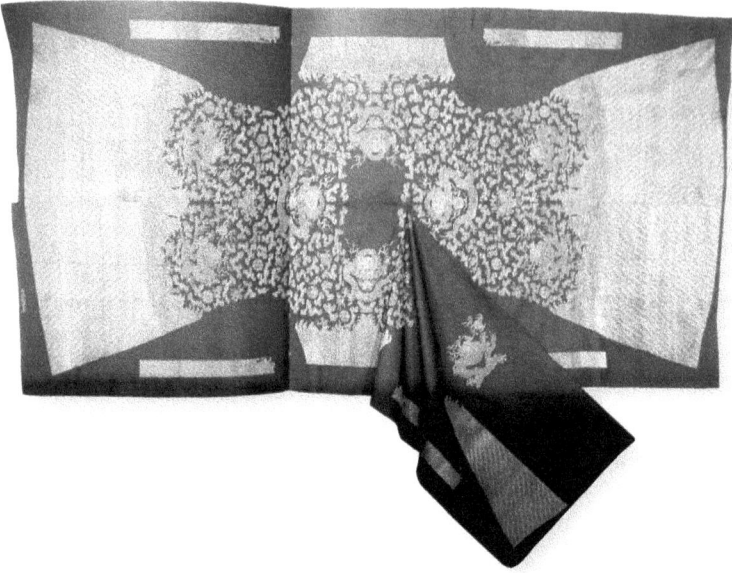

Embroidery was usually done flat on a frame first. Deep blue silk and gold robe, embroidered in two pieces, matched centre front and back ready to be cut out and made up into a robe.

The T'ang Dynasty, 618–907 CE, was considered to be a Golden Age and the capital at the time was Chang An. It became a centre for woven and embroidered textiles and thousands of women were employed as seamstresses and embroiderers and every opportunity was taken to decorate clothes and household items. The Old Kingdoms of Qi in Western Shandong and Linzi were especially renowned for their exquisite embroidery.

The court was controlled by an intellectual, usually aristocratic, civil service. These men had won their place through the examination system or by various nefarious means. It could be well worth the risk, as court appointments were the entrée to wealth and power. Embroidered rank badges identified the hierarchy. The Imperial family's circular rank badge represented Heaven and depicted a three- or five-clawed dragon, while court officials and mandarins wore square badges, representing Earth. The mandarins' rank was clearly visible on his hat button and the square rank badge on his gown. The wives of both military and civil service officials wore similar patches on formal occasions to those of their husbands.

Hand embroidered peacock rank badge lying on a polychrome silk satin fabric with butterflies and pale turquoise medium weight corded silk. Dyed blue pongee silk has a warp of Bombyx mori and the weft of tussah silk. The two silks take the dye differently resulting in a pleasing, slightly uneven colouring.

The Catalogue of Ritual Paraphernalia of 1766 set out the clothes that were appropriate for each rank of official. For really formal occasions, the Emperor had to wear a dragon or *chifu* robe, with a pleated skirt in the correct Imperial shade of yellow, with blue for the Qing Dynasty and red for the Ming Dynasty. Over the *chifu* he wore a plain dark-blue silk coat with an embroidered or appliquéd badge, split in two at the centre front opening.

Symbolic motifs from many philosophies and rituals were often incorporated into embroidery and some were puns or word games. The word for bat sounds like the word for happiness, so the bat became the symbol for happiness. Ancient symbols were incorporated into the Emperor's robes, including the sun, moon, stars and heavenly mountains. The dragon and pheasant motifs were reserved for the Emperor and Empress and symbolized the Emperor's responsibility to create a harmonious empire. Other symbols include birds and animals, the parasol, conch shell, double fish of endless knowledge, butterflies, peaches, chrysanthemums, peonies, bamboo, fire, axes and *fu* symbol for good fortune and happiness.

Embroidery styles can be regional, international and often ancient. It was traditional for young girls to do embroidery, and as the fame of a particular style spread, the techniques were widely copied and have continued to the present day. Bian embroidery was a court style found mainly in the Northern Song capital of Bianliang, now Kaifeng in the Henan Province. It uses rich, bright colours and is exquisite and elegant. Shu embroidery is also known as Su or Suzhou and has developed over the last 2000 years. Typically, it depicts joyful subjects like garden scenes, panda bears or fish lazily swimming and is done in brightly coloured silks using extra-fine satin stitch. It can be breathtakingly beautiful because it is often reversible, sometimes with two entirely different scenes, both appearing to be the right side. Yue, or Cantonese embroidery can incorporate twisted peacock feathers, stitched so they shimmer and glow. Xiang embroidery is considered one of the four great embroidery styles of China. It has been practised since the Warring States period between 475 BCE and 221 BCE, especially around Changsha, the capital of Hunan Province where examples of embroidery have been found dating back more than 2300 years. The random or uneven nature of this stitching means that colours and textures are mixed together to great effect to highlight, for example, a landscape with a tiger that seems to leap, three-dimensionally, out of the silk. The fall of the Manchu government in the late nineteenth century brought many changes and fully embroidered garments became too expensive, even for the court.

Chinese clothing

The Chinese have always dressed in a very distinctive style and although their clothing has evolved through the ages, it has kept its own integrity. The earliest tomb paintings show people of all ages wearing similar garments and it was the quality of the fabrics and colour rather than differences in style that distinguished the nobility from the commoner. Beautiful jewellery, including jade pendants and rings, earrings, necklaces and combs, are depicted with wedding, ceremonial and bereavement clothes. During the Han Dynasty, women wore either a loose, V-necked top or short jacket with a long skirt and an extra-long, decorative belt. Men, whatever their status, wore a short jacket that closed left to right

Above: Embroidered cats, double sided embroidery where the two pictures can be completely different and neither show from the other side. This is achieved by placing the very fine satin and stem stitches directionally, and hiding the thread ends within the work, both designs keeping within the actual boundaries.

Right: Mother, maid and six children, Tang, 618–908.

over their trousers. They also wore a short overskirt, a style that remained popular during the Song, Yuan and Ming periods.

Yang Guifei, 719–756, was the powerful Precious Consort of Emperor Xuanzong. She was beautiful, manipulative and the Emperor was so besotted with her that he could deny her nothing, including gorgeous silks. In one picture she is shown wearing a sleeveless jacket, shorter at the front than at the back, specifically designed for energetic horseback riding and hunting. In other pictures she wears a high-waisted gown with a little shawl and silk shoes with padded toes, decorated with flowers and phoenix. Even before the tenth century, aristocratic women had believed tiny, bound feet to be beautiful and had exquisite little silk lotus shoes embroidered to fit. They wore their hair coiled high in a bun, with

Silk in China

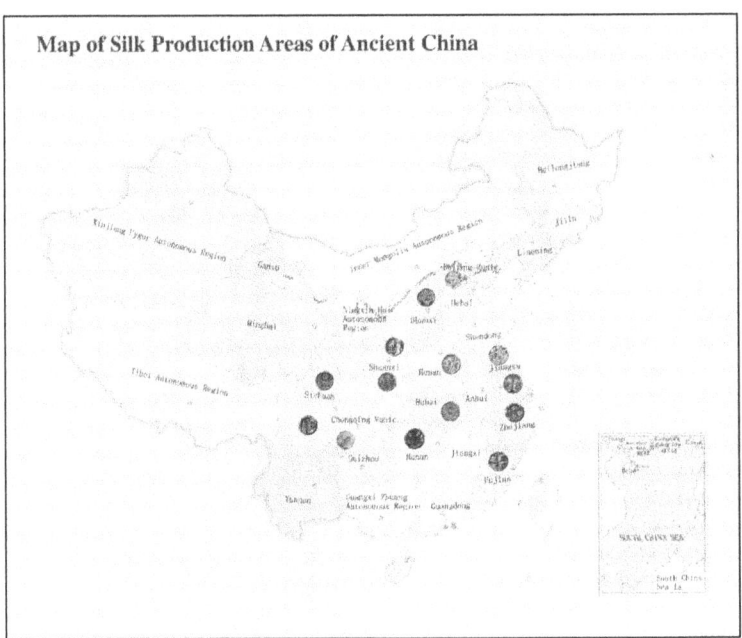

Map of sericulture regions.
Source: Foreign Language Press.

such names as 'gazing-gods bun' or 'cloud bun'. Noblewomen of the Yuan Dynasty, 1271–1368 CE, wore long, loose gowns with wide sleeves and narrow cuffs, made from red and gold embroidered silk brocade, often trimmed with fur.

During the Yuan Dynasty, court officials wore a gown with a round collar, made from fine silk satin, woven with a cloud design. The sleeves were long, with the distinctive Manchu horse-hoof cuffs that covered the knuckles. By the late Qing period, women began wearing highly decorated matching skirts and pants or the slim-fitting Qi robe or *cheongsam*. There are over 50 different tribes incorporated into China and all have their own distinctive dress and style with beads, embroidery, patchwork and headgear, but these days, village people all over China wear the ubiquitous short jacket and cropped pants.

Canton and Pearl River Delta regions

There has been sericulture in the Canton and Pearl River Delta regions for generations. The tropical climate produced a labour-intensive but productive lifestyle and there was work for everyone. Traditionally in this region, girls around the age of 10 or 11 joined girls' clubs. For the next six to twelve years they continued to eat with their families and work in their fathers' fields, but they spent most of their leisure time in the close company of their girlfriends, chaperoned usually by an older widow. It was highly interactive, and some girls learnt to read and deep bonds of friendship often formed. They heard songs and stories of the past, traditions and legends, and the girls considered themselves sisters and sometimes a certain amount of resistance built up to any overarching male and parental control.

By the early twentieth century, village life had dramatically changed. Sericulture had continued to expand and the countryside was now dotted with hundreds of silk-reeling factories or filatures, using steam-power to mechanically reel silk yarn for export. The filatures were staffed by village women and girls who, for the first time, were being adequately paid. Working outside the home gave the girls a new feeling of independence, yet they understood their family's expectations. They knew that they would contribute their wages to the family, be married off to a local boy and would live and work for the rest of their life under their mother-in-law in his family home.

The silk-producing area of the Pearl River Delta had some rather unconventional marriage arrangements. In the nineteenth and early twentieth centuries, many young silk workers who had grown up belonging to girls' clubs were earning sufficient wages to refuse to marry altogether. If coerced, they could refuse to leave their family home and move into their husband's home, bringing, it was felt, shame to both families. Sometimes a bride refused to consummate her marriage, and she negotiated instead to pay the groom's family a sum of money to be used to acquire a concubine for the young man. Underlying this, there could be some serious conflict as to which family could claim her wages.

With steady jobs in the silk factories, some silk girls moved out of

Advertisement for 'Two Girls' products, the cheongsam was part of the promotion of their products.
Source: The House of Kwong Hong Ltd, HK.

their family homes into spinster houses or Buddhist vegetarian halls and many formed sisterhoods. Some even took the final step, the *sou hei* ceremony or vow of celibacy to eschew marriage altogether. The vegetarian and spinster halls were a powerful base for the girls and offered stability, safety and companionship, as well as a religious justification for their way of life. It also helped to secure their financial future and care in old age.

In 1926, there were over 200 filatures operating in the silk district of Quangdong, but by 1935, in the aftermath of a worldwide depression, only 21 factories were still operating. The silk industry slumped and 36,000 workers were laid off. Both the output of raw silk and the price went into a downward spiral. Streams of unemployed silk workers migrated to Hong Kong and South-East Asia as labourers, mail-order brides and prostitutes. Many took their bonds of sisterhood with them and managed to retain their independence, staying single and working within a family as an amah or domestic servant.

For centuries, peasants had farmed their own small pockets of land. They observed traditional practices, festivals, banquets, and paid homage to their ancestors. Following the revolution of 1949 and the establishment of the People's Republic of China, nearly a third of the land once devoted to mulberry cultivation was absorbed into Mao's great plan. It was known as the Great Leap Forward and gave the state a monopoly over all agriculture to enable it to finance its massive plan for industrialization. This policy led to the farmers' total loss of their livelihood along with their small plots of agricultural land. The policy's failure between 1958 and 1966 led to terrible disintegration within society and, for some, even death in the Great Famine that followed.

China and the World Trade Organization

Slowly, during the 1970s, China began to reform its economy and set its sights on the big prize of being accepted as a member of the World Trade Organization. This organization required many fundamental changes to China's political, agricultural, even cultural way of life. The initial applications failed, until 2001 when China

Mao's happy, healthy, willing workers, 'Setting out on Campaign', poster by Wang Shun 1975, Renmin Meishu chubanshe.

was finally successful. China saw sericulture as an opportunity to advance a product in which they had a supreme advantage and they concentrated on improving all aspects of sericulture. They had the history, the land, the people, the infrastructure and the funds and they increased their output until it virtually flooded the market.

Initially, China did not understand how their silk, the cheapest in the world, was being rejected on the international stage. Their understanding was that if they could supply the greatest quantity of silk at the cheapest price, they would control the market, but international trade can be rather more subtle. China did not appreciate that price alone was not the determining factor and it was quality, not quantity, that was valued. The most sophisticated buyers of silk were only interested in top-quality fibre, and price was almost irrelevant. This was because in the sophisticated world of high fashion and design, the computerized machinery used to weave and finish these superb fabrics would only accept the finest grades of silk.

There were other ramifications because as China repeatedly dropped the price to try to capture the market, other silk-producing countries could not compete and their sericulture industries failed. The calamity was worldwide, and one country after another ceased growing silk, destroying families, lifestyles and associated industries.

China's spectacular drive to industrialize has had its successes. People's expectations and standard of living have risen, but there have been terrible costs. China still plans to support and fund all aspects of sericulture, to be the leader in new research, invest vast amounts in science and technology, respond to the market and expand its international trade.

There have been many instances where the use of land and water has been fundamentally changed and often severely damaged by China's policy of taking agricultural land to expand urbanization. The key silk-producing region surrounding Shanghai is just one example of the state sponsoring vast, new cities, built on land formerly used for agriculture and mulberry trees. While farmers have been leaving sericulture and their land and moving to the cities for decades, often illegally, the new state plan is to relocate 21 million people a year into these new cities, with almost unfathomable consequences. 'China is experiencing urbanization at a speed and scale that is unprecedented in human history,' said Helen Clark, UNDP Administrator, at the launch in 2013 of the report on 'Sustainable and Livable Cities: Towards Ecological Civilization'. There are now more people living in China's cities than in its countryside, so the question must be asked: What is the future for sericulture and China remaining the world's greatest supplier of silk?

Alternative products, mulberry tea, three nourishing drinks made from enzymes developed from the pupa, mulberry ice-cream, mulberry soap that can include silk fibre, crushed mulberry leaves or pupa oil, Jim Thompson's canned pupa.snack.

CHAPTER TWELVE

Science and the Future

In recent years there have been massive, worldwide changes in the silk industry. Sericulture has expanded dramatically in some countries, and in others it has been abandoned and now many countries only concentrate on manufacturing and finishing imported silk. Almost all countries involved in sericulture have put resources into education, technology and scientific development to improve the quality and yield of their mulberry trees and silkworms. While China dominates the world in both growing and manufacturing silk, many countries appreciate that sericulture does not have to be exclusively for the production of thread and textiles. With sericulture there is no waste and a vast array of alternative products can be developed and can help maintain viable communities and anti-poverty programmes. Silkworms are protein packed and so can make a real contribution to the health and welfare of society, so this chapter concentrates on the changes and future for silk.

Properties

The properties of this natural fibre can be imitated but not surpassed and in today's world of valuing a natural product, silk is worth protecting and promoting. Silk's special lustre, its strength,

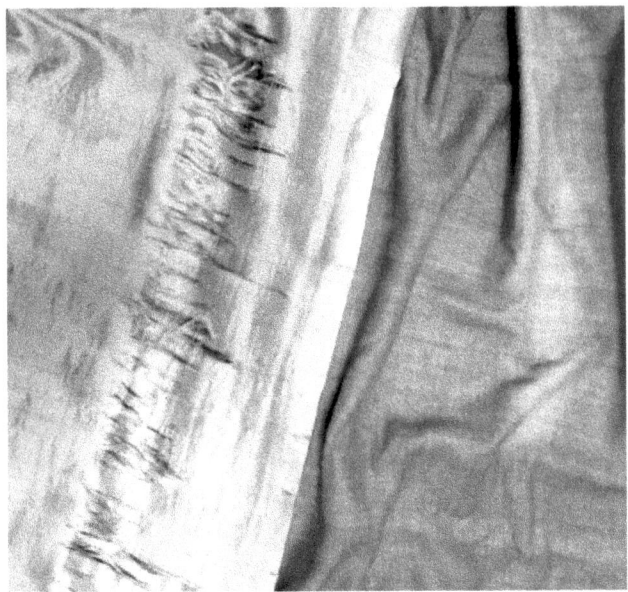

Two examples of destroyed silk. Dupioni curtains shattered by sun and condensation and a handwoven eri silk wrap, badly faded by the sun.

elegance, affinity for dyes, both natural and chemical, ability to absorb moisture up to 30 times its weight, to be warm in winter and cool in summer, make it one of the most comfortable fabrics to wear. It is relatively robust, easily washed, wrinkles hang out when it is worn and it dries quickly. Silk can be destroyed by sunlight, condensation and perspiration, especially in combination, so whenever possible garments should be rinsed out in warm water and mild soap, and silk curtains lined with cotton or polyester. Silk is also hypoallergenic and the medical profession have long used silk for suturing and protecting wounds. Today, the scientific push is towards expanding its use into alternatives and food products.

Technically, silk is fire retardant and if a flame is applied down the side of a piece of silk it will travel slowly, leaving a burnt edge with a string of shiny black bobbles that crush easily leaving a sulphurous smell like burnt hair. In contrast, an imitation silk may leave a black charred edge, but the shiny black bobbles will be hard and uncrushable. Silk used to be measured in deniers, but these days it is measured in mommes. It is 'the number that equals the weight in pounds of a piece of silk if it were 45 inches wide and 100 yards in length'. The higher the weight in mommes, the more durable the weave, and the more suitable it is for heavy-duty use. Habutai, paj, chiffon and fine China silk are between 3 and 8 mommes, while heavier charmeuse and dupioni silks are up to 30 mommes.

Diseases

Silkworms are fragile creatures and it is a constant battle to protect them from diseases caused by viruses, protozoa, fungi and bacteria. The most common are flacherie, grasserie, pébrine and muscardine and an infestation can destroy a whole industry and community. In addition, there are animal and insect predators like uzi fly, birds and mice that can eat the silkworms, or lay their eggs in the pupae and contaminate the cocoons. These losses affect everyone — the farmers and all the associated crafts and industries. Hygiene is the key and education can raise the standard in the rearing shed, and in some developing countries this can also lift the standard of hygiene for the families as well. Most of the diseases are worse during the rainy season and winter, but fungal spores multiply during periods of high humidity and contaminate rearing houses, silkworms and litter, increasing the problems, so contaminated worms and litter must be burnt or disposed of promptly. The rearing beds and often the silkworms too are dusted with lime powder and the whole area,

Dusting the silkworm beds with lime powder to control diseases.

floors, walls and equipment are washed and sprayed frequently with disinfectant or peroxide. The mulberry trees can also suffer from mealy bug, leaf roll, root rot, stem canker and leaf blight, and the farmers sometimes need help to recognize and control these diseases.

Changes

Sericulture is an agricultural activity and because silk is such a small part of most countries' national income, it attracts only limited financial, scientific and government support. Most countries see the need to make changes and are developing better and more appropriate disease-resistant strains and hybrids of silkworms and mulberry trees, specifically for all the different stages of growth, soils and climate. *Bombyx mori* silkworms eat only mulberry and to produce high-quality consistent fibre they need a source of high-quality mulberry leaves. Japanese scientists led the world in producing an artificial food, made up of powdered mulberry leaf, reconstituted and mixed with soy, yeast, sucrose and trace elements. It looks like a muesli bar but it is expensive to produce compared with fresh mulberry leaf, but more convenient in some industrial situations. It is acceptable to the silkworms and they thrive on it, but only if they have never tasted the real thing.

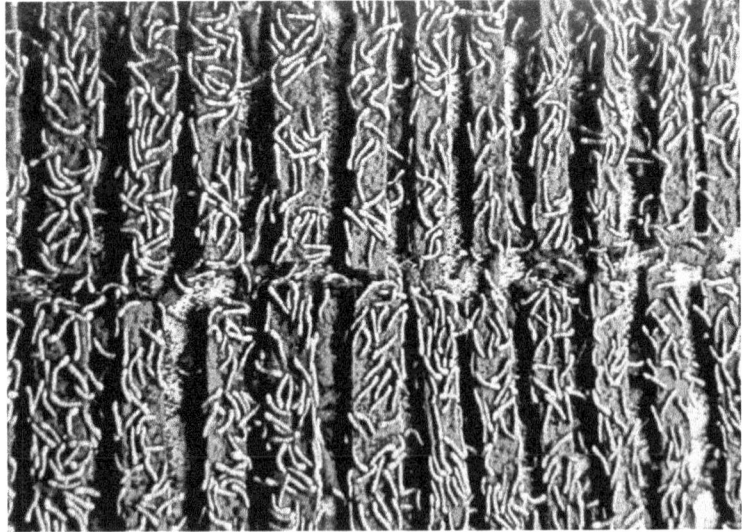

Silkworms feeding on 'meusli bar' style processed mulberry feed.

In today's scientific age, traditional ways no longer produce silk of sufficient quality and quantity and so education to teach the latest methods of care are essential. Some countries have outdated buildings and systems for transport, distribution, storage and industrial plant that require a major capital investment to improve and bring them up to standard so they can compete in the international market.

Some countries are increasing their use of machinery on the larger commercial units and there are changes in the proportion of land given over to sericulture. In India, the land area has fallen significantly, but production has increased due to the introduction of more productive mulberry varieties, improved silkworm hybrids and more efficient silkworm rearing and silk reeling. Traditionally, sericulture thrived in humid and subtropical regions between the 30° and 45° northern latitude, and this area has expanded with successful production levels up to the 60th latitude. The limit here is less the latitude than the cost of labour.

Sericulture is labour-intensive, seasonal and fits in well with rural life. Traditionally, it has involved the whole family under the control of the farmer. These days there is some recognition that women can run their own lives and businesses very efficiently, in ways that will relieve poverty and ensure the income returns to the village. Some women have difficulty in gaining clear title to land or a 'no objection letter' from their husband or landowner that would allow them to make decisions, apply for grants and sign contracts in their own right.

Many towns and cities have become manufacturing centres, offering a variety of jobs in mills and filatures, weaving plants, and garment factories. Regrettably there are still aspects of low value, poor pay, sometimes appalling conditions, whether in the countryside or city. In general it is still men who control the industry, arrange the loans, sign the contracts, control the hours worked and the pay offered. Sometimes better education for management is required to be able to function in the industry and the high-powered atmosphere of international trade and marketing.

Uses

There is no waste with sericulture and silk fabrics range from the lightest organza used to replace glass windows in some villages to heavy upholstery and carpets. Silk was also used for parachutes and tyre linings for racing cycles, elastic webs, electrical instruments, fishing lines and ropes. Silk has gone full circle. In ancient China it was used for light armour, to stop arrows penetrating the body, and make them easier to withdraw. Today the military has an increasing interest in developing special silk fibres to make bulletproof vests.

One of the most exciting developments in recent years has been to utilize abandoned mulberry orchards and generations of expertise in sericulture in ways other than making yarn. The pupa has a wide range of uses. It is rich in oil, proteins, minerals and vitamins E and K. The oil is used in soaps, cosmetics and creams, and the pupa is eaten in Asian countries as a snack, freeze-dried or pan-fried. It is also being used as a scientific medium in Korea to grow a variety of spores, fungi and enzymes that are later developed into nourishing and strengthening drinks, syrups, whisky and Nuegra, a natural alternative to Viagra. The skin of the tussah pupa, known as 'chiton', has been developed as a natural health food, with wide claims to lower cholesterol, assist weight loss and improve digestion.

Sugared wild mulberries Sentab, Uzbekistan.

In medicine and surgery, hybrid silk is used to make artificial blood vessels, bandages and sutures for wounds. Mulberry roots, bark and leaves are used in herbal medicines. Mulberry fruit are rich in minerals and vitamins, and many claims are made for its anti-oxidant function. It is also valued as a laxative and to treat sore throats, depression, fever and high blood pressure. A whole range of food products and additives have been developed by drying and crushing the mulberry leaves to make herbal teas or by using the powdered leaves to make pale-green, mulberry-flavoured ice cream. The silkworm can be dried and powdered at the fourth instar to make a highly nutritious, protein-rich 'flour' that is added to bread, cakes, biscuits and pasta and is especially valued as a protein supplement.

Man working with mulberry wood in Hotan, China.

Science and the Future

Display of mulberry papier-mâché painted dolls, Samarkand.

Mulberry timber is resistant to termites and can be used for house-building, fence posts, cheap gun handles, walking sticks, toys and sports gear including cricket bats. The branches can be stripped to make paper or used for fodder for animals, fuel for stoves. Furniture and agricultural implements are made and bowls and spoons carved from the wood. The trees are often planted on embankments to stabilize soil erosion, or grown as an inter-crop, offering shade. The silkworm litter is burnt to produce bio-gas and as fuel for cooking in rural areas and to feed fish and ducks. They are later eaten or sold, and the silt from the duck ponds applied to the land as fertilizer before the ponds are flooded again to grow rice.

Spider silk

There are over 34,000 species of spiders, as well as ants and mussels that can spin a silk thread. The spinnerets on most spiders are located on their abdomen but the zebra tarantulas from Costa Rica have their spinnerets on their feet, and that helps them to climb up vertical surfaces. Medical, pharmaceutical and military research departments are hoping to harness the strength and flexibility of spider silk, as it is stronger than steel and more elastic than rubber. It is the protein in dragline silk that lets spiders drop and helps

Golden silk spider, *Nephila clavipes* found in Central, Southern and North America. It grows up to 40mm in length and there has been considerable interest recently, much of it directed toward their potential for bio-engineering high performance fibers.

the web to catch its prey. The researchers see insects as inexpensive and easy to genetically engineer. Unfortunately, spiders in captivity become stressed and resort to cannibalism and must be separated and milked individually, making them far more labour-intensive than silkworms. It takes 425 spiders to spin enough silk to create a square metre of cloth, so farming spiders has not been profitable so far.

Cape made from Golden Orb Madagascan spider silk in 2009. Eighty-two people worked for four years to collect and milk over one million spiders to make the cape.

To increase the quantity and ease of collection, scientists are experimenting on goats, cows and hamsters by inserting spider-silk genes into their cells in an attempt to create proteins similar to those of spider silk. The military have been funding a programme to develop transgenic cloned goats to produce milk that contains silk proteins and these fibres have been sold under the name 'BioSteel', but it takes 600 gallons of milk to produce a single bulletproof vest. The distinctive toughness of spider silk could be used to improve materials that protect wounds and aid healing, and to produce artificial ligaments and tendons for surgical implants. A whole range of ecological materials could emerge from the industrial production of these special aspects of spider silk.

So far, engineers have had limited success trying to spin silk on silicon micro-spinnerets. The fibres produced are too wide, with diameters ranging from 10 to 60 mm, compared with diameters of 2.5 to 4.0 mm in natural fibres. The results have been promising but are still a long way from matching naturally produced silk.

Science

In the 1950s, Nobel Laureate Linus Pauling identified the basic structure of silkworm silk. Since then, there have been impressive developments in the field of cellular therapy and tissue engineering. Genetic modification of the silkworm has led to obtaining disease-resistant lines and hybrids that inhibit viruses, along with improved absorption of the protein in the mulberry leaf and quality and length of silk fibre.

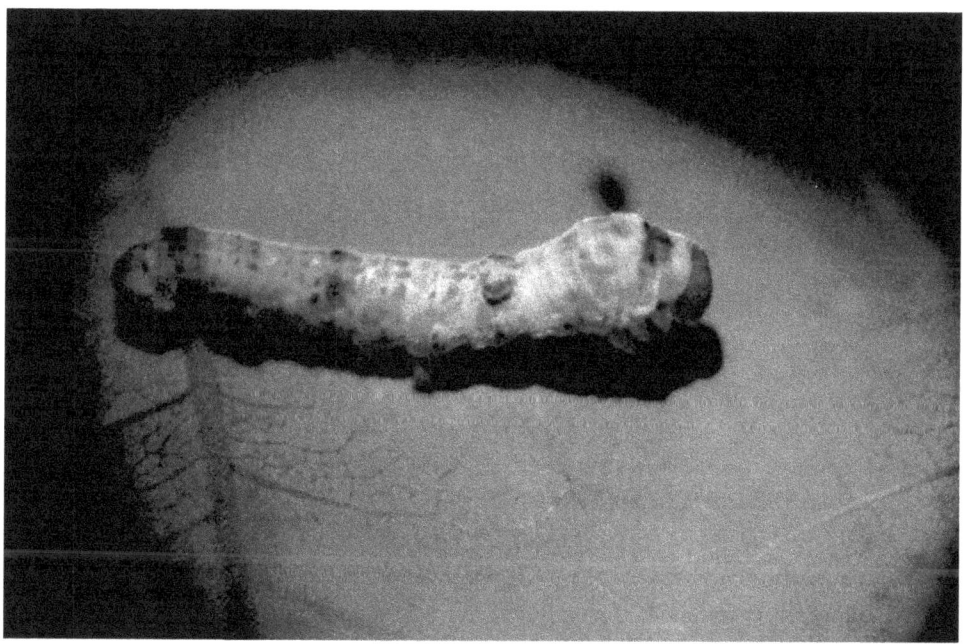

Trans-genetically modified fluorescent silkworms are being developed to track their genes to manipulate their properties.

Scientists so far have developed around 3000 genotypes of *Bombyx mori*. There has been great interest in developing transgenetically modified silkworms to spin green fluorescent silk. When ultraviolet light shines on the silk glands of infected larvae, the glands glow with an eerie green colour. Studies are continuing in many areas for practical applications, especially in the production of veterinary vaccines.

Unfortunately, sometimes there have been catastrophic outcomes to the use of 'good' chemicals. One of the valued agrochemicals that was believed to be safe and widely used in the countryside and farming communities for the control of pests, had a hidden effect. It was very effective when sprayed on crops but it was found that it took only one part in 30 million of the chemical to drift onto mulberry leaves or into rearing houses to affect the gene that triggers the next stage in the silkworm. This trigger stops the silkworm eating after the fourth stage and begin to look for somewhere to spin a cocoon. Without this trigger, the silkworm does not stop eating and implodes and dies, without spinning its cocoon. This means that it never pupates or metamorphoses into a moth, mates or lays eggs and the result is the total collapse of the whole industry.

Future

With labour costs ever increasing and countries like China able to set a low price due to their enormous scale of production, some of the most exciting developments are in alternative products for sericulture, as well as textiles. Today the production of raw silk in the European Union is very low, while the demand for high-fashion textiles is high but it is an uncertain market and silk is subject to fashion whims and trends.

Organisations such as the International Silk Association (ISA), the Black, Caspian Seas and Central Asia Silk Association (BACSA), FAO, World Bank and the Global Organic Textile Standard (GOTS) are just a few of the many groups focused on the promotion, expansion and attaining higher standards that will lead to a better quality of life for all people involved in sericulture.

In future, production of silk for fabrics will probably continue to move to developing countries in tropical and subtropical regions. There, labour costs are still relatively low and sericulture can contribute to anti-poverty programmes, to improve incomes, living standards and quality of life for rural people. It would be a mistake to expect sericulture to bring in quick returns or profits, as technical developments require extensive educational programmes and funding. With worldwide marketing, financing and supply, the demand for silk is annually increasing by 5 per cent, but there is fierce competition from synthetics, so the main drive is to diversify and utilize silk and sericulture in the most efficient way to produce quality silk and improve the lives of the greatest number of people, because there is a strong future for silk in our world today. It would be a sad day indeed if this natural, versatile and luxurious fabric was no longer available to contribute to world health and welfare and for us to experience the joy of wearing silk.

Ocean Deep, a silk chiffon blouse and jacket made from the same chiffon, but torn into strips and knitted.

CHAPTER THIRTEEN

Practical: Sewing with Silk

Silk has its own unique quality and, like a holograph, even the tiniest piece contains within it the essence that is silk — precious, luxurious and unique. Silk is a joy and a delight, and as a natural fibre adds an indefinable quality of luxury and style, but many people are just a bit scared of using silk, cutting into expensive fabric with no guarantee of success. Overcoming fear and incorporating silk will enhance your work and add great value too. It could lift it above all other and put you ahead of the game, especially if you are hoping to exhibit and sell your work.

Some of the objections people have to using silk include: it is very expensive and hard to find, it frays badly and slips, is hard to cut and sew, and, worst of all, what if one makes a mistake and wastes all that gorgeous fabric? So, start by making something small, hemming a length to make a scarf, or shawl, or incorporating silk into patchwork. These are terrific places to start and you will have a precious gift to keep or give away. Once you get the feel of the different silks, your courage will mount and in no time you will be choosing a pattern and be right into sewing with silk.

Silk has an enormous advantage with its lovely lustre and subtle texture. It dyes beautifully, ranging from the most subtle watered

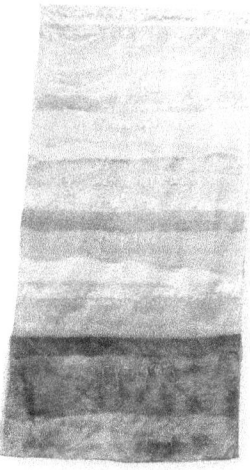 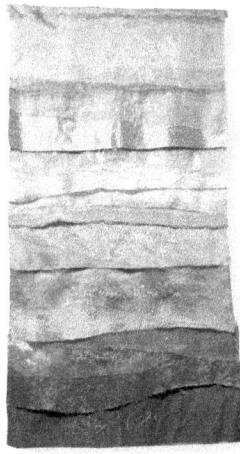 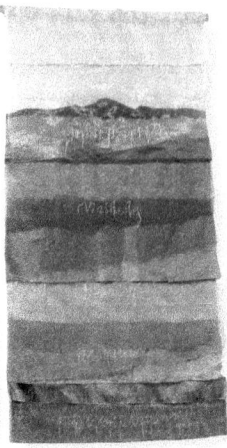

The "Auckland Series' of wall hangings from the Exhibition at the Depot Artspace Gallery, Auckland. 1: North Shore Beaches. 2: Volcanic Auckland. 3: Islands of the Gulf. All are layered silk and mixed sheer fabrics, with the names of the bays, mountains and islands around Auckland, embroidered on them.

effects to the most brilliant glowing colours. It is warm to the touch and breathes so it is comfortable to wear, summer or winter. The first trick is to get to know and recognise the different silks and understand what they can and cannot do. While there is a relatively small range of silk fabrics available in our shops, most weaves come in a variety of weights and colours, especially the dupioni silks. Paj, habutai, chiffon or organza can be very fine, while noil and burette are tough and can handle like cotton. Taffeta and shantung are crisp and very stable, while soft satins and crepes are more fluid and ideal for draping. Unfortunately, not all silks, even of the same type, are equal. Some countries have higher quality standards and the old 'you pay for quality' is still a safe guide.

Specialist shops keep a range of new silk fabrics and many designers import short lengths of unique silks and have an annual sale of remnants, a real treasure trove. There is also the internet to explore and the joy of choosing, ordering and waiting for the parcel to arrive. Nevertheless the greatest fun can be had from scouring charity shops for old silks, discarded Indian saris and Japanese kimono, crumpled old silk shirts and skirts, drapes, wedding and evening dresses. Don't discard a garment because it is stained or faded, as

Baches at the Edge of the Ocean, large silk quilt, machine stitched and hand quilted with marine life and haiku, evoking the secluded nature of many New Zealand beaches set against a vast ocean, exhibited at The Depot Artspace Gallery, Auckland.

you can usually work around those parts. Everything can be washed or overdyed to become the absolutely perfect silk for your project.

Handling different silks

Some silks should be treated with caution and perhaps not used for your first garment or quilt. Chiffon can be impossibly flimsy and some silks are so cheap, sleazy and badly woven, they will fray at the first touch. Some very expensive silks with metallic or other mixed threads, lots of added decoration, tinsel, sequins, ribbons and fringing could be a bit tricky, as can very heavy gritty, wild silks used for upholstery.

Soft silks will drape beautifully, but can be rather flimsy if woven too loosely. Test it by pulling it gently crosswise, on the bias, to see how it handles. If it springs back into shape, it might be strong enough to make pants or a skirt, flexible enough for a soft blouse or dress or at its best as small pieces in a patchwork quilt. To deal with sleazy, unstable silks or excessive fraying, consider stabilizing it by ironing a lightweight fusible knitted or woven backing onto the silk before cutting it out.

Finishes for silk. Bias cut silk satin slip, hand embroidered with buttonhole stitch scalloping around the neck. To right: heavy silk tweed with bias binding to finish the edge, blue hand-dyed fine twill weave with overlocked edge, silk satin slip with French seams and narrow hem, turquoise chiffon with overlocked seam and finest stretched zig-zag edge to make it frill, medium weight corded silk with flat fell seams.

A fusible lining is especially useful when patchworking, but test it first because some iron-on backings leave tiny glue spots that show on the surface, especially very lightweight scarf and lining habutai, China silk or paj. A lightweight nonfusible interfacing or muslin might be better. Whenever possible, allow at least a 1 cm seam allowance for patchwork and 2 cm for general sewing to give plenty of room to manoeuvre and finish the edges. That could take some adjustment if you are used to using quilters' cottons with a quarter-inch seam allowance, but the wider seam really helps to eliminate wobbly stitching or seams fraying apart.

To finish the seams you could overlock each piece, or use a spray to seal the edges, or just put it together as quickly as possible, complete the seams and finish the edges with a minimum of handling. The preferred method for most light- and medium-weight silks is to make a French seam or use a flat fell seam that gives a double row of stitching with all the fraying edges tucked neatly inside. Very fine chiffon and scarf silk look great when the raw edge is hand or machine rolled or finished with a tight zig-zag or narrow overlocking. Some medium-weight silks like shantung are just fine with a pinked edge and some heavy silks can have their edges covered with bias binding. There are lots of possibilities depending on the weight of the silk, style of the item or garment and the amount of expected wear and washing.

The grainline

The grainline is critical and ignoring it is the cause of many failures in working with silk. If it is a garment piece, it must be placed on the straight grain unless otherwise directed. To find the straight grain, whenever possible tear the silk to get a true grainline and everything else can be measured off against this. Some silk does not tear well and the edges are untidy and stretched and the fibres may even pull and run back into the fabric, and so other choices need to be made.

If it does not tear easily, then cut a short nick of about 1 cm through the selvedge and pull a thread just sufficient for it to slightly wrinkle the fabric right across and show the grainline. The thread doesn't have to be pulled out — it's just a guide — and this will give a clear cutting line. If many strips are required, then cut nicks in the selvedge at exactly the width of strip you require, then pull the threads, and this will give you multiple cutting lines. Cutting a corded or ribbed silk is also easy — just follow the thicker threads.

The exceptions to cutting selvedge to selvedge are satin and dupioni silk because they both fray badly if cut across the weft. Much better is to cut along the length of the fabric, parallel to the selvedge. This is because they are unbalanced weaves with the weft either thicker as in dupioni silk or a surface faced weave, as in satin.

Sericulture Jacket, silks and mixed fabrics, with the story of sericulture, built on felt with appliqued motifs and butterflies.

Be aware that some silks, like velvet or plush, have a nap, or an up and down, to the texture or design that must be taken account of, and a printed design, even stripes and checks, may not be printed on the true grainline. You will then have to make a decison as to whether to follow the grain or the printed patten. If it is well off grain, try first to wet and then iron the fabric and see if it will pull back into shape, otherwise put the silk aside to use as small pieces in patchwork, because larger areas will droop or twist and never lie flat.

Cutting out

If the silk is really slippery, a helpful way to cut the fabric accurately is to tape the length of silk down onto the cutting surface, and carefully draw cutting lines around each shape or use a ruler and mark out each strip for as many strips as you need. Alternatively, taping down an old sheet onto your cutting table as a cutting base will certainly help to stop the silk slipping around, especially when cutting different shapes and pattern pieces.

It is very disappointing, but most silks are very difficult to cut using a rotary blade, as the silk just disappears into the cutting mat without cutting through, so a really sharp pair of long-bladed scissors is essential. You will also need other small pairs of scissors for any fiddly bits and individual small pieces, and medium-weight silks cut very well with sharp pinking shears. Most sharp dressmakers' scissors will be just fine, but any sign of earlier poor handling, like your family using them to cut paper or — heaven forbid! — wire, will leave the blades with little nicks that will snag the silk, making it impossible to cut cleanly. Whenever possible, treat yourself to a pair of quality scissors and use them only for silk. Hang a label or tassel on them and threaten allcomers with dire consequences. Good scissors will repay you with a lifetime of good service.

Designing and sewing silk garments

With its lovely drape, silk can be very feminine and slimming. If you are not sure whether a style will suit you, drape some of the silk around yourself in front of the mirror and then plan a fun day with a friend and go window shopping, and try on lots of garments of a similar weight to the silk you want to sew. It will be a great day and just think what you will have learnt about yourself, your shape and the best style and weight of fabric to suit you and your purpose.

You will now be well ahead for choosing a pattern. Silk can be fluid and tricky to handle so choose a pattern with simple lines and avoid complicated detailing because unpicking will leave marks. A slightly looser fit will not put strain on the delicate fabric and seams, and will slide over the bulges and angular bits and will usually be more flattering. A neat waist, a generous skirt, a draped bodice will all look good. 'Ease' is the extra allowed for the body to move and feel comfortable when you sit or lift things. Patterns have this extra allowance for ease built in and you can add a little extra at the sides to make fitting easier and more accurate.

Many styles will require either a separate underlining if the silk is sheer, to give body and to control transparency, or an interfacing, either fusible or sewn in to firm up the edges and details like collars and cuffs. Many garments also need a lining sewn separately or attached in places to cover up the construction and help the fabric to sit smoothly and not bag or sag.

Although some people prefer to pre-wash and iron all their cottons, this is not always necessary for silk, unless the colours are dark and there is some apprehension that they could run. Dip the length of fabric into clear, warm water, part-dry on the line and iron while still quite damp, pulling and checking it is on true grain as you go. Be aware that washing can dull the brilliance of the colours and change the texture, so if the garment will always be drycleaned, you might prefer not to pre-wash it.

Place the pattern pieces on the fabric and pin into the seam allowance to avoid pin marks, and using long smooth strokes, cut around the pattern. Keep your finest pins and needles just for silk and use a fine machine needle between 65 and 80, or 9 to 12, and change it after every major project. It is perfectly acceptable to use a good-quality sewing thread, but if you can find a matching silk, it does make all the difference. Silk thread comes as filament silk and spun silk thread, and both glide through the fabric. The main problem using a cotton or polyester thread is that the seam may wrinkle and if you dye the item, the thread will not take up the dye in the same way and might stand out.

Bias is the exact diagonal line between the corner on both the warp and weft. It takes great care to cut bias strips and a whole bias-cut garment is really only for the experienced sewer. Extra care is needed placing the pattern, extra pinning within the seam line to stop the fabric shifting while you cut, and care in sewing as either the top or bottom fabric can twist and slip. While bias-cut edges should not fray, they can very easily stretch and distort, and if the garment is hung up, it can stretch alarmingly, so allow an extra 3 cm on the side seams. Even a super-lightweight zipper can make a bias edge stretch and wobble. Seam puckering can be caused by an incorrect or blunt needle, tension too tight, or the foot on the machine not exerting the correct pressure. Tear-away strips and tissue paper may not be worth the bother, but they might work well for you and your machine. When it comes to putting up the hem, hang the garment overnight, then put it on and get a friend to measure around the bottom with a measuring stick, and pin a straight line for the hem. It will be amazingly wobbly, even with all that care, so cut along an 'average' position between the pins to get an even curve. The wider the flare, the narrower the hem: 0.5 cm for a circular skirt and up to 3 cm for a straight skirt.

Properties

A silk lining could be perfect, but is not always practical because silk will rot through repeated contact with perspiration, condensation or strong sunlight, especially with all three. In summer, perspiration and strong sunlight will weaken a gorgeous silk blouse and an antiperspirant could leave white powdery marks. The easiest way to combat this is to rinse the blouse in warm water after each wearing, roll it in a towel and iron it while it is damp. It is so easy and your blouse will look fresh and last for years and years. Heavier garments can be put in a mesh wash bag after hand washing, and spun in the washing machine to remove the water. It is important not to drip-dry the garment or it may drop or droop; better to part-dry it as quickly as possible, out of direct sun, and iron immediately. Strong sun and condensation destroy curtains, so again, a polyester or cotton lining is preferred.

Silk is warm in winter and cool in summer, which in practice means that while others around you are putting their jackets off and on, you will probably not notice the changes in temperature at all. The only thing better than a layer of silk in the winter is two layers of silk, because they double the insulating qualities. Because silk breathes, this works in summer too, and a light silk blouse or dress can be the most comfortable to wear, even when the temperature and humidity are high. Usually, light creases will hang out when the garment is worn, but silk can build up static electricity if it is tumble-dried and that can be a bother in a lining or underslip.

Lustrous, glossy silks can absorb grease and dirt very easily, so clean hands are essential. Even if you have been gardening or doing

The Golden Road to Samarkand, silk quilt and mixed fabrics including felt and actual paper money from Uzbekistan, suggesting the road leading to Registan Square in Samarkand, and the terrain to be crossed, high mountains, sun-bleached deserts, jungles and deep lakes. Machine stitched and hand quilted and embossed.

something that roughens your hands, please do not be tempted to put handcream on just before you handle the silks. Silk will absorb the grease and the marks cannot be removed, and worse, they still remain even if you dye the silk. Much better is to keep handcream or lotion beside the sink and apply it frequently after your hands have been in water so they will always remain soft, and snagging and grease marks will be avoided.

Washing and drycleaning

Almost everything — blouses, shirts, scarves, lightweight skirts and pants, nightwear and undies — can be handwashed. Just test wash a little bit first, like an unobtrusive part of the inside pocket or hem, and if it seems fine, then go ahead. It is much better not to leave the silk to soak as it dulls the colours and occasionally some excess dye may run. A tablespoon of vinegar in the last rinse should deal with any excess dye. Most silks can also be machine-washed using a cold or warm wash and a mild detergent. The harsh detergents designed for washing machines have extra brighteners and stain removers, so avoid them, along with chlorine and other bleaches that turn the silk yellow. A liquid detergent is preferable to a powder, just in case the powder does not dissolve completely, in which case it will leave powder specks on the silk.

Usually, washing silk is not the problem. It is the combination of interlinings, facing and stiffenings that all shrink or react differently that destroy the pristine shape and style of the garment. Items with a mixed-fibre content — heavily tailored jackets, quilts, wedding or evening wear, those with a high lustre, very loose weave, a heavy, gritty texture or lots of embellishments — should be drycleaned. Also, any major stain, wine or grease is best left to a specialist drycleaner because you cannot dab at a spot to remove a stain off silk, as it usually leaves a nasty ring mark.

Manufacturers usually place a 'Dryclean only' label on their silks, as much for their own protection against people who mishandle their garments by washing them in really hot water or tossing them in the washing machine with work clothes. Most of us will follow the drycleaning advice for the first few times, but then try a gentle handwash and find it works just fine. After washing a heavy garment it can look really dreadful so it should be taken to the drycleaner for the final pressing, at half the price and twice the value because it is professional pressing that make the garment look like new again.

It is very difficult sometimes to iron out wrinkles in silk, so the secret is to always iron silk while it is still quite damp, then hang it up to air before putting it away. If the silk does get too dry, there are a number of options. You can either rinse it again, quickly in clear water without soap, and this time iron it well before it dries, or you could wear it as it is, if it will be covered with a jersey or coat. Another option is to loosely wrap it up and put it in a plastic bag and leave it overnight in the freezer to chill, and then iron it in the morning. A label might be worthwhile so you can identify it some months later after you have long since forgotten where you put that nice blouse.

When ironing, choose the silk setting and test the temperature. A steam iron is not necessary because the item should be ironed

Homage to Escher, Sea Birds Jacket, built on felt, silk and beads, part of the exhibition at The Depot Artspace Gallery, Auckland.

damp. Old steam irons sometimes spit and leave brown stains, but a pressing cloth offers some protection and is necessary for heavier silks. Some old silks water spot even in the rain and so cannot be sprayed to damp them down, so silk needs to be completely dipped in water, and partly dried and then ironed. Crepe is a bit unusual as it can crinkle up and appear to shrink before your very eyes. This is the nature of crepe, and it will iron back to its correct size. High-lustre satins and fancy weaves need to be ironed on the back rather than the front, but take care with the seam lines. Slip a piece of light card under the seam allowance and then the marks will not show through when it is ironed. If you press the seams from the right side the outline might show so use a pressing cloth or parchment paper.

Antique fabrics are a special case, and if the item is very valuable, it is wise to contact a museum or seek the advice of a textile conservator. If a quilt or hanging needs freshening up, the conservators very gently vacuum it, on the lowest setting and with a piece of clean muslin over the vacuum funnel so as not to draw the fabric up into the tube. It is worth doing because silk can be destroyed by dust and grit.

In principle, antique fabrics cannot be washed and hung up and must be supported at all times. To wash an antique item, the conservators use a very large shallow tray, large enough to take the whole garment laid out flat. The garment is placed on a fine mesh and warm water is added to the tray and the fabric or garment is allowed to soak for a specific length of time. The water is drained off and fresh water of the same temperature is added. The process is repeated, but requires extreme care. Finally the textile is lifted, still on the mesh frame, and patted dry, but not moved or hung, and allowed to dry flat away from direct heat and light but in a warm atmosphere.

Use a padded hanger for your silk items or refold them each time in a different way for storage so the fabric is stressed in a different place. Layer it with acid-free tissue paper and, if appropriate, wrap it around a wide cardboard tube. Rolling it up loosely is infinitely better than folding it into a sharp fold. A box that can be sealed is much better than plastic bags that might sweat if the humidity is high.

Patchworking and quilting with silk

As with all sewing, there are two distinct threads to the story. Some items, incorporating patchworking and quilting, are made within the home as a necessity or for pleasure, and there are quilts made for exhibition, or in specialist ateliers on commission, to be bought by the wealthy. They could be whole cloth quilts that relied on exquisite and complex stitching patterns for their effect and to keep the various layers in place, or they could be pieced or appliquéd quilts made up of scraps, special fabrics or ribbons. Quilts vary in size from vast full bedcovers to knee and foot coverlets, children's quilts, and miniature dollshouse quilts.

In the medieval period, the quilted vest was not a fashion item but a necessity to keep the person warm and to stop the armour that a man may be wearing from chaffing the skin. It proved to be such a comfortable garment that quilting was used in various everyday and fashion items — doublets, trunk hose, bombasted sleeves, waistcoats, petticoats and under-coats. During times of poverty, quilts could become a necessity, or maybe a gift, a treasure made for a hope chest, a child, a beloved relative or friend. Every tiny scrap left over or cut up from discarded garments would go into a kaleidoscopic design. Women have always gathered to chat and stitch, make quilts, exhibit them, enter them in competitions, use

Ngataringa Bay miniature quilt picture, the view from the studio, looking over the grass, sand and mangroves, across the deep blue harbour to the Waitakere Range and the sky.

them to raise money, and some quilters, both men and women, have earned their living quilting.

In general, most silk fabrics can be used in patchwork and some extraordinary quilts and garments have been made, including crazy patch quilts and wearable art. There is no reason why silk cannot be combined with cotton and other fabrics, as long as a few points are taken into account. For the best results, combine fabrics of a similar weight, neither heavier nor lighter than the rest of the fabrics, so a medium-weight dupioni silk, habutai, shantung, pongee, satins and twills are fine. Chiffon, organza, fine paj or scarf-weight habutai are best avoided unless they are backed, or the rest of the fabrics are also very fine. These silks are perfect for embellishment, ruching, gathering, rosettes, and so on. Likewise, very heavy upholstery fabric or silk suiting is best combined with heavier calico, blanket or furnishing fabrics. Crepe and knitted silk fabrics are rather different because their flexibility make it harder to combine them with other materials, but they could be wonderful as a binding around the edge where flexibility would be an advantage.

In the early days, wax was sometimes used to mark a cutting line and seal the edges but that is not recommended, as it will permanently mark the silk. With small motifs, a better way could be to use an

Silk Road Jacket, silk, quilted featuring the vast changing landscape travelling across China, Uzbekistan to the West, Shore Stitchers' Exhibition, Auckland.

iron-on lightweight fabric to stabilize the patch. If the quilt is to be hung, do sew Velco or a similar product right across the top so the whole width will be supported and add a label with your name and the history of this quilt.

The choice of batting for quilting or jackets is also yours. Silk batting can be very expensive and may not be warranted so experiment with different weights of polyester, dacron, cotton and wool, and choose the one that feels best for your project. A good choice to make quilted silk jackets look and feel luscious and cosy, is to buy the thick polyester batting used in duvets and split it back to the exact thickness for a particular garment. Everyone has their own special techniques for quilting — using a frame, running or stab stitches or having it machine quilted. A favourite with silk is to make quilts and jackets reversible and quilt through the batting but not through to the other side. It is not too dense and does not feel like double the work and it is an easy, fun way of stitching without the anxiety of having to match it on both sides. We all have our little ways. Quilting is great fun and it could be your entrée into the world of silk.

Bibliography

2000 Years of Silk Weaving, Los Angeles Museum of Art, E Weyhe NY 1944

Aksit, ilhan, *The Mystery of the Ottoman Harem*, Aksit publishing 2010
Alexander, Alma, *The Secrets of Jin-Shei*, Harper Collins, 2004
Arizzoli-Clementel, Pierre, *The Textile Museum*, Lyon, 1990
Aruga, Hisao, *Principles of Sericulture*, Translated from the Japanese, New Age International (P) Publishers, New Delhi, 2001
Ashelford, Jane, *The Art of Dress, Clothes and Society 1500-1914*, National Trust Lond. 1996
Askari, Nasreen & Liz Arthur, *Uncut Cloth*, Merrell Holberton London, 1999

Balfour-Paul, Jenny *Indigo*, British Museum Press, 1999
Bailey, Adrian, *Passion for Fashion, Three Centuries of Changing Styles*, 1988
Baker, Patricia, *Islamic textiles*, BM Press 1995,
Croom Helm, London, 1977
Banerjee, Mukulika and Daniel Miller, *The Sari*, Berg 2003
Barbar, Elizabeth Wayland, *The Mummies of Urunchi*, Macmillan, 1999
Barham, Henry, *An Essay Upon the Silkworm*, 1719
Baricco, Alessandro, *Silk*, Panther1997
Battersby, Martin, *Art Deco Fashion*, Academy editions
Berg, Maxine, *The Age of Manufacturers, 1700-1820*, Fontana 1985.
Bergreen, Laurence, *Marco Polo From Venice to Xanadu*, Quercus, London 2008
Bertin-Guest, Josiane, *Chinese Embroidery*, Traditional Techniques, B T Batsford, 2003
Black, David, ed *World Rugs and Carpets*, Country Life.
Black, J Anderson, Madge Garland and Frances Kennett, *A History of Fashion* Orbis 1990
Blunden, Caroline & Mark Elvin, *Cultural Atlas of China*, Phaidon, 1983
Bonavia, Judy, Sarah Jessup, & Edward Juanteguy, *The Silk Road from Xi'an to Kashgar*, Passport Books, NTC Publishing Group, Lincolnswood, Ill. USA1993
Boraigh, Dr., G. ed, *Lectures on Sericulture*. SBS Publishers Distributors, Bangalore, 1994
Boucher, Francois, *A History of Costume in the West*, T&H 2004
Boulnois, Luce, *Silk Road: Monks, Warriors & Merchants*, Odyessy 2003
Breward, Christopher, Edwina Ehrman, Caroline Evans, *The London Look, Fashion from the Street to Catwalk*, Yale University press, Museum of London, 2004
Brockett, L P *Silk Industry in America* Reprint Prepared for the Centennial Exposition 1876, Uni of Michigan University Library
Broudy, Eric, *The Book of Looms*, Studio Vista, London, 1979
Browne, Clare, *Silk Designs of the Eighteenth Century*, Victoria and Albert Museum, London, Thames & Hudson, 1996
Brown, Gail, *Sensational Silks*, 1993
Bull, Anna, and Paul Corner, *From Peasant to Entrepreneur, the Survival of the Family in Italy*, Berg, Oxford/Providence 1993
Buss, Chiara, ed *Seta, il Novecento a Como*, Fondazione Antonio Ratti, Silvana Edit, 2001

Cansdale, C H C, *Cocoon Silk, A Manual for those employed in the Silk Industry and for Textile Students*, Sir Isaac Pitman & Sons, Ltd, London, 1937
Chan, Charis, *The Odyssey Illustrated Guide to China*, Odyssey, 1994
Chinese Sites:, *Dunhuang*, 2006
Noble *Tombs of Mawangdui, Art & Life of the Changsha Kingdom, 3rd to 1st c BCE* Hunan Provincial Museum, 2008
Chung, Young Y, *The Art of Oriental Embroidery, History, Aesthetics and Techniques*, Bell & Hyman 1980
Chung, Young Yang, *Silken Threads, A History of Embroidery in China, Korea, Japan and Vietnam*, Abrams, NY 2005
London Boston & Henley, 1982
Claxton, William, *Silk & the Silk Workers, Rambles among our industries* Blackie & Son Ltd 1913,
Cogukoba, Hacpuca et al, *National Uzbek Clothes (XIX-XX centuries)* 2003

Collins, Louanne, *Silk Museums in Macclesfield,*1989
Collins, Louanne & Moira Stevenson, *Silk Sarsenets, Satins, Steels & Stripes, 150 Years of Maccelsfield Textile Designs,* c20026
Coleman, Teresa, *Dragons and Silk, From the Forbidden City, The Genius of China, A Close-up Guide,* Odyssey Publications, HK 1999
Constantine, Mildred & Laurel Reuter, *Whole Cloth,* The Monacelli Press, 1997
Contini, Mila, *Fashion from ancient Egypt to the present Day,* Paul Hamlin 1965
Conway, Susan *Thai Textiles,* BM Press, 1992
Cook, J Gordon, *Handbook of Textile Fibres,* Merrow Publishing 1960
Cossalter, Elisabeth, & Jean-Marc Vlache, *Au fil de la Soie,* Didier Richard, 1996
Cotterell, Arthur, *China: A Concise Cultural History,* Guild Publishing, London 1988
Crotch, W J B, *The Silkmoth Rearer's Handbook,* The Amateur Entomologist's Society 1965
Cunnington, Phillis, & Catherine Lucas, *Costume for Births Marriages and Deaths,* Adam & Charles Black, London, 1978

Dalby, Liza, *Geisha,* University of California Press, 1983
Dalby, Liza, *Kimono,* Vintage Bks, London 2001
Dalby, Lisa, *The Tale of Murasaki,* Chatto & Windus, London 2000
Dandin, S B & Jayant Jayaswai, K Giridhar, *Handbook of Silk Technologies,* Central Silk Board, Bangalore, 2001
Dean, Jenny, *Wild Colour, How to grow, prepare and use natural plant dyes,* Michael Beazley, 1999
Debin Ma *The Modern Silk Road: The Global Raw-Silk Market, 1850-1930*
De Koning-Stapel, Hanne Vibeke, *Silk Quilts, From the Silk Road to the Quilter's Studio,* The Quilter's Digest Press, 2000
Downer, Lesley, *Geisha, The Secret History of a Vanishing World,* Headline 2000
Drege, Jean-Pierre and Emil M Buhrer, *The Silk Road Saga,* Facts on File, N Y, Oxford, 1989

Ehrman, Edwina, *The Wedding Dress, 300 Years of Bridal Fashion,* Te Papa Press, 2011

Fagan, Brian, *New Treasures of the Past,* Guild Publishing 1988
Fairbanks, John K and Edwin O Reischauer, *China Tradition and Transformation,* George Allen and Unwin, London, Boston, 1979.
FAO Manuals on Sericulture, Mulberry Cultivation (Manual 1, 1995),
Silkworm Rearing (Manual 2, 1995) ,
Silkworm Reeling (Manual 3, 1996),
Non-mulberry silks Manual 4, 1987), Central Silk Board, Bangalore, India
Fashion, Kyoto Costume Institute, *A Fashion History of the 20th Century,* Taschen, 2012
Fashion, 100 Years of Fashion, Twentieth Century in Pictures, Ammonite Press, 2009
Fau, Alexandra, *Histoire des Tissus en France,* Editions Ouest-France 2006
Favier, Jean, *Gold & Spices, The Rise of Commerce in the Middle Ages,* Holmes & Meier, NY, London 1998
Federico, Giovanni, *An Economic History of the Silk Industry 1830-1930,* CUP 1997
Fei, Hsiao-Tung, *Peasant Life in China,* Routeldge & Kegan Paul, London, 1980
Feltwell, Dr John *The Story of Silk,* Alan Sutton, 1990
Fitz Gerald, Pamela, *Warm Heritage Old Patchwork Quilts and Coverlets in New Zealand and the Women who made them,* David Bateman 2003,
Flanagan, J F *Spitalfields Silks of the 18th & 19th centuries,* F Lewis, Leigh-on-Sea, 1954.
Fletcher, Joan, *Silk in New Zealand,* NZSW&Woolcrafts Soc Inc
Footprints of Foreign Explorers on the Silk Road, China Intercontinental Press,2005
Franck, Irene M & David M Brownstone, *The Silk Road, A History,* Facts on File, NY, 1986

Gaddum, H T, *Silk,* H T Gaddum & Co 1979
Ganga, G & J Sulochana Chetty, *An Introduction to Sericulture,* Oxford & IBH Publishing Co Pvt New Delhi,
Gardiner, Brian O C, A *Silkmoth Reader's Handbook,* The Amateur Entomologist, 1982
Garfield, Simon, *Mauve,* Faber & Faber, 2000
Gelber, Harry, *The Dragon and the Foreign Devils, China and the World, 1100BC to the Present,* Bloomsbury 2007
George, M Dorothy, *London Life in the Eighteenth Century,* Penguin Books1963

Gillow, John & Nicholas Barnard, *Traditional Indian Textiles,* Thames & Hudson, 1992
Gillow, John & Bryan Sentence, *World Textiles, A Visual Guide to Traditional Techniques,* T&H London1999
Ginsburg, Madeleine, *The Illustrated History of Textiles,* Studio editions 1991
Gleeson-White, Jane, *Double Entry, How the merchants of Venice shaped the modern world, and how their invention could make or break the planet,* Allen & Unwin, 2011
Goodden, Robert, *The All Colour Book of Butterflies,* Ocotopus
Goodwin, Jill, *A Dyers Manual,* Pelham Books London 1982 SC 746.6
Gordon, Beverly, *Shaker Textile Arts,* University of New England Press, 1983
Gordon, Maggi McCormick, *The Quilter's Resource Book, the definitive book on quiltmaking traditions from around the world,* Chrysalis, London 2004
Gostelow, Mary, *Embroidery, Traditional designs, techniques and patterns from all over the World,* Cavendish, 1982
Gostelow, Mary, *Art of Embroidery, Great Needlework Collections of Britain and the United States,* Dutton, NY 1979
Gostelow, Mary, *The Complete International Book of Embroidery,* Simon & Schuster, 1977
Groves, Sylvia, *The History of Needlework Tools and Accessories,* David & Charles, 1973
Gwynn, Robin D, *The History and Contribution of the Huguenots in Britain,* Huguenot Heritage, Routledge & Kegan Paul, London 1985

Hao, Qian, & Chen Heyi & Ru Suichu, *Out of China's Earth, Archaeological Discoveries in the People's Republic of China,* Frederick Muller Limited London and China Pictorial Beijing
Harris, Jennifer *5000 Years of Textiles* BM Press, 2006
Heden, Sven, *The Silk Road,* George Routledge & Sons, London, 1938
Hibbert, Christopher, *The English, A Social History 1066-1945* Guild Publishing, 1987
Higgins, Clare, *The Spitalfields Silk Industry in the mid 19th century,* MA Thesis, May 1989
Hiney, Mary Jo, *Simply Silk,* Krause Publications 2007
Hopkirk, Peter, *The Great Game, On Secret Service in High Asia.* Oxford University Press, 1990
Hopkirk, Peter, *Foreign Devils on the Silk Road,* Oxford University Press, 1980
Howell, Georgina, *In Vogue, Six Decades of Fashion,* Allan Lane, 1976

Illustrated Ladies Dress of the Qing Dynasty, Dutotime, HK China,
Inalrik, Halil with Donald Qualaert, *An Economic and Social History of the Ottoman Empire, 1300-1914,* 1994

Jacques, Anne, *The Wardle Story, A Victorian Enterprise,* Churnet Valley Books, 1996
Jardine, Lisa, *Worldly Goods, A New History of the Renaissance,* Macmillan, 1996
Jardine, Lisa, *Ingenious Pursuits, Building the Scientific Revolution,* Abacus 1999
Johnstone, Pauline, *Three Hundred Years of Embroidery, 1600-1900,* Treasures from the Collection of the Embroiderer's Guild of Great Britain, Wakefield Press, 1987

Keay, John, *The Honourable Company, A History of the East India Company,* Harper Collins, 1993
Kerridge, Eric, *Textile Manufacturers in Early Modern England,* M U Press, 1985
King Brenda, *Dye Print & Stitch, Textiles by Thomas & Elizabeth Wardle,* England 2009
King, Brenda, *Silk and Empire,* Manchester University Press, 2005,
Kolander, Cheryl, *A Silkworkers Notebook,* Interweave Press, 1985
Kosode in Edo-Period Japan, When Art Became Fashion, Los Angeles County Museum of Art, 1992
Krefeld, City of Velvet & Silk, 1992
Kyoto Costume Museum from 18th to 20th century, Icons, Taschen, 2004

La Belle Epoque, Fifteen euphoric years of European History, 1900-1914, William Morrow & Co Inc NY 1978
Lattimore, Owen & Eleanor, *Silks, Spices and Empire, seen through the eyes of its discoverers,* The Great Explorers series, Tandem Books, 1973
La Seta in Europe, Secc XIII-XX 1993, incl articles by Donald King V&A NB.94.
Le Coq, Albert von, *Buried Treasures of Chinese Turkestan,* Allen & Unwin 1928
Lee, Chong-Sik, *Korea, the Land of the Morning Calm,* Doubleday, 1988
Legends in the Weaving, Thailand, 2001

Le Ver de soie, BT Nature
Liming, Wei, *The Land of Silk,* Foreign Languages Press, Beijing, 2002
Liu, Xinru, *Silk & Religion, An Exploration of the Material Life and the Thought of People. 600-1200*, OUP Dehli, 1996
Liu, Xinru, *The Silk Road, in World History* OUP 2010.

Maxwell, Robyn, *Textiles from South East Asia, Tradition, Trade and Transformation,*
Maxwell, Robyn, *Sari to Sarong, Five Hundred Years of Indian and Indonesian Textile Exchange,* National Gallery of Australia, 2003
Mei, Hua, *Chinese Clothing, Costume, Adornment and Culture,* Cultural China Series, China Intercontinental Press, 2008
Menz, Christopher, *Morris & Co,* Art Gallery of South Australia, Adelaide, 2002
Merson, John, *Roads to Xanadu, East and West in the Making of the Modern World,* BBC, 1989
Meyer, Karl & Sharleen Brysac, *Tournament of Shaddows, The Great Game and the Race for Empire in Asia,* Abacus, 1999
Mohanty, P K *Tropical Tasar Culture in India,* Daya Publishing House, Dehli 1998
Mola, Luca, *The Silk Industry of Renaissance Venice,* Johns Hopkins,
Money, D C *China, The Land and the People,* Revised Ed., Evans Brothers, London, 1990
Munsterberg, Hugo, *The Japanese Kimono, Images of Asia,* OUP HK 1996
Muqi, Che, *The Silk Road, past & present,* Foreign language Press 1989
Murray, Stuart, *Shaker Heritage Guidebook,* 1994
Macartney, Lady, *An English Lady in Chinese Turkestan*, Oxford University Press, Hong Kong, Oxford, 1985

New Archaeological Finds in China, Discoveries during the Cultural Revolution, Foreign Language Press, Peking, 1973
Newby, Eric, *The World Atlas of Exploration,* Macmillan

O'Brien, Sandra, *Great American Quilts, 1990,* Oxmoor House, Birmingahm AL
O'Hara Callan, Georgina, *The Thames & Hudson World of Art Dictionary of Fashion & Designers,* 2007,

Pafford, Elizabeth and John, *Employer and Employed,* Ford Ayrton & Co Ltd, Silk Spinners, 1870-1970, Passold Research Fund, Ltd, 1974
Paine, Sheila, *Embroidered textiles, Traditional Patterns from Five Continents,* Rizzoli, 1990
Parker, Julie *All about silk, A fabric Dictionary and Swatchbook,* Rain City Publishing, 1991
Parker, Rozsika, *The Subversive Stitch, Embroidery and the making of the Feminine,* The Women's Press Ltd, 1984.
Parry, J H *Trade and Dominions, European Overseas Empires in the 18th Century,* Cardinal 1974
Peterson, Barbara Bennett, *Notable Women of China, Shang Dynasty to Early 20th Century* Sharpe London 2002
Ponting, K G, *A Dictionary of Dyes and Dyeing,* Mills & Boon, London 1980
Potter & Corbman, *Fiber to Fabric,* Gregg Publ. 1957

Qingxin, Li, *Maritime Silk Road,* transl William W Wang, China Intercontinental Press, 2006
Quilters Guild Heritage Search, UK Quilt Treasures, Kangaroo Press, 1995

Reeve, John, *Living Arts of Japan,* BM 1990
Reischauer, Haru Matsukata, *Samurai and silk,* Charles E Tuttle, Tokyo 1986
Ribeiro, Aileen, *Dress and Morality,* B T Batsford, London, 1986
Ribeiro, Aileen & Valerie Cumming, *The Visual History of Costume,* Batsford, 1989
Rice, David Talbot, *Islamic Art, World of Art Library* T&H BCA 1975
Roberts, Claire, & Huh Dong-hwa, eds, *Rapt* in Colour, Korean Textiles and Costumes of the Choson dynasty, Powerhouse Museum, Sydney, Australia and the Museum of Korean Embroidery, Seoul, Korea. 1998
Roberts, Claire, *Evolution & Revolution, Chinese Dress 1700s -1990s,* Powerhouse 2002
Rutherford, Judith & Jackie Menzies, *Celestial Silks, Chinese Religious & Court Textiles,* Art Gallery of NSW 2004

Sancar, Asli, *Ottoman Women, Myth and Reality,* Tughra Books, 2009
Schoeser, Mary, *World Textiles, A Concise History,* T&H World of Art,
Schoeser, Mary, *Silk,* Yale University Press, 2007
Scott, Philippa *The Book of Silk,* Thames & Hudson, London 1993
Seagrave Stirling, Dragon Lady, *The Life and Legend of the Last Empress of China* MacMillan London, 1992
Sericulture Manuals, FAO   1: Mulberry Cultivation, 1995
                             2: Silkworm Rearing, 1995
                             3: Silk Reeling, 1996
Sharples, Jennifer, *Thai Silk,* 1994
Sherman, Jean, 'Spinning Silk Threads for Embroidery' in *Spin Off,* Summer 1994
Shrine, C P *Chinese Central Asia, An Account of Travels in Northern Kashmir and Chinese Turkestan,* OUP 1986
Silber, Julie, *Amish Quilts of Lancaster County*
The Silk Book, Silk & Rayon Uses Association, Incorporated, London 1951
Silk Manufacture, A Treatise on the Origin Progressive Improvement and Present State of the Silk Manufacture, Longman's, London,
Silk & Stone, The Art of Asia, Hali, 1996
So, Alvin Y *South China Silk Districts,* State University of New York, 1986
Sodikova, Naphisa & Hacpuca Cagbikoba, *National Uzbek Clothes of Bukhara and Samarkand XIX-XX BB*, Taskent, 2006
Sonwalkar, T N, *Hand Book of Silk Technology,* New Age International New Delhi, 2001
Spence, Jonathan, *The Search for Modern China,* Norton & Co NY 1990
Spring, Chris & Julie Hudson, *Silk in Africa,* Fabric Folios, BM Press, 2002
Steele, Valerie, *Paris Fashion, A Cultural History,* OUP 1988
Steele, Valerie, *The Corset, A Cultural History,* Yale University Press
Steele, Valerie, & John S Major China Chic, *East Meets West,* Yale University Press, New Haven & London, 1999
Stein, Mary Frost 'To Utilize Every Idle Hand: Silk Culture in the United States', in *Spin-off* Summer 1994
Swan, Susan Burrows, *Plain and Fancy, American Women and their Needlework 1700-1850,* Holt Rheinhart & Winston NY 1977
Synge, Lanto, *The Royal School of Needlework. Book of Needlework and Embroidery,* Collins, 1986

Textile Museum of Lyons,
Thompson, Paul, *The Works of William Morris,* Heineman London 1967
Tie-dyeing & Batik, Octopus Books 1974
Tsukiyama, Gail, *Women of the Silk,* St Martins Press, NY 1991
Tsukiyama, Gail, *The Language of Threads,*

Vainker, Shelagh, *Chinese Silk, A Cultural History,* BM Press, 2004
Vollmer, Keall, Nagai-Berthrong, *Silk Roads China Ships,* ROM, Toronto, 1983
Vollmer, John, *Silks for Thrones and Altars, Chinese Costumes and Textiles, From Liao through the Qing Dynasty,* publ. Myrna Myers
Von Le Coq, Albert, *Buried Treasures of Chinese Turkestan,* Oxford University Press, Hong Kong, Oxford, New York, 1985

Walker, Annabel, *Aurel Stein, Pioneer of the Silk Road,* John Murray,
Waller, Maureen, *1700 Scenes from London Life,* Scepter 2000
Walvin, James, *The Quakers, Money & Morals,* John Murray, London 1997
Warner, Sir Frank, *The Silk Industry in the UK* (1932)
Warner, Marina, *Indigo,* Chatto & Windus, London, 1992
Warner, Pamela, *Embroidery, A History.* Batsford, (London, 1991),
Warren, William, Jim Thompson, *The Legendary American in Thailand,* Jim Thompson Thai silk Company, Bangkok, 1983
Waters, Charlotte, *An Economic History of England,* OUP London, 1947
Watson, William, *The Genius of China, An Exhibition of archaeological finds of the People's republic of China,* held at the Royal Academy London Sept 1973

Watt, James, CY, & Anne Wardwell, *When Silk was Gold, Central Asian and Chinese Textiles,* Abrams US
When Art Became Fashion, Kosode in Edo-Period Japan, Los Angeles County Museum of Art, 1992
White, Palmer *The Master Touch of Lesage, Fashion Embroidery Paris,* Chene 1988
Whitfield, Susan, *Aurel Stein on the Silk Road,* BM Press 2004
Whitfeild, Susan, *Life Along the Silk Road,* John Murray, London 2000
Wiesner, Merry E, Guilds, Male Bonding and Women';s Work in Early Modern Germany, in *Gender and History Vol 1 No 2 Summer 1989*
Wilson, Elizabeth & Lou Taylor, *Through the Looking Glass,* BBC, 1989
Wilson, Verity, *Chinese Dress,* V&A Far Eastern Series, 2001
Wood, Frances, *The Silk Road, Two Thousand Years in the Heart of Asia,* BL, 2002
Wrigglesworth, Linda & Gary Dickinson, *Imperial Wardrobe,* Ten Speed Press Berkley 2000
Wright, Grace, *Sericulture, The Proper Employment of Women in 19thc China,* 2005

Xun, Zhou & Gao Cunming, eds *5000 Years of Chinese Costumes,* China Books & periodicals, 1988

Yang, Shaorong, *Traditional Chinese Clothing, Costumes, Adornments and Culture, Arts of Asia,* Long River Press, SF, 2004
Yang, Sunny, *Hanbok, The Art of Korean Clothing,* HollyM 1997
Yarwood, Doreen *European Costume, 4000 years of fashion,* Batsford 1975
Yiping, Zhang, *The Story of the Silk Road,* Transl. Jia Zongyi, China International Press, 2005
Yung, Peter, Xinjiang, *The Silk Road: Islam's overland route to China,* OUP1986

Zhijuan, Liu, *The Story of Silk,* Foreign Language Press, 2nd ed 2007

Index

A
Abolitionists 143, 149, 150
Abr-Ikat 135-8
Africa 197-9
Agriculture 43,77,83,102,127-8,143-8,202, 219-22, 226, 234
Albania 129-30
Alexander the Great 124,135
Alhambra 190
Alternative products 59-61, 222, 224-6
Alum 68,177
American Revolution 145-6
Andalucia 190
Andra Pradesh 67, 76-80
Angkor Wat 103
Aniline dyes 177
Anaphe infracta, A moloneyi, 199
Animals 52, 58, 66-7,93, 108, 130, 199, 206, 213
Antheraea pernyi, A. mylitta, A.polyphemus, A.proyeli A. ricini, A. yamamai 21-22,77, 113, 157, 202
Aao ba ba, ao dai, ao tu than 98-101
Appliqué 211, 242, 249
Apprentice 69, 120, 172, 174
Arabs, states 122, 189
Archaeological sites, 45, 83, 99, 209
Arkwright 163
Armenia 120-1, 130-1
Armour 29, 228, 232, 249
Artificial food 9, 226
Artificial silk 11, 39, 122, 159, 169, 174,183
Arts & Crafts Movement 170
Asku period 26
Aspinwall, Dr Nathan 143
Assam 21, 63, 69, 77
Astana 206
Aticas luna 113
Attacus atlas 22
Auction 12, 79-80, 148
Awase 35
Azerbaijan 131-3

B
Babur, Mohammed 64
Backstrap loom 49, 67, 69, 99, 108-9, 114, 205
Baji 44, 46, 54
Balkans 117-127
Ballets Russes 180,185
Bamboo 26, 89, 114, 204, 213
Bandha 67
Bangalore 78
Ban Krua 89,90
Banknotes 207
Banks, Charles S 106
Banpo 203
Barbier, Georges 180
Batik 75, 110, 114, 131
Batting 251
BCSCA 130, 234
Beads 52,72-4, 99, 186
Benares 65
Bengal 62, 71, 170
Bias 177, 187, 239, 240-4
Bicycle spinning wheel 196
Bihar 77
Bizarre silks 118,
Black and Caspian Seas and Central Asian (BCSCA) 234
Bleaches 17, 247
Bo 52
Boiling off 16, 82, 101
Bodo 63
Bolivia194
Bollywood 73
Bolts of silk 34, 48, 209
Bombazine 174
Bombyx mandarina Moore 202
Bombyx mori 9, 18, 20, 50, 63, 75-81, 112, 118, 189-90, 198, 202, 213, 226, 234
Bombyx mori linneus 84,94
Bone rank 47
Books of silk 17
Borocera madagascariensi, 198
Bound seams 240
Bounties 142
Bragança 191-2
Brahmin 68,77
Braintree 163-7, 178
Bratac 194
Brazil 192-3
Bribery 38
Bride, 26, 71, 92, 113-4, 138, 178, 217-19
Brin 12
Brocade 30,62,73-4,85, 104-8 126, 132,150, 189, 204-5, 211
Brocatelle 165
Broderie anglaise 66
Bronze 83, 204, 211
Buddhism 48, 52-3, 63, 88, 92-3, 99, 110, 114-15, 211, 219
Burma 63, 84-5, 88,103,111-12
Bursa 118-9, 121-2
Buttons 168
Byzantine Empire 117

C
Calendering 18, 177
California 157
Calligraphy 57, 139, 201
Cambodia 64, 83-5, 103-6
Camels 208
Canada 158-9
Candling 14,95
Can Shu, 'Book on Sericulture' 202
Canton and Pearl River Delta 217-19
Canut 181
Capullos de Encino 195
Caravanserai 125, 131-2
Carding 18-19, 77
Carolina 142-3
Carpet 80,116, 122, 126, 131-2, 206, 228
Ceremonial robes 46, 52, 104, 197
Chacim 191-2
Chakla 72,
Chanel, Coco 186, 188
Chastity 58, 92
Chemicals 14, 32, 40, 69, 74, 80, 96-7,126, 183, 234
Cheney Brothers, 146, 152-5
Cheongsam 100, 106, 110, 216-18
Chiang Mai 83, 88
Chiang Shinawatra 88
Chiffon 70-5, 225, 236-9, 240, 245
Chifu or dragon robe 213
Children 26, 47, 54-7, 66, 76, 92, 96, 108, 136, 142, 149-153, 155-6, 161, 173-4,
Chima 44, 54, 58
China 20-25, 43, 46-8, 51,54, 59-61, 66, 76, 82-5, 99-106, 117-8, 122-4, 130,139,141, 147-9, 155-9, 169,177-8, 183, 188-9, 194, 198, 200-21, 251

258 THE WORLD OF SILK

Chinai 66
Chirimen 29
Chiton 228
Chogori 54, 58
Choli 73
Chosen Period 45, 52-3, 59
Christianity 66, 68, 124-5,197-8
Chrypy 132
Clark, Helen 221
Climate 23, 26, 49, 64, 73, 76, 91, 94, 102, 109, 112-3, 127, 130, 133, 193-4, 217, 227
Clothing 28, 45, 48, 52,54-8,86, 100, 108, 112, 131, 187, 213-6
Cocaine 194
Cobden Free Trade Treaty 164
Cochineal dye 130-1
Cocoons 9-16, 76-80-3, 94-5, 101,106-8, 118,122-4, 126-8, 130-4, 139, 145-6,148, 152,157, 193-5, 199, 201-3, 225
Cocoon Inn, Koza Han 122
Coffee 102,199
Coggeshall 165
Colombia 194
Colonies 141-6
Comb, Combing 18,55
Como 188-9
Concubines 56, 201, 207, 217
Condensation 224, 245
Confucianism 47,52-3, 57
Congleton 169
Connecticut 143-6
Conservation 248-9
Corsets 186
Cos 122
Cosmetics 15, 37, 55, 113, 139, 205
Cotton 6-7, 26, 37, 55, 57, 64-67, 70, 73, 88, 92, 99, 110, 112, 115, 118, 126, 142, 152, 158, 161, 183, 224
Count Hilaire de Chardonnet, 183
Court 27-8, 56, 64, 72, 85, 100, 103-5, 122-4, 205-7
Courtauld 172-4
Courticelli Company 154
Courturiers 178, 184-5
Crape 166, 174-7
Crepe de Chine 18, 29, 35, 66, 73,106, 113, 118, 154, 186, 238, 248-50
Criollo 195
Cutting out 242-3

D
Damask 50, 106, 162, 165
Damyo 28
Daoism 48, 211
David Evans & Co 177
Debata 41
Debenham 167, 178
Debts 39-40, 163
Delhi 74-5
Denier 224
Department stores 32, 59
Department of Sericulture 61,86
Depression 40-1, 88, 128, 184, 188, 191, 219
Deserts 210-11, 246
Desho 36
Design 40-1, 65, 67, 74-5, 83-5, 90, 93, 108, 114, 126, 131, 179, 183-4, 197, 220, 243
Destroyed silk 224, 250
Dhoti 74
Diadem 52
Diapause, hibernation 10,80
Disease-free eggs 14, 42, 94, 109, 127, 183
Diseases 11,14-5,81,95,118, 128, 143, 182, 225-6
Disinfection 9, 14, 17, 226, 233
Distribution 124, 127, 227
Don Quixote 190
Dormitories 39, 121
Doucet, Jacques 186
Dowry 72, 114, 131
Drape, Drapery 190, 239, 243
Drawboy, Drawloom 30, 41, 65
Dress 26, 29, 31-2, 86, 97, 100, 118, 124, 130, 184-8, 216, 239
Dried and powdered silkworms 61, 228-9
Drinks 61,79, 222, 228-9
Drycleaning 246-7
Dunhuang 210
Dupioni 89, 94, 107, 224-5, 238, 241
Durumagi 44-6, 54
Dyes, Dyeing 19, 33, 42, 54,67-9, 74-6, 82-92, 104, 106-7, 110, 114-116, 125-6, 130, 137, 150, 162, 170-1, 177, 183, 186, 188-90, 194-6, 199, 201, 224, 237
Dynasties 200-2, 210-14

E
Ease 243
East India Company 65,162
Edit of Nantes 161, 189

Education 48, 53, 86, 153,223-7
Eggs, Graine, Seed 9-14, 25, 42, 61, 76-7, 80, 90-1, 102-9, 118, 127, 133-4, 136, 143, 157, 183, 190, 195, 225
Eki 29
Embroidery 29,35-6,46-8,50-2, 55, 57, 64, 66, 70-2, 74, 84, 108, 114, 118, 121, 126, 130-1, 138, 154, 160, 169, 170-2, 186, 197-9, 200, 203-16
Emperors 25, 31,33, 201-7, 213
Employees 30, 86, 127, 138,169
Empress 56, 185, 200, 213
England,65-6, 80, 84, 96-7, 117, 125, 141, 145,155, 160-79
Enzymes 13, 222, 228
Eri, *Samia cynthia ricini*, 21, 37, 63, 69, 76-7, 199, 224
Erté 186,
Essex 163-5, 173
Ethiopia 197,
Europe 31, 40, 69, 80, 85-7, 117-19,125-9,130-1, 134, 157, 183, 189-90, 234
Evil eye, spirits 69
Exhibition 7, 172, 237-9,248-52
Exports 65, 87, 97,102-3, 110, 124, 127-136, 143

F
Fabric 26, 61-7, 77, 99, 102, 110, 112, 131-6, 151, 174, 228, 238, 240, 248
Factories 39, 90, 119, 129, 130, 136-8, 141-2, 145-6, 169,174, 184, 192, 217
Families 26, 33-4, 37-9, 68-9, 72, 76-8, 82, 91-2, 105, 113-4, 126-9, 132-4, 143-4, 163, 196, 199, 212, 217, 220, 225-7, 231
Famine 219
FAO 130
Farmers 9,42-3, 48, 50, 53, 94, 102, 105, 109, 121, 124, 127-8, 132-6,142-3,148-9, 183,193-4, 199, 219-21
Fashion 30, 58,75, 97, 110, 118, 143,160, 164, 175-178, 181, 184-7, 220, 206, 234
Ferghana Valley 135
Fertilizer 13,15, 23, 94,102,130, 230,190
Fibroin 12
Filament 12,18, 80, 103, 152,

194, 244
Filature 14,17, 38-43, 88, 102, 145-6, 152, 194, 217-19
Finishing 188, 223
Fish 15,94,114,159,190,213,228
Flacherie 157, 183, 225
Flapper era 177, 186
Floss 12,16, 131,169, 209
Fluorescent silkworm 233-4
Foods 60-1, 92, 113, 163, 205, 224, 227-9
Forests 20-1,76, 102, 109
Fortuny, Mariano, 186
France 40, 70, 117-8, 126, 134, 141-4, 150-1,157, 161-4, 180-9, 192, 198, 209
Franklin, Benjamin 144-5
Fraud 148-9
Freeze-dried pupa, 15, 61, 94
French seams 240-1
Furisode 24, 32
Fustanella, 130

G
Gaddum, H T & Co 169
Garments 30, 49, 56, 73, 74-5, 86, 90-2, 97, 102, 105-6, 118, 122-4, 129, 158, 176, 186, 198, 208-9, 214-16, 231-2, 238, 241, 249-51
Gauze 50,52, 66,106, 176,204-5
Geisha, Maiko 36-7,185
General Wang Kon 49
Genetic modification 127, 233
Georgia 127-9
Georgia US 142-3
Geonotypes, phenotype 129, 234
Germany 96,134,150-1,155,189
Gervex, Henri 185
Ghagra choli 73
Ghana, Asante and Ewe 197-8
Gifts 25,44,47,55,63,71-2,92-3, 103, 107, 114-5, 125, 130, 142, 186, 198-9, 206-11, 249
Girls' Clubs 39, 217
Gisaeng 56-7
Global Organic Textile Standard, (GOTS) 96-7, 234
Goats 123-2
Gold 30,50-2, 55,62-5,71,73-7, 83, 88, 92, 103-4, 107-12, 126, 130-1,186-8, 198, 212
Goodden, Robert 179
Goreum 52, 54-5
Government 29, 40-2, 52, 69, 72, 78, 80-1, 105, 115, 121-2, 127, 131-4, 134-9, 142-5,

146, 158, 161, 183, 195-6
Gowns 27, 29-30, 52, 56,174-5, 184-5, 204-5, 209, 215-16, 226
Grainline 241-2
Great Exhibition166
Great Game 209
Greige, raw silk yarn 188
Greece, Soufli 13-4, 122-4
Grosgrain 106, 155
Guilan 125
Guilds 42, 119-20, 162
Gujurat 65, 67-8, 71-3
Gum arabic 18, 71
Gunma 38-9, 43
Gut, fishing line 22,190, 228
Gypsy moths, *Lymantria dispa* 157

H
Haberdashery 154, 184
Hainan Island 22
Hair 30, 45, 56-8, 186, 215
Haircutting ceremony 39,50
Hanbok 46, 54-6, 58
Han Dynasty 99, 208-9, 214
Hanks, Rodney & Horatio 145
Hargreaves, James 163
Harmonists 149-152
Hart Dyke, Lady Zoe 178-9
Hatcheries 9, 10, 14, 77-8, 118, 193
Hats 26, 46-8, 52, 54
Haute Couture 75,1 84-9
Harem 119
Heaven 51-2, 212
Hemp 26, 45, 54-5, 59
Herodotus 124,
Hill, Samuel Lapham 153-4
Hindus 68, 73,78,99,108,111-14
Honiton Lace 178
Hook-and-tulip motif 139
Horses 205, 207, 215,
Huguenots 161,169, 172
Humidity 11,95,225,245,249
Humphreys Weaving Co 167
Hwang Jini 56-7
Hybrids 10,23,95,127,194,229
Hygiene 11, 118, 183, 191,199, 225

I
Ice cream 60-1, 222, 229
Ikat 32, 66-8, 84-5, 93, 104, 108,111
Immigrants 45,66,82,155-6,193
Imperial Silk Workshop 25, 28

Independence 72,130-4, 138
India 10, 20, 62-81, 84, 102-3, 108, 126, 130-5, 139, 170-1, 183,1 98
Indigo 64,69,88,114,177,183
Indonesia 88, 107-9
Industrial revolution 161
Industry 69, 75-7, 118-9, 126, 131, 155,162,186,193-6, 219-21
Immigrants 155-6
Instars 10, 229
Interlinings 239, 240, 244,245
Iran 124-127
Iribe 186
Ironing 68, 242, 247-8
ISA 234
Islam 67, 189-90
Italy 102, 126-8, 141,155, 157, 182, 187-8, 198, 186

J
Jackets 26, 45-8, 54, 93, 100, 132, 187-9, 204, 210-14, 247-8, 251
Jacquard, Joseph-Marie, loom, 40-1, 69, 146, 150, 163-7,181-2
Jains 64, 68, 77
Jamdani 62, 70
James I 141
Jammu & Kashmir 76, 80-1, 170-4, 177,
Japan 22-43,80-6,96, 106, 108, 110, 118-9, 155-8, 177, 182-3, 187, 196, 226
Java 84, 109
Jeogori 44
Jewellery 46-7, 55, 72, 83, 86, 93, 121, 152, 155-8, 214
Jews 191, 198
Journeymen 162
Juhgori 54, 58
Juni hitoe 27, 29

K
Kanoka 34
Karnataka 70, 73, 76-8
Kasaya 210
Kashmir, 65, 76, 80, 170, 177
Kay, John 163
Keeper of the Caves 198
Khorat Plateau 88, 93 ,96
Kimono 24-37, 106, 185, 238
Kings 48 50-1,56, 85-7,167,188
Klongs 85, 88-9
Knitting, Knitwear 31,188, 236, 250

Korea 25, 41-61, 199, 228
Korean silk fabrics 50, 59
Kozabirlik 121
Kray brothers 174
Krefeld 189
Kumar, Ritu 74
Kutch 68, 70, 72
Kymer 84, 103
Kyoto 30-1, 40

L

Labour 102, 142, 155-6, 173, 227, 234-5
Lac, *Lacifer lacca* 65
Lacquerware 57, 204-5
Lady of the Silkworms 201
Lady Dai 204-5
Lianoning 22
Lam Dong 102
Laos 88-9, 93, 103, 112-15
Lavin, Jeanne 186
Leek, Leek embroidery 168-172
Leodian 168
Lesarge 187
Levant Trading Company 162,
Levies 142
Liberty & Co 167
Libya 197-8
Life cycle 8-11, 183
Lime powder 225
Lisle 158
List 163
Lombe, Thomas 163
London 128, 162-3, 167, 186-7
Looms 32, 42, 45, 49, 64, 67, 69, 87-9, 92, 105, 110-2, 115, 156, 165, 173, 180, 190-2, 198, 203
Lullingstone 178-9
Lungi, *lon-gyi* or sarong 74, 111
Lun taya acheik 111
Lustre 18, 20, 77, 94, 183, 223, 237, 245
Lyon 40, 85,118,128,176,181-2

M

Macclesfield 163-8, 178
Machine Twist 153-4
Madagascar 197-9, 232
Madder 177
Magazines, *Farmer & Gardener, Silk Culturist, Farmers' Register, New England Farmer, Woman's Exponent, The Lady Gazette Du Bon Ton, The Needlewoman.* 90, 142, 148, 151-2, 160, 168, 176, 184, 186
Malacate 196

Malay, Malaysia 110-111
Malong 104
Management 81, 96, 109, 111, 127, 227,
Manchester 168
Mansfield 143-4, 146 Manufacturing 90, 96-7, 124, 139, 141, 145-6, 150-5, 161-5, 175, 182-4, 223, 227
Manuscripts 65, 112, 115, 123, 201, 210
Mao 219-20
Maps 164, 202, 205, 216
Margilan 135-6
Market 70, 80-1, 95-6, 105,115, 127, 135, 152, 158, 220, 235
Marriage 39,49,58,91,114, 121, 201, 207, 217
Masham 203
Mashru 70,
Mating 14,21
Matmi, Matami 84, 91, 93
Mawangdui 202-5
Mawata caps, hankies 20
Medicine 61, 229-30
Mehmet II 117
Meiji 31-2, 37, 40
Mekong 105,
Mengikat 66-7
Merchants 12, 53, 69, 117, 191, 198
Metamorphosis 6,12, 234
Mexico 22,195-7
Middle east 84-5
Migration 91,112
Military 28-9, 47, 53, 57, 87-8, 130, 155, 208, 212, 228, 230-2
Mills 39-43, 69, 119, 120-4, 140, 145-6, 150, 153-6, 168-9, 170-7, 198, 227
Ming 100, 203, 211-15
Mirrors 55, 203-4
Missionaries 195
Mommes 224-5
Mon,crest 33, 35
Mon-Khymer 112
Monastery 92
Mongol 49, 50, 125,
Mordant 68, 115, 177, 183
Mormons 149-52
Morocco 197
Morris, William 170-2
Motifs 55, 114, 213
Moulting 10,12
Mourning 54,174-5, 188
Mud-mee 93,
Muga, *Antheraea assamensis*, 21,

63, 74, 76
Mughal 64-6, 74
Mukta 77
Mulberry 22-23,26,38,45,50-1, 61-3, 76-80, 83-4, 81 ,87, 91-6, 102-9, 112-19, 122-4, 127-8, 130, 133-9, 141-6, 147-9,151-7, 179, 192-6, 198, 202-7, 219-21, 223-9, 230, 233
Multicaulis 22, 147-9, 146, 152
Mulberry paper 112, 115, 123, 138-9, 201, 230
Multi-loom 163
Mummies 211
Murals 46
Murasaki Shikibu 27
Muromachi 28,
Murcia 190,
Museums 68,90,103-4,124,128-9, 145, 167, 189, 191, 209
Music 28, 33,57,92,203
Muslims, 65, 67, 70-1, 79-84, 88-90, 108,125-6, 128, 198-9
Myanma 103, 111-12
Mysore 70, 73, 78, 80

N

National Council of Women 151
Needles 203, 209-10
Neolithic Period 46, 201
Netherlands 107
Netherworld 202, 205
New Jersey 144-5
New York 90, 149, 155, 158
Nigeria 197-9
Nishijin 40, 42
Nivi 73-4
No theatre 40
Nobility 58,
Noil 19, 23
Nonotuck Silk Company 154
Norigae 55
Northampton 140, 148-9, 152-4
Nuegra 228

O

Oak tussah, tasar 77,195, 202-3
Oaxaca 195-7
Obi, cord, dome, sash, scarf 30-3, 37
Object d'art 57
Odhni 72-3
Oil 15, 61,94
Organic silk, 94-7
Organza 58-9, 104, 174, 228,

Index 261

238, 250
Organzine 17, 118, 192
Orissa 67-9, 76-7
Ottoman Empire 117, 121, 174

P

Paquin, Jeanne 185
Padding 54,
Painting 30, 32-3, 46, 48, 57, 67, 73, 83,112, 131, 205, 209
Pakse 104
Paleolithic 100
Pallau 73
Pantaloons 86, 93, 185
Pants 26, 30, 57, 100, 110, 204, 214-16
Paper 57, 77, 115, 176, 201
Parachutes 121, 134, 158, 178, 228
Paradise Mills 169
Parasols 110, 166, 198, 213
Paris 142, 144, 185
Parse 66-8
Partnerships 194
Pasteur, Louis 42, 97, 118,183
Patchwork 58, 72, 150-1, 210, 216, 237,239-40, 242-6, 249-50
Paterson NJ 155-6
Patola 66-7, 85, 104
Pattern 33-4, 68-9, 71, 85, 93, 205, 91, 93, 104-10, 149, 176-7, 180, 198, 243-4, 249
Pauling, Linus 233
Paulownia 24
Peacock standard 97
Pearls 65,74
Peasants 26, 38, 53-5, 65, 183, 195, 219
Pebrine, *Nosema bombycis* 42, 81,87, 109, 118, 123, 129,181-3 191,225
Peduncle 21
Pelliot, Paul 209
Pennsylvania 142-8, 151, 155
People's Republic of China 219
Perek Man 99,
Periplus Maris Erythreae 64,
Perkin, William 177, 183
Persia 85, 124-6, 162, 189
Persperation 224, 245
Peru 194,
Pha chong kaban, Pha hang, Pha nung, Pha sabai, Pha sa- rong, Pha sing, 82-7,104
Pheromone 13, 21
Phetchabun, 94-7
Philadelphia 144, 146, 150

Philippines 106-7,147
Philosamia ricini, eri 113,
Phnom Penh 104
Piedmont, California 157
Piedmont, Italy 188, 192
Pilgrims 211
Pinyo 58
Pirates 51,84
Pit loom 69-70
Pliny the elder 122
Polo, Marco 135
Poirot, Paul 185
Polychrome silks, 188, 200, 205-6, 213
Pongee 50, 203, 213
Ponzelar 189
Portugal 84, 191-2
Post-Soviet States 127-139
Pottery 83, 99, 204
Poupee 185
Poverty 63, 92-3, 112, 223, 227, 235, 249
Predators 10, 225
Pregnancy 39
prêt-à-porter 75, 189
Princess 25, 26, 32, 34, 49, 50, 166, 207
Printing 68, 74-5, 83, 170, 177, 183, 189, 202
Properties 223-5, 238, 245
Prostitutes 53, 56, 219
Protein 15,22, 61, 113, 130, 223, 229, 233, 238-33
Punjabi suit 73
Pupa, chrysalis 9, 12, 15, 61, 94, 113,130, 197, 222, 225, 228-9,234
Purses 54-5
Puyo 45
Pyong yang 45

Q

Quakers 149-152
Quality control 70, 81, 220, 235
Queens 47-8, 56, 867, 97, 165, 175,178-9
Quilts, Quilting 54,140,149-151
167, 203-5, 239, 246-51
Qum 126
Quotas 127, 135-6

R

Rajasthan 68
Ramie 50, 54, 57-61
Ramanagaram 78
Rank badges 58, 212
Rapp, Gertrude 151

Raw silk 16, 18, 76, 89, 97, 102-3, 125-6, 136-2, 141,143-4,183, 219, 223-4
Rayon 159, 174
Ready to wear 75
Rebozos 196
Reeling 12, 15-17, 21, 40, 50, 64, 80, 87-8,94-6, 100-2, 105-6, 118, 122, 127, 129, 131, 134, 149-152, 159, 192, 217
Religious communities, 150-2, 201
Research 111-12, 119, 127-8, 132, 150, 191
Ribbons 52-6, 146, 150, 155-6, 168-9, 176, 184, 205, 249
Rice 89, 91, 94, 105-6
Rituals 52, 86,120,113,128, 230
Robes 27,52,57,106,200,207-11
Roger I Sicily 122
Rokumeikan 30-1
Rotary blade 243
Royal silk 110-11,191
Russia 22,17, 117, 127-8

S

Salon 185-6
Salwar sharmees 73
Samarkand 135, 139, 246
Samfoo 110
Samia cynthia ricini 21
Samurai 28-30, 40
San Diego 157
Sangtu 45
Sari 62, 66-7, 72-5, 110, 238
Sarong 84, 93, 104, 110
Sassanian Dynasty 125,
Saturnia pyretorum, 22,
Saturniidae, 20,202,
Satin 24, 70, 75, 126, 150, 162, 174, 207, 213-16, 238, 240
Schapping 20
Schiaparelli, Elsa 186-7
Scholars 53, 56-7
Schools 48, 57, 86, 100-2, 106, 110, 132,136,174, 178, 188,192
Science 48, 80, 93, 128, 134-6, 205, 222-235
Sculpture 48,73
Sericin, gum 18-20, 78,105,193,
Sericulture 10-23, 26, 38, 41-3, 61-3, 64, 67,70, 75-8, 80, 82,88, 90-2, 94-7, 100-3, 106-10, 115-19, 121-8, 130-3, 139, 141-5, 148, 150-52, 156-7,189-97,201-2, 216-18,

220-3, 227, 234,242
Sericulture Research Institute 119, 121, 128, 132,
Sewing 237-51
Sewing Twist 146, 153-4, 169, 171, 244
Shah Abbas I of Persia 125
Shakers 149-52
Shamanism 48
Shanghai 201, 221
Shantung Shandong, 22, 33, 207, 241, 250
Shawls 56, 66, 74, 93, 108, 151, 175, 195, 199, 215, 236
Sheki 131-3
Sherwani 74
Shibori 24, 29, 34
Shichao 207
Shin Saimdang 56
Ships 84,106
Shirts 74, 93, 102, 110, 114
Shoes, 26, 46, 58, 86, 144, 209, 215
Shogun, 30,31
Shot silk, 89, 92,107
Silk Association of Great Britain and Ireland 71
Silk Girls 37-9, 217-19
Silk glands 12
Silk moth 8-14, 22, 42,76-7, 94, 120, 157
Silk Road, Routes 84, 117, 125, 128, 131,139, 208, 251
Silk Ships, Trains 106,157-8
Silk Stockings 106, 158-9, 177
Silkworms 26,50-1, 56, 61, 76, 80-4, 91,94, 105-6, 111-3, 129, 202-3, 118, 122, 129-131, 136, 141-6, 147-8, 151-2, 157, 178-9,182-3, 190-5, 225-6, 229, 232-4
Silver 30, 45, 48, 65, 71, 88, 93, 103-4, 112, 186, 188, 200, 207
Singer Sewing Machines 152-3
Sinh 114-5
Sisterhoods 219
Skirt, 26, 46, 54, 72, 74, 87, 93, 100, 102, 106-8, 176, 213-16, 238, 243, 246
Slaves, 25 45, 53, 125, 142, 149, 150, 195
Smithsonian Museum 144
Smuggling 127
Soap 17, 222, 224, 228
Soda ash 20
Songket 88, 108
South America 192-4

South-east Asia 99-102, 110
South Manchester 146
Spain 189-191, 195
Speculation 147-9
Spider silk 230-3
Spies 209
Spindle, drop, wheel 45, 92,108
Spinneret 12
Spinning 12, 18, 92, 114, 169, 192, 196
Spinning jenny 192
Spinster houses 218
Spitalfields, 161-7, 172-4, 178
Spun silk 77,80, 152
Srinagar 80
Stain removal 245-7
Stamping 84
Steam-power 168-9, 173, 217
Stifling 12,15, 88
Stiles, Rev Dr. 143
Strength 223
Sudbury 165-8
Sumptuary law 26, 48, 58, 108
SUPPORT organization 97
Surgical sutures 130, 134,158, 190, 224, 229
Suwon Symposium 60-1
Suzhou 17
Suzanni, 138-9
Swan's quills, paper tubes, prins 162
Symbols 56, 108, 110, 114, 125-6, 131, 197, 213
Syria 183

T

Tabi 37
Taffeta 106, 175, 188, 209, 238
Tai 83-4
Tai Deang 114
Tajikistan 124,134-9
Tale of Genji 27
T'ang 47-8, 205, 208-15
Tapestry 30, 93, 206
Tattoo 26
Tax 26, 48, 53,64, 105, 120, 125, 127,130, 183, 206,
Technical 223
Tekke 132
Tentering, 155,165
Tenum Pahang Diraja1 10
Test for silk 224, 239
Textiles 40, 47-8, 67-9, 85-6, 92, 96, 104-5, 107-110, 128, 165, 172, 197-8, 189, 191, 205-11, 223-4
Texalis ventalis 64
Thailand, Siam 10, 82-97

Thigh-roll 77
Thompson, Jim 88-90, 96
Throwing 17-18, 96, 105, 127, 169, 178
Throwster 79, 162, 172
Tie-dye 24, 66-8, 104, 137
Tinting 17
Tiraz 198
Tobacco 106, 142
Tokyo 31, 40-1
Toledo 190-2
Tombs 47, 201-11
Tomesode 33
Tomioka 39-40
Tourist 72, 138, 194
Trade 47, 66, 84-8, 99, 108,117, 122-3, 131, 144, 122-5, 158, 207-9, 227
Trade Unions 174
Transportation 145-6, 183, 227
Trás-os-Montes 191-2
Treasures 100, 205-6, 208-11, 238
Tribute 207
Trimmings 145, 177, 186
Tripoli 198
Trousseaux 91,118
Truck system 163
Tuk Tuan Keraing Aji 110
Tunisia 197-8
Turkey 117-122, 183
Tussah, Tasar, Tassar 9, 20-22, 63, 68-9, 75-8, 113, 195, 203

U

Ukraine 133-4
Umbrellas 159, 166
Uncut cloth 73, 111
Underground railway 149-150
Unemployment 127, 181, 219
Unified Shilla 48-9
United States 96-7,141-159, 187 189
University 86, 131,127-8, 134, 158, 194
UNOPS 111
Unseemly bottomless pants 100
Upholstery 69, 97,228, 237, 250
Uses 228-230
Utah 150-2
Uzbekistan 135-9, 228, 246
Uzi fly 11

V

Valentino 90
Vanners 166
Varanasi 65
Vegetarian Halls 218-19

Velvet 64,71, 84, 106, 126, 131,150-55, 162, 167, 186, 206, 242
Vernet, Marie 185,
Vietnam 88-9, 99-102
Villages 16,75-6, 80, 91-4, 105, 108, 113-4, 122-3,126, 131,134, 191, 196, 199, 209, 217, 227
Vionnet, Madeleine 87
Virgina 141
Vodiy Ipagi, or Valley Silk 136
Voltine, uni, bi, multi 10,14, 20, 78-9, 94, 105, 113, 196

W

Wada Ei 47
Wages 38-9, 155-6, 173-4, 209, 217, 227
Walters, Stephen & Co 165
Wang Kon, General 49
War 31-2, 40, 64, 85, 88, 104-8, 112, 115, 117-9, 121-9, 134, 154-9, 164-6, 173-4,177, 181, 186-7, 191, 195, 201
Wardle, Lady Elizabeth 171-2
Wardle, Sir Thomas 170-1, 80
Warners 167
Warp 49-50, 66-70, 94, 108, 137
Warring States period 201
Washing 77, 177, 224, 246-9
Waste silk 18-20, 77, 97, 131, 152, 188, 223
Weavers' houses 161,165
Weaving 41-2, 48-9, 64, 68-9, 76, 79-89, 90-3, 110, 115, 102, 105, 108, 111-13, 117, 122-6, 134-7, 154, 161-3, 169, 173, 179, 181-4, 189, 195, 205-11
Weddings 32, 54-5, 66-9, 72, 92, 100-1, 114, 121, 152,166, 178-9, 198, 238, 247
Weft 50, 66, 93-4, 111
Weighting 179, 183, 189
Whisky 61, 228
Whitchurch Mill 174
Whitmarsh, Samuel 148-9
Wild silk 20, 21, 76, 91, 111-13, 122, 171, 195-9, 202-3
Wilson, Mrs Woodrow 145
Women's work 26, 38-40, 92, 101, 105, 108-11, 115, 120-1, 144, 151, 155-7, 217, 227
Women Who Weave 196
Workshops 64, 67, 108, 122, 126, 178, 189, 205

Workers of the World 156
Worth, Frederick 185
W T Organisation 219-21
World Bank 234
Wright, Susannah 150
Wu-di 47

Y

Yangban 53
Yang Guifei 215
Yarn 61, 97, 102, 105, 108, 111, 117- 8, 197, 228
Yi Dynasty 54, 56-7
Yodgorlik factory 138
Yokohama 35
Yuan 50, 93, 216
Yutaka 35, 43
Yuzen 32, 34, 43

Z

Zari 70-1
Zodiac 56,
Zoroastrian 66
Zori 37
Zwaardecroon, Hendrick 107

www.ingramcontent.com/pod-product-compliance
Lightning Source LLC
Chambersburg PA
CBHW080246030426
42334CB00023BA/2721